# POWDER AND BALL
# SMALL ARMS

*Dieu n'est pas pour les gros bataillons, mais
pour ceux qui tirent le mieux.*
God is not on the side of the heavy battalions,
but of the best shots.
*Voltaire*

"...no thing is so hard as Killing of men."
*Trooper Edward Stilman, 1743*

LIVE FIRING CLASSIC MILITARY WEAPONS IN COLOUR PHOTOGRAPHS

# POWDER AND BALL SMALL ARMS

## MARTIN PEGLER

The Crowood Press

First published in 1998 by
The Crowood Press Ltd
Ramsbury, Marlborough
Wiltshire SN8 2HR

**British Library Cataloguing
in Publication Data**
A catalogue record for this book is
available from the British Library

**ISBN 1 86126 185 3**

Edited by Martin Windrow
Designed by Frank Ainscough,
Compendium
Printed and bound in China

**Dedication**
To Katie, for all the time I've not
been there; and to Martin, for his
patience, especially where
computers are concerned.

**Note on photography**
Unless specifically credited otherwise, photographs reproduced in
this book are copyright Martin
Pegler 1998. All were taken with
either a 650 or 1000 Canon EOS
camera; lenses were Canon USM
100-300, 28-80, and a 50mm
Macro for close-ups. The 650 has
a five-frames-per-second capability,
which I found out the hard way is
not fast enough to catch the
complete firing sequences of a
wheel lock or flintlock. Natural light
was used wherever possible in
conjunction with a dedicated flash
and slave unit; a tripod was
employed at all times. All print film
was Fuji Velvia, either 100 or
200 ASA; Fujichrome was used
for transparencies.

## Author's Preface

The history of firearms development is the story of a complex process of trial and error pursued by a large number of usually anonymous people over a long period of time. The technology that we accept so casually today would have been incomprehensible to our pre-industrial forebears, living as they did in a world where change came about with infinite slowness. It is all too easy for us to underestimate the revolutionary impact that the invention of practical firearms had upon society; it is no exaggeration to say that it changed the course of history. And probably because of their importance, firearms have become the object of more half-truths, misinformation and exaggeration than most other areas of technological endeavour.

This book sets out to take a brief look at how the muskets, rifles and pistols of the 15th to 19th centuries - those which threw a ball propelled by powder - were developed; but mainly to describe in non-technical language how they actually handled and worked, their accuracy (or lack of it), and their practicality as battlefield weapons. It closes with a chapter on the first metallic-cartridge weapons, whose loads still employed black powder and a solid lead bullet.

What was actually involved in loading, firing and hitting a target in previous ages of warfare has often been the subject of ill-informed guesswork (except in Hollywood, of course, where sheer fantasy has always been good enough). For this book - as for the other titles in this series - each of the most significant types of weapon has been loaded and fired in as consistent a manner as possible, to give the reader some idea of the practical handling and the battlefield limitations of each class of firearm. It is not meant to offer a general history of firearms (of which there are arguably too many already), nor a series of thorough technical analyses (which are available to the specialist reader elsewhere). Naturally, in the less specialised world of our ancestors many basically similar weapons were used by both sportsmen and soldiers in many countries. However, military firearms are useful to the commentator in that armies are deeply conservative institutions and usually have only adopted types that were tried and tested - and which consequently offer a convenient guide to the chronological and technical progress of the most important patterns of black powder weapons.

It is worth stressing at the outset that many of the results obtained were not what would have been achieved on the battlefields of Europe between one hundred and five hundred years ago. Modern technology has given us reliable black powders which have been properly mixed and stored, and lead bullets which are perfectly spherical and correctly sized for the bore. The guns we used were quite pampered, in that their mechanisms and bores were kept as clean as possible during shooting - probably the single most important factor in ensuring reliable functioning and accuracy.

Gunpowder is a wildly impractical propellant, each charge fired leaving in the bore a clinging residue of oily black soot, which in a smoothbore can make reloading extremely difficult after as few as five shots (the problem is exacerbated in rifles, whose tight-fitting bullets can jam in the bore once the rifling grooves are clogged by fouling). The soldiers who used these weapons in earnest did not have the luxury of a quiet test range, and the fact that they managed to keep their longarms functioning at all is something of a miracle.

Where accuracy is concerned, the results that we obtained should be treated only as a guide to what each specific type was *probably* capable of; they certainly should not be taken as finite proof of the consistent capabilities of any given type. The results obtained can (and did) vary dramatically depending on the individual weapon and the quality of powder used, the ability of the shooter, even the weather conditions. Although wherever possible original examples were used for test firing, genuinely authentic replicas were used in many instances for practical reasons (aside from the embarrassing risk of returning a priceless original to its owner as a box of component parts, replicas do not suffer from worn bores, weakened springs and years of mishandling, and are thus safer and more consistent). Original guns have been used for most of the photographic sequences in this book, and the data compiled is based on information gleaned from trial-and-error shooting with both replicas and originals. Any factual errors in the text are mine.

Although the firearms described fall into separate categories which we now associate with specific periods of history, it should be emphasised that these weapons often overlapped in use, and at no period can it be said that one particular type entirely replaced another. In the world before industrial mass production the process of invention and change was a very slow one, and innovations were only adopted gradually and unevenly. For instance, armies of the 1640s made simultaneous use of matchlocks, wheel locks and flintlocks despite the fact that, in theory, one type had superseded another technically. Guns were too valuable to simply be discarded because something better had come along, and change was regarded with suspicion; the unquestioning acceptance of technological advancement as A Good Thing dates only from the 19th century.

While a number of different types of firearm are covered here, until the advent of the rifle the technical history was really one of ignition development. For most of its long life the hand gun or musket was merely a metal tube loaded with powder and a projectile; for four hundred years the story of the gun was really a series of attempts to get the powder to explode reliably rather than to project the ball with any great accuracy. The methods used to achieve this - heated wire, matchcord, pyrites, flints, fulminate caps - marked stages in a long process of trial and error. As writers and gunmakers both understand, knowing what you want is one thing - attaining it is another.

## Acknowledgements

A great many people assisted with the writing of this book, giving their time and advice unstintingly. I would especially like to thank the many excellent re-enactors who posed for me, and the following in particular: Chris Otterburn of the Chapter of St Bartholemew, Nick Hodson and Mark Goodman of the Fairfax Battalia, Graeme Charlton of the 68th Durham Regiment of Light Infantry, Lloyd Day of the Southern Skirmishers Association, Steve Barker of the 95th Regiment, and Marc Meltonville for his splendid bronze gun. Thanks as well to Charles Kightley and Chris Gravett, whose ability to find obscure quotations was nothing short of amazing, and Russell and Paula Wright for the use of their house and grounds for many location shots, and my apologies to Fen for making so much noise. Also to Chris Howard for holding the Colt beyond the limits of endurance, and Peter Smithurst for providing a splendid pair of hands. Thanks too to those collectors who did not wish to be named, for allowing me to photograph their ammunition and guns – you know who you are… . I would specifically like to thank John Waller for permission to use the 1st Battalion (Combat) Interpreters, in particular Alan Eyles, Sally Hague, Frank Hammond and Adam Des Forges, without whom… and so on.

Special thanks to Graeme Rimer for the benefit of his limitless knowledge of firearms, and for letting me loose in the collection of the Royal Armouries Museum. Lastly, very grateful thanks to Tony Barton, acting unpaid Casting Director, Locations Manager, Tailor and Costume Historian, without whose enthusiastic help many of the photographs in this book could not have been taken. To anybody else I may have forgotten to acknowledge, I offer my sincere thanks.

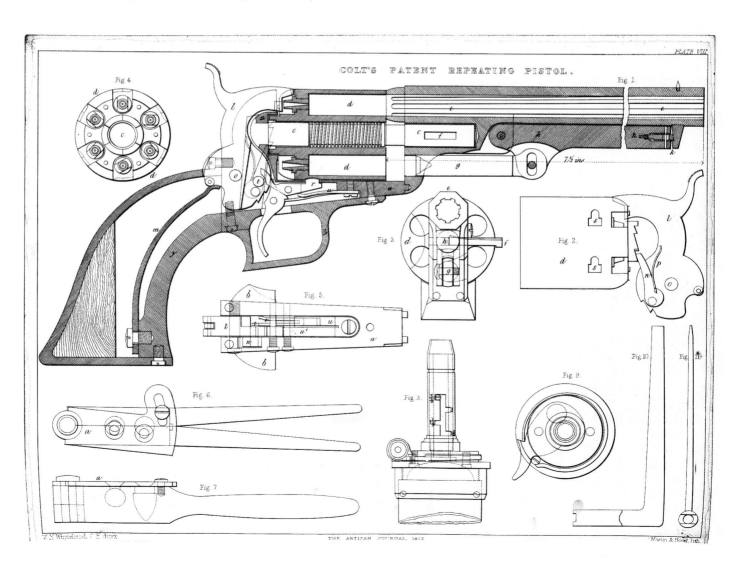

# CONTENTS

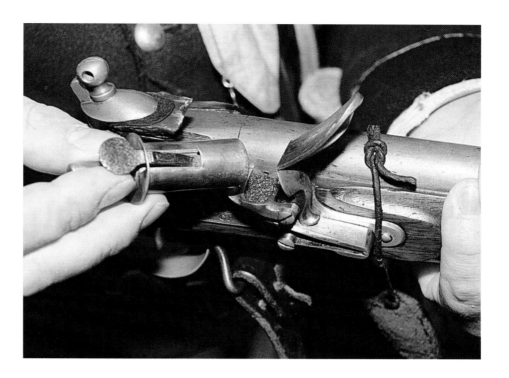

# GUNMAKING and GUNPOWDER: A brief introduction

An interesting display of the uses of gunpowder in the mid-15th century, from a German volume entitled The Firework Book. A cannon of stave-and-hoop construction fires a ball; it has a four-wheeled carriage complete with yoke attachments for a draught team and a trail-chest for ammunition. The group in the right foreground are using both crossbows loaded with incendiary bolts and an early hand gun. The defenders are also equipped with guns, which can be seen protruding from the embrasures; and some try to dislodge the fire-arrows from their wooden roofs with hooked poles. (I-34; A8/418; The Board of Trustees of the Royal Armouries)

The manufacture of most arms and armour, from the Middle Ages onwards, was controlled by guilds - voluntary associations of craftsmen who banded together to create monopolies in their own self-interest. They jealously guarded their particular skills, and as time progressed they expanded to cover a number of different manufacturing processes. Initially the makers of the earliest hand guns and cannon were armourers and blacksmiths who understood the techniques of forging iron, and had some idea - doubtless gained at the cost of many fatal accidents - about how to construct barrels that could withstand the pressures and temperatures generated by gunpowder. By the mid-15th century gunmaking had evolved into an art of its own; but such was the hold of the guild that in London, for example, the gunmakers were not permitted to break away from the blacksmiths to gain a charter as a Worshipful Company in their own right until 1637 during the reign of Charles I, by which date little armour was still being made for military use.

The trade of gunmaking had its origins in Western Europe in the early 14th century, and by the 15th there were major centres of production in Italy, at Brescia and Milan; in Germany, at Nuremberg, Dresden, Suhl and in the Rhineland; and in Bohemia, where both Carlsbad and Prague flourished. Many firearms were imported into France and England during this early period; but by the early 1600s a large provincial gun industry had sprung up in France, in Brittany, Normandy, Picardy, Burgundy, the Champagne, Alsace and Lorraine as well as in Paris. In Belgium, Liége was to become one of Europe's major manufacturing centres, and had adopted a system of barrel proofing in 1672 - one of the earliest in the world.

In the England of Henry VIII (r.1509-1547) there was a surge of interest in firearms, partly due to the king's own enthusiasm, and London became the main manufacturing centre for nearly a century. Birmingham had long been the home of a thriving metalworking industry, and in the decades following the English Civil War (1642-51) the Birmingham gun trade began to supply increasing numbers of arms to the government. By the 18th century large contracts were being given to this regional trade to supply the army with muskets.

The industry in the United States is of particular interest. A small manufacturing base had sprung up by 1810 in and around Worcester, Massachusetts, which by that date was producing one third of the 65,000 arms being manufactured in America. The industry boomed, and by the middle of the century large industrial plants had been built in many areas, but particularly around Hartford and New Haven, Connecticut, producing firearms on the revolutionary new production line method, later to be copied by all the world's industrialised nations. Indeed, by 1862 there were no less than 239 factories producing firearms in the United States.

This huge expansion in firearms manufacturing around Europe and later the USA depended not only on demand, but on the ability to supply a reliable product. Unless universally high standards could be enforced on the makers of locks, stocks and barrels, then the end product could be at the very least unreliable, and at the worst deadly. The greatest threat to life and limb was that of weak barrels, and by 1638 the London Gunmakers Company had taken to stamping all its own barrels - and those of foreign imports - with marks to certify that the materials and workmanship were of an accepted quality. Thereafter all gunmakers were required to submit their arms for proof at the Proof House. The system used for proving a firearm was quite simple: the barrel was loaded with about three times the standard powder charge and the gun was fired. If the barrel was weak it would rupture; if it survived it was stamped by the Proofmaster with a distinctive mark. This was a vital process; purchasers naturally looked for the proofmarks on any gun offered for sale, and any without a marked barrel would have been almost worthless. After 1813 this requirement was enshrined in law by an act of Parliament, which was reinforced in 1868, and similar standards were adopted world wide during the 19th century. It says much for the quality of the products offered by the gun trade in Britain that the failure rate has been estimated at 0.000003% ...

## Gunpowder

For those unfamiliar with the propellant common to all of the guns featured in this book, a brief explanation of the history and properties of gunpowder may be of interest.

Nobody knows exactly who invented the volatile mixture of saltpetre, charcoal and sulphur which makes up gunpowder, or when and where it first appeared. A tantalising passage in a work written in the late 2nd century AD by Philostratus has long been quoted as one of the earliest accounts of the use of gunpowder, and as one of the reasons why Alexander the Great failed to conquer India:

*"The Oxydracae dwell between the rivers Hyphasis and Ganges. Their country Alexander never entered, deterred not by fear of the inhabitants, for they come not out of the field to fight those who attack them, but these holy men ... overthrew their enemies with tempests and thunderbolts shot from their walls. It is said that the Egyptian Hercules and Bacchus ... attempted to conquer them; they in the meantime made no show of resistance, appearing perfectly quiet and secure, but upon the enemy's near approach were repulsed with storms of lightning and thunderbolts hurled upon them from above."*

Charming though this is, it is no longer regarded as a reliable account of anything but a bad electrical storm. It is quite feasible that an early knowledge of gunpowder, allied to its use in some form of cannon, may have existed on the Indian continent at this time, but exactly where that knowledge came from is a mystery. Its invention has at various times been ascribed to the Arabs, Greeks and Chinese, and it is quite possible that its use as a crude pro-

*Attempting to storm a castle - another illustration from* The Firework Book *full of facinating details of mid-15th century warfare. As the attackers scale ladders (note wheels at top and spikes at bottom) the defenders drop some form of barrel-shaped incendiary device on them. These may have taken the form of grenades, although it is possible that they contain a flammable compound other than gunpowder. The right hand scaler seems to carry a pavise shield. Between the crossbowman and armoured halberdier at the foot of the ladders stand two handgunners with early wooden-stocked guns. They are basically unarmoured, and both carry falchions as sidearms. (I-34; A8/416; The Board of Trustees of the Royal Armouries)*

pellant was discovered in several different countries at roughly the same period. Certainly a form of it existed in China around the 11th century, long before its appearance in Western Europe; it was undoubtedly known and used as a propellant for fireworks from around the latter half of the century. A gun barrel of Chinese manufacture has recently been dated to 1332, giving at least an indication that the use of gunpowder for firearms was well known by that date. These early guns, known as '*huo ch'iang*', were simply reinforced hollow bamboo tubes, sealed at one end and bound round with wire to prevent their thin walls bursting. The type of projectile fired is unclear, but could have been a hard clay ball.

The most likely route for the formula to have arrived in Europe was from the Middle East via Moorish-occupied southern Spain; the Arabs had been trading with the Chinese for centuries, though there is no firm evidence for these links being the conduit for the knowledge of gunpowder from East to West. Neither is there any clear proof of its use prior to the latter half of the 13th century, although there are isolated mentions of gunpowder being used at the siege of Belgrade in 1073 and during the Arab-Iberian war in 1147. There is a specific mention of artillery at the battle of Toulouse in 1218, although at this date its psychological impact was probably still more valuable than its tactical effect.

There is slightly more evidence to support at least an approximate date for the introduction of black powder to England at some point between 1257 and 1265. A Franciscan friar named Roger Bacon (1214-1294) recorded its formula as a complex anagram in a work entitled *De Secretis Operibus Artis et Naturae et de Nullitate Magiae*. Puzzlingly, however, this anagram appears only in later editions of the book; perhaps he did not learn of gunpowder until later than the date generally accepted for its introduction? It must also be said that Bacon did not make any specific mention of the use of gunpowder in firearms. This code was not understood until 1904, when it was eventually translated by Lt.Col.H.Hime as: "*But take seven parts of saltpetre, five of young hazelwood [charcoal] and five of sulphur; and so you may make thunder and lightning, if you know the trick.*"

Even now there is much controversy over the date of Bacon's work, for although it appears in a 16th century copy of his book a totally different code, as yet unbroken, appears in an earlier manuscript. There are other claimants apart from Bacon for the title of 'Inventor of Gunpowder'. The claim of a monk named Berthold Schwarz ("Black Berthold") of Freiberg is sufficiently honoured in his home town to warrant a statue, though sadly unsupported by hard evidence. Other early contenders include Marcus Graecus (c.1300), St Albert Magnus (c.1280), and an anonymous Arabic treatise dated to about 1460. Whatever the truth, gunpowder was certainly firmly established in chemical form, if not in function, by 1267, when in his *Opus Tertium* Bacon described its powers:

"*By the flash and combustion of fires, and by the horror of sounds, wonders can be*

**ABOVE** *The man at bottom left seems to be boiling or steeping matchcord; another rolls it into balls, and a third man with a tray carries away finished rolls. At top left we see matchcord rolls being packed into barrels. The man at top right is packing some sort of tied bags - almost certainly pre-measured powder charges for cannon, which are also shown in slightly later Swiss chronicles. (I-34; A8/424; The Board of Trustees of the Royal Armouries)*

**ABOVE RIGHT** *Weighing prepared powder, and packing it into cast balls of iron or clay. The man in the foreground is making slow match, which is being inserted into the balls to provide a fuse. (I-34; A8/417; The Board of Trustees of the Royal Armouries)*

**RIGHT** *Four different types of gunpowder. At left is very fine "serpentine" of the type used in the Middle Ages. Second from left is modern fine (FFFFg) for priming; then medium (FFFg) for use in pistols and smaller calibre muskets and rifles; and finally coarse (FFg), used primarily in large calibre longarms and cannon.*

*wrought, and at any distance we wish - so that a man can hardly protect himself or endure it. There is a child's toy of sound and fire made in various parts of the world with saltpetre, sulphur and charcoal of hazelwood. The powder is enclosed in an instrument of parchment the size of a finger, and since this can make such a noise that it seriously distresses the ears of men, especially if one is taken unawares, and the terrible flash is also very alarming, if an instrument of large size were used no one could stand the terror of the noise and the flash. If the instrument were made of solid material the violence of the explosion would be much greater."*

Gunpowder, or black powder as it is more commonly called today, has a number of properties which make it quite unsuitable as a propellant for firearms. It is hygroscopic, absorbing moisture from the atmosphere like a sponge until it eventually becomes so damp as to be rendered useless. Even modern powder, carefully stored, sometimes fails to ignite on the ranges simply because of a morning's exposure to damp conditions. When fired it leaves a thick, acidic carbon residue behind which chokes barrels, and if left unattended causes serious corrosion of metal parts. Handling loose powder for any length of time inevitably gets it into the mouth, which makes the shooter desperately thirsty - easily remedied on a range, but not so on a waterless battlefield. It also has the distinct tactical disadvantage that igniting powder creates 300 times its own volume in dense and highly visible white smoke.

Its burn rate is very different from modern smokeless powders, and the velocities produced are generally lower; bullets travel at sub-sonic speed, giving the gun a 'booming' report very distinct from the familiar 'crack' of modern weapons. Unlike modern high explosives such as TNT or ammonal, gunpowder is in fact a *low* explosive; these terms are often used incorrectly by laymen, but have precise meanings. The chemical property of all explosives is

*continued on page 14*

*Reconstruction of an English cavalry trooper of the 1640s-50s, holding an "English lock" flintlock pistol of the type which became popular during the English Civil Wars. Its overall length is 23.5ins (596mm), its barrel length 15ins (381mm), and its weight 2lbs 10oz (1.2kg).*

The pistol copies the form of the earlier wheel lock in having a rounded lockplate, even though this was no longer necessary to accomodate the wheel lock's internal spring. Unlike the less practical snaphaunce, which had the striking steel mounted on a separate swivelling arm ahead of the pan, the English lock has a spring-loaded steel and pan cover ("frizzen") made in one piece.

The trooper did not carry the musketeer's bandoleer of powder bottles, so relied on either a flask or pre-prepared paper cartridges. Here he fills the priming pan from his flask, which has a spring cut-off in the nozzle; then he snaps the cover closed, to retain and protect the priming while loading continues. The flint in the jaws of the cock is wrapped in a strip of leather to give a secure grip.

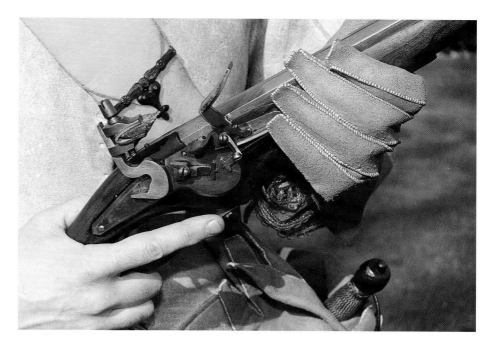

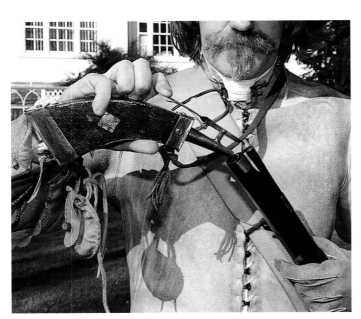

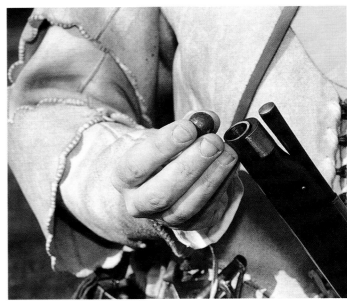

*The trooper pours the main charge into the muzzle; we used a charge of 40 grains. This early flask has no measuring capability, so 17th century soldiers would have relied upon an experienced eye to get the charge more or less consistent.*

*Dropping the large ball into the barrel, he rams it firmly down. This ball was an extremely good fit in the .62in (15.7mm) bore and did not require wadding, although usually this would be necessary to prevent loss or movement of the bullet when the loaded pistol was stowed in a saddle holster.*

that on ignition they rapidly create gas under pressure; high explosive gases blow apart from each other so quickly that they force any surrounding material to give way, hence the fact that artillery shells explode into fragments. Low explosive creates gas more slowly, and it always takes the line of least resistance, which makes it excellent for propelling a projectile down a barrel.

The recoil is also far more gradual and softer than with modern firearms using cordite or nitrocellulose-loaded cartridges, making shooting a comparatively large calibre such as a .75 inch musket quite feasible. Attempting to shoot a bullet of this calibre using modern smokeless powders would result in a visit to an osteopath, as the recoil would be punishing in the extreme. Having recently fired a modern .55 inch anti-tank rifle, I can assure readers that a day on the range with a Brown Bess is a far more pleasant experience.

The composition of powder has altered somewhat from its early form, and is now generally mixed to a ratio of 75% saltpetre, 15% charcoal and 10% sulphur. The charcoal and sulphur mixture is quite harmless until saltpetre is added, for its chemical property produces oxygen when it is heated, which fuels the other two elements. In its original form black powder was produced as cakes and ground down by mortar and pestle into grains of very fine powder. This fineness caused it to form a compact mass in the barrel; consequently it burned quite slowly when ignited, giving lower bullet velocities.

This form of powder was usually known as "meal" or "serpentine". As an experiment to see just how efficient it was we mixed sulphur, hazelwood charcoal and saltpetre into a fine powder and set it alight. Instead of the near-instantaneous flash, blast of heat and grey mushroom cloud of smoke that one gets from modern powder, the meal fizzed, and burned very slowly in a quite controlled manner - so slowly, in fact, that it appeared unlikely to be able to persuade any projectile to leave a barrel, as the pressure build-up appeared to be too gradual. Such powder undoubtedly worked; but - allowing for our lack of expertise in manufacturing - the experiment does suggest why such large charges were used in early guns, generating so much powder smoke. A large charge was simply the only method of providing sufficient energy to launch a projectile with any effectiveness.

The most important change in the manufacture of gunpowder was not to come about until the late 1550s, when the process of "corning" or "granulating" was introduced. This involved mixing sulphur, saltpetre and charcoal in a wet paste, and drying it into a hard cake of gunpowder which was then forced through a sieve. This produced larger grains of powder than the fine mix previously used, which when loaded into a barrel did not form a solid mass but was separated by tiny air gaps between the individual grains. This gave faster ignition and more powerful chamber pressures, increasing range, velocity and accuracy.

Selection and care of powder was vital to ensure that ones firearm would function properly when needed, and much advice was given on the matter. One of the most descriptive passages comes from a translated treatise by a German author called Kabel, published in 1619 and confusingly titled *Military Fireworks*. The author advises:

*"For a souldier must ever buy his pouther [powder] sharpe in taste, well incorporate with satlpetre, and not full of coal-dust [charcoal]. Let him accustome to drie his pouther, if he can, in the sunne, just sprinkling it over with aqua vitæ or strong claret wine. Let him make his titch [touch] powder, being finely sersed and sifted, with quick-pale, which is to be bought at the powder-maker's or apothacarie's ... This preparation will at first touch give fire, and procure a violent, speedy and thundering discharge. Some use brimstone, finely powdered, in their touch powder, but that furs and stops up your breech and tutchole."*

Modern production methods give us uniform mixtures of component chemicals, and a choice of varying grain sizes. These are classed from very coarse - referred to as "Fg" - as used in cannon, through medium FFFg for use in small calibre muskets, to FFFFg, a very fine powder whose texture makes it ideal for priming but not for use as a main charge. The size of grains affects the rate of combustion and breech pressure, which in older guns was of some importance, as breech explosions are not a recommended experience.

The guns fired during the research for this book were all of comparatively large bore, and were loaded with either coarse or medium powder. All measurements have been given in grains, partly because this is more precise than drams, but also for practical reasons: most dispensing flasks and measures these days are made in Italy or America, where drams are not used as a unit of measurement. When loading we always erred on the side of caution as regards charge sizes, particularly for original firearms. For those readers who are interested a conversion chart will be found at the end of the text.

It is interesting to speculate how early hand-gunners determined the correct charges for their weapons other than by a sometimes lethal process of trial and error. A rule-of-thumb method which was still in use in the percussion era was to take a musket ball in the palm of the hand, and pour powder over it until the ball was totally covered by a pyramid of powder. This was regarded as a reasonable starting point for determining the size of charge. The effectiveness of this would rather depend on the efficiency of the powder, but as a rough guide it seems to have had some validity.

There is little doubt that the unaccustomed, shattering report of gunpowder and clouds of dense smoke on the 14th century battlefield must have had a profound moral effect on the soldiers, to say nothing of their horses. It is not surprising that the production of gunpowder was referred to as the Black Art, and was likened to alchemy. What is perhaps more surprising is that such an unsuitable chemical substance should have survived to the present day as a popular propellant for firearms.

*Although this lock was smooth to operate it took two hands to bring the cock back to the fully cocked position.*

*The trigger is pulled; the cock strikes the flint against the steel, simultaneously knocking it forward and releasing a shower of sparks into the priming powder, which flares through the touch hole, setting off the main charge in the barrel.*

# THE HAND GUN

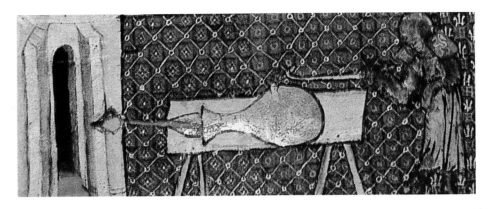

One of the earliest illustrations of a gun, from the Milemete Manuscript of 1326. It is being fired from a table top, apparently without any means of restricting its recoil, and the projectile is an arrow. (MS 92, The Governing Body of Christ Church, Oxford)

The cast bronze Loshult gun, pre 1400 - probably the earliest known example of a hand gun, it is very similar in type to that shown in the Milemete Manuscript, though only 11.75ins (298mm) in length. It may originally have been attached to a step cut into the end of a simple wooden pole, to help absorb recoil. (Courtesy The National Historical Museum, Stockholm)

There is little doubt that, in one form or another, the firearm was in military use in Europe by the first decade of the 14th century. However, no real proof has been found to establish this prior to a mention in documents surviving in Florence dated 1326, when the Council of Florence appointed two officials responsible for the manufacture and supply of "metal cannon and iron projectiles". The reference to projectiles is not specific, and may refer either to bullets or arrows. Later the same year there is another reference to payment being made for cannon, iron balls and gunpowder. (At this time all mechanical engines of war such as catapults, mangonels and trebuchets were referred to by contemporary chroniclers as "artillery", and the historian must be particularly careful to establish the exact meaning of primary sources.)

An illustration of the type of gun to which the Florentine papers refer appeared in a manuscript dated 1327 produced by Walter de Milemete. It was one in a series of instructions produced for Edward III, and shows a mail-clad soldier firing what appears to be an elongated vase which rests on a wooden table. Exactly how accurately this represents the original is open to debate, but it is generally accepted to be at the very least a reasonably accurate artist's impression based on first hand descriptions, particularly as other illustrations by the same author show a similar, larger gun. The shape would indicate that these guns were swollen at the base or breech end to strengthen them, enabling them to withstand the high pressures created during ignition, and this certainly indicates a reasonably sophisticated understanding of the mechanics of firearms construction. Despite their shape the internal bore of these guns would have been cylindrical, in the same manner as modern firearms.

Finding evidence for use of the gun in England in the first half of the 14th century is not so easy. There is an account dated 1333 from the Privy Wardrobe - which was the royal arsenal for the English crown in the latter half of the century - recording the purchase of sulphur and saltpetre for the purpose of manufacturing gunpowder. A more important reference appears in 1345 which specifically lists a number of guns, and refers to repairs of *"gunnis cum saggitis et pellotis"* (guns with arrows and pellets). The interesting mention of repairs indicates that this was not a new weapon.

From this date the frequency of references to guns and accessories increases dramatically. Records survive dating from 1346 which detail items stored at the Tower of London. These include very large quantities of lead ingots, lead shot and, in one instance, 912lbs of saltpetre and 886lbs of sulphur - sufficient raw material to manufacture a considerable quantity of powder.

Actual descriptions of the guns themselves are tantalisingly inconclusive. Some are described as having "tillers", most probably a simple form of gun stock along the same lines as a crossbow; and some of the materials used in construction are also mentioned. One is "cupro", which translates literally as copper but could equally have been either brass or bronze. Iron is also recorded, and accessories include such items as brass moulds, iron ladles and metal ramrods. There is no clear indication as to what size of gun is referred to.

The first documented use of the term "handgone" in England is dated 1338, in a list of stores kept on a vessel of Edward III's fleet. This includes mention of *"iii canons de fer ove v chambre"*, and *"un handgone"* (three cannons of iron with five chambers, and a hand gun). This presumably refers to a very early form of breech-loading gun as well as to a smaller portable type, and is one of the earliest existing indications of a clear division between large guns served by a crew and smaller pieces designed to be fired by an individual.

The earliest surviving example of a handgun is from Loshult in Sweden and dates from c.1350-1400. It is flask-shaped, of bronze alloy, and bears a strong similarity to that illustrated by Milemete. Barely 11.75ins (298mm) long, it has a comparatively large bore of 1.4ins, and at its breech end a touch hole is drilled. Clearly it would be almost impossible to hold, aim and fire such a weapon, but some clue as to how it may have been used can be gleaned from other rare surviving examples. These, in collections around Europe (and specifically from Germany), show a broadly similar style, which in its simplest form was no more than a cast bronze or iron barrel of between one and three feet in length, attached to a thick wooden pole or stock. The stock has a channel cut into it to take the barrel, and a step behind it against which the breech of the gun rested, the barrel being held firmly in place by one or more iron bands.

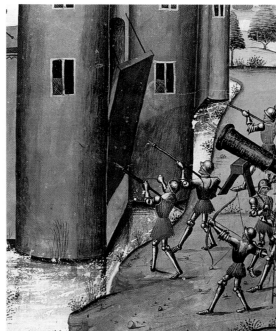

Reconstruction of an English hand-gunner of c.1460. The bronze barrel is fitted to a wooden stock or "tiller" closely resembling that of a crossbow. (Photograph Robert

A classical scene imagined in contemporary dress: a manuscript illustration of c.1468 showing Macedonian soldiers attacking a Persian fort armed with cannon and hand guns. The guns appear to be of the bronze or iron tube type, similar to the two shown below; they are fired with hand-held match while the pole stock is held under the right armpit and the weight is supported by the left hand. (Burney MS 169, by permission of the British Library)

Two examples of bronze hand guns, possibly of French origin, from the late 15th century. The upper gun has a side-mounted touch hole and pan, the lower example a pan centrally mounted on top of the breech. The touch holes of these early guns could be extremely large, some examples measuring .35in (8.8mm) across. (XII.959/960; A2862; The Board of Trustees of the Royal Armouries)

Barrels for these very early guns reveal several different methods of manufacture. The most common, if they were brass or bronze, was to cast the gun in one piece. If they were made of iron then forging or building-up was preferred. Building-up was a process similar to that of making a wine barrel, but instead of using wooden staves lengths of iron were held tightly together to form the barrel, with steel hoops forged around it to provide reinforcement. Towards the latter part of the 15th century a new method of manufacture evolved; the barrel was made as a hollow tube, with a separately made breech plug screwed into one end. This made for an extremely strong barrel assembly, and was particularly well suited to iron barrels, as a result of which the use of bronze or brass gradually declined.

There are very few specific references to the early use of handguns, or even the forms of projectiles used. The Letter-books of the City of London dated somewhere between 1337 and 1352 show that there were in the chamber of the Guildhall *"six instruments of latten [brass], galled gonnes"* with five *"tillers"* for the same, as well as four hundredweight of lead pellets and 32lbs of powder. The description of lead pellets would indicate that these were a form of hand gun rather than cannon, and it is quite likely that they were of the type illustrated in the Burney manuscript (above right).

\* \* \*

For these early guns the use of spherical lead bullets was no guarantee of accuracy, since the

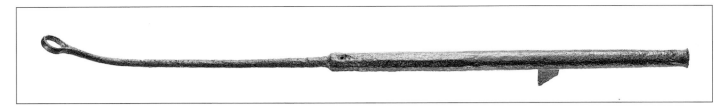

One of the earliest known illustrations of a matchlock gun, from a manuscript dated 1411; it shows the simplest form of matchlock, with a very early stock. Although uncomfortable to shoot, it was a considerable improvement over earlier types. (Codex Vindobana 3069; Austrian National Library, Vienna)

most fundamental problem associated with smoothbore firearms was that of windage. This is the term given to the escape of propellant gas past the bullet due to the poor fit between the bullet and the bore of the gun, and it was a major obstacle to achieving any reasonable accuracy with a smoothbore weapon. To use an exaggerated analogy, upon firing the bullet would bounce up the bore like a golf ball in a drainpipe and emerge from the muzzle at an extremely unpredictable angle. Within one hundred yards or so it would probably be anything from several inches to several feet out of line with its point of aim. Neither was that the only problem that the hand-gunner had to contend with, for there were other forces at work on the bullet.

When fired, a projectile is subjected to the forward thrust of the explosion countered by the air resistance that it meets, which inevitably slows it down. There is also the downward pull of gravity, which gives the bullet its trajectory or flight path; because of gravitational pull this is always a gradual curve back towards the surface of the earth. The bullet itself also contributed to its own instability in flight; lead castings were never perfect and a bullet always had imperfections, making it heavier on one side or another. When fired this caused it to veer off line, an effect naturally compounded by windage.

Nobody now knows who first discovered that the effects of windage could be lessened by the use of a wad of paper or a patch of thin cloth, but this proved the best solution until the advent of the rifle in the 19th century made it unnecessary. Although there is no clear evidence from this early period the patch was probably lubricated with grease, which aided loading and also helped to keep the fouling residue soft, making it easier to clean out. The patch was wrapped around the bullet before it was rammed down into the barrel, ensuring a fairly tight fit between the ball and bore which acted as a crude but reasonably effective gas seal.

That Milemete should show an arrow being fired may seem at odds with the radical new concept of the firearm; but medieval habits of thought were basically conservative, and longbows and crossbows represented a familiar and reliable technology. Writings of the 14th century frequently refer to the manufacture of arrows for guns, and until well into the late Middle Ages they remained in common use alongside ball projectiles. These arrows were similar in shape and size to crossbow bolts, made with oak shafts, iron heads, and - since the heat of discharge obviously made feather, parchment or leather impractical - fletchings of brass or possibly iron. Although two fletchings were normally used on crossbow bolts, three were fitted to shafts for use in guns to give added stability, and the arrow was provided with a simple gas seal in the shape of leather washers around the front of the shaft. These not only sealed the chamber but also supported the arrow so that it was central to the bore when fired (otherwise it was as likely to embed itself in the ground or climb towards the heavens as to threaten the enemy). Several contemporary illustrations show a type of fire arrow being shot from crossbows, so this crossover of technology to arrows being fired from guns was not as outlandish as it may appear to us.

Of course, the best solution to the problem of windage would have been to ensure that the lead balls were a perfect fit for the bore of the gun, but this was impractical because of the speed with which black powder fouled a barrel: after a few shots it would no longer have been possible to ram a tight-fitting bullet down the bore. The science of bullet manufacture was also in its infancy, and perfect size could never be guaranteed. The bullet therefore had to be undersized simply to ensure that it could be rammed home. Partially solved with the advent of breech-loading weapons, the problem was not entirely eradicated until the introduction of the metallic cartridge.

There are few accounts of the effectiveness of these early weapons, and one of the rare examples, unfortunately anonymous, is from *The Chronicles of England, Part II*. It describes the death of one of the more notable English casualties at the siege of Orléans in June 1428: *"As [the Earl of Salisbury] was inspecting his dispositions with a view to attack, a wicked rascal inside the town fired a gun, and a ball struck the Earl a fatal blow."*

While undoubtedly a lucky shot, this does indicate that the gun, at least in defence and presumably fired from a steady rest, was already considered a serious anti-personnel weapon. Another account, by William Gregory, of their use by Burgundian mercenaries at the Second Battle of St Albans in 1461, also has a respectful tone: *"They had handguns which could shoot both pellets of lead and arrows of an ell [about 45ins] in length with six feathers, three in the midst and three at the end, with a mighty peece of iron at the head, and would fire withal."*

In fact the use of firearms was much more widespread in the early 15th century than many people realise. The Council of Frankfurt am Main had decreed as early as 1431 that all citizens capable of bearing arms should have a gun, which would number over 2,000 individuals. Within 20 years they had further ordered that the campaign wagons accompanying the army should each carry, as standard equipment, two hand guns and a breech-loading gun (probably a small cannon). As there were in the region of 1,000 wagons in the army this added up to a considerable quantity of firearms.

In a little-known work excitingly entitled *A History of the Arrival in England of Edward IV*, another anonymous chronicler relates how the subtle art of gunnery had not yet been entirely mastered during the Wars of the Roses. In April 1471 Edward IV and his army had encamped while pursuing the Earl of Warwick's men: *"The Earl of Warwick had many more [guns] than the King, and so the Earl's army shot guns almost all night, thinking to do great damage to the King and his host. But, thanks be to God, it so happened that they always overshot the King's army and did them no harm, because the King's army lay much nearer than they thought."*

During the 14th century three distinct types of handguns had appeared, all of roughly similar form. These comprised a cast bronze or brass barrel strapped onto a wooden stock; a wrought iron barrel with an integral metal "tail" (both types of which we test fired); and a short, rather massive, vase-shaped barrel of the so-called Loshult pattern with a wooden stock fitted to it. None would have been particularly comfortable to hold and fire; most illustrations show these early guns being fired from the waist, which our tests actually found to be the most practical way of using such weapons.

There was no attempt at standardisation of bore sizes, which vary from about .5in (12mm) to 1.5ins (36mm). These sizes were doubtless based on the practical maximum that a man could comfortably carry and shoot. The wooden stock was clearly of limited use in controlling the recoil, and it was probably not until the mid-15th century that a short spur appeared beneath the barrel, permitting the gun to be rested over a parapet or palisade which would absorb some of the recoil of firing. More importantly, it also enabled the shooter to attempt to aim, although probably to little avail.

Igniting the weapon was at best an awkward procedure, using either a heated wire or a piece of matchcord being thrust into a touch hole - sometimes surrounded by a shallow saucer-shaped depression for priming powder - in the top surface of the barrel; this left the firer balancing the gun precariously with one hand and arm at the moment of detonation. The use of a wire was clearly impractical unless the gunner was in a fixed defensive position with access to a heat source such as a brazier, so a piece of burning cord became the more usual means of igniting the primer. The gradual adoption of a short wooden stock led to another method of firing. One or two contemporary manuscripts illustrate hand-gunners with the stock balanced on top of the shoulder rather than being held in to the side of the waist, which is quite sensible in view of the shape of these early stocks.

One of the most important improvements came about during the first decade of the 15th century (the earliest known illustration is dated to 1411) when a simple S- or Z-shaped lever, called a "serpentine" from its snake-like shape, was attached to the side of the stock on a central pivot. A small pair of screw-clamped jaws at the top of the lever held a length of the smouldering matchcord; when the lower end of the lever was squeezed upwards with the fingers the top end pivotted down, allowing the match to descend onto powder in a priming pan incorporating a touch hole through the top or side of the barrel. It was a simple and effective solution to the problem of ignition, enabling the gunner to hold his weapon with both hands, point it in the rough direction of the enemy, and fire with just the pressure of his fingers. Unfortunately no complete original examples of this early form of matchlock are known to survive.

Having developed the very earliest form of matchlock, technology raced ahead with almost indecent speed, taking the hand gun out of the realms of the simple tube loaded with ball and powder. The term "hand gun" had gradually come into more common use by the mid-15th century, but writers of the period relied on phonetic spelling. Allied to a very loose grasp of technical terminology, this caused immense confusion among later generations of firearms historians. Mention can be found of *gonnes, gunnes* (in many different spellings), *cannon, bombardes, sclopus* and *hackbuts*, each of which may refer to any size of weapon. The last term is a corruption of the German *Hackenbüchse* or hook gun, which referred to the style of early gun fitted with a wall hook to reduce recoil, although writers did not always bother to differentiate between those with and without this attachment. The French also borrowed the word, turning it into the far more elegant *harquebus*, which was subsequently borrowed back by the English in the 16th century as *arquebus*, neither having any reference to the original German meaning.

As with many of the types of firearms mentioned throughout this book, there were considerable periods of overlap when two, three or more types could be found in simultaneous use around Europe. There was never a clearly defined point at which one form of firearm supplanted another, and the earliest types of hand guns were to remain in use until nearly the end of the 15th century alongside the more sophisticated "first generation matchlocks". Gradually attention turned towards improving the new mechanism, and its technical development will be looked at in the next chapter. The longbow - the dominant projectile weapon from the early 14th to the end of the 15th century - had served England famously well; but proficiency with the bow required years of very demanding training. The appearance of practical hand guns from the late 15th century onwards signalled its death knell, although the bow was to remain an important military weapon into the 16th century. Despite the increasing use of the firearm for both war and sport there was considerable reluctance on the part of the government to accept the inevitability of technological progress. As late as 1513 Henry VIII made a proclamation praising the longbow and reaffirming the Statute of Winchester, which made it a legal requirement for men to own and practice with the longbow. Thirty years later the failure of the law to force Englishmen to continue with their longbow training and the momentum gained by the hand gun were acknowledged in another royal proclamation of 1544:

*"...some number of his subjects skilled and exercised in the feat of shooting in handguns and hagbusshes...gives licence and liberty to all and singular his majesty's subjects born within in his grace's dominions being of age of sixteen and upwards, that they and every of them*

*Detail from the Schilling Chronicles of c.1474, showing hand-gunners - top right, and in upper boat - firing with the stock held on top of the shoulder. They are represented as light skirmishing troops operating in the van of the Burgundian heavy armoured cavalry alongside crossbowmen. The ordinance of St Maximin de Trèves, a document of 1473 giving the exact company composition of Duke Charles the Bold's standing army, specifies one hundred each hand-gunners, crossbowmen and pikemen as the infantry of each 900-strong mixed company. (Die Grosser Burgundischer Chronik; MS A5, Zentral Bibliothek, Zurich)*

*An early matchlock gun, possibly German, of about 1500; the serpentine is missing. (XII.1787; A4/475; The Board of Trustees of the Royal Armouries)*

*Hand-gunners at the siege of Alesia, 1533; detail from a painting by Melchior Feselen. It is interesting to note that although they have fully stocked matchlocks of at least two different types, they are all firing from the waist. The central figure is applying a hand-held match to a gun almost identical in type to the early German gun illustrated on page 19. They have both powder horns and small round flasks for priming powder. (INV.686, Alte Pinakothek, Munich)*

*henceforth may lawfully shoot in handguns and hagbusshes without incurring forfeiture loss or damage for the same.”*

This concession was to a great extent due to the constant threat of war with France, and when peace eventually broke out in 1546 the proclamation was revoked. The royal government was clearly worried about the possible effects of letting the mass of subjects loose with lethal weapons which, unlike the bow, required no great skill to master. This situation would recur on more than one occasion in British history.

**Technical Specifications**
(*Note:* In this and the other panels throughout this book, data quoted refer to the actual weapons fired during the course of tests rather than to a general type. The powder charge is that which was judged to have provided the optimum performance, rather than a possible maximum.)

**Iron medieval hand gun:**

| | |
|---|---|
| **Overall length** | 35.25ins (895mm) |
| **Barrel length** | 11.75ins (298mm) |
| **Calibre** | .50in (12.7mm) |
| **Weight** | 6.8lbs (3.1kg) |
| **Charge** | 40 grains |
| **Ignition** | Matchcord |

**Bronze medieval hand gun:**

| | |
|---|---|
| **Overall length** | 47ins (1194mm) |
| **Barrel length** | 29ins (737mm) |
| **Calibre** | .50in (12.7mm) |
| **Weight** | 7lbs (3.1kg) |
| **Charge** | 80 grains |
| **Ignition** | Matchcord |

**Early matchlock hand gun:**

| | |
|---|---|
| **Overall length** | 60ins (1525mm) |
| **Barrel length** | 38ins (965mm) |
| **Calibre** | .61in (15.5mm) |
| **Weight** | 24lbs (11kg) |
| **Charge** | 65 grains |
| **Ignition** | Matchcord |

**Firing the hand gun**

We were fortunate to be able to obtain three different types of replica handguns for testing. The earliest is a forged iron copy of a gun known to have been widely used around 1450. The other two are of a slightly later period, one being a bronze hackbut of the late 15th century, of a type illustrated in the Schilling Chronicles. The last was a simple matchlock pattern of a type widely used by e.g. Burgundian troops at the end of the 15th century and beyond. It is this type that is primarily found in illustrations of the period, and which was to survive in a modified form well into the 17th century.

As the numbers of available shooting replicas are very small, the chance to compare these types was not to be missed. It was not possible to gather all three together on the same day, so the shooting was spread across a period of time. As there was no reliable contemporary data available to guide us in judging the initial charges, loading these guns was clearly going to be a series of exercises in trial and error. As with many modern replicas, the guns used were generally better made than the originals. Most importantly, they had accurately bored straight barrels - original examples are quite crudely bored, and must have produced an interesting flight path for their projectiles.

It is possible with all smooth bored weapons to load a loose or "rolling" ball, and this may well have been the method used for these early guns. This means that once the powder charge has been poured in, a loose ball with no patch was dropped in on top, and the butt of the gun rapped smartly on the ground two or three times to ensure that it was firmly seated. This is not now regarded as a safe practice; as the bore becomes fouled there is a strong chance that the ball will not rest firmly on the powder, allowing an air gap between the two. This often results in a breech explosion, which can have the most serious consequences when it occurs six inches from your face and eyes; so for safety we always used a ramrod.

As accuracy was never going to be a strong point of the short **iron gun** we were more interested to see how effective it would be when fired against steel plate, mainly to determine its ability to penetrate armour.

With a charge of 50 grains of coarse powder poured into the barrel, and a close-fitting ball rammed down, it was held horizontally at the waist while a small measure of priming powder was poured into the pan. The limitation of this type of weapon become immediately apparent when the stiff breeze immediately blew most of the priming powder away. Reprimed, and with the metal stock held tightly into the waist, the second shortcoming of the hand gun became clear: the entire weight has to be borne on one arm, as the left hand tried vainly to locate the touch hole. This was not too uncomfortable with this small iron gun, but would have been much more so with a larger, heavier weapon.

It also proved impossible to prevent ones eye from moving away from the target and looking down to the priming pan to see what the left hand was doing with the match. Eventually the slow match was successfully applied, and the resultant smoke and flame were nothing if not spectacular, although the recoil was almost negligible. The main problem with the waist-held guns was simply trying to ensure that the target was hit at all, so a "spotter" was employed to peer downrange from behind the shooter and direct his aim.

Three sheets of 2mm steel plate were bolted together with about one inch between them, and an aiming mark put in the centre of the top sheet; they were then placed at the 30 yard point on the range. The .50 calibre iron gun was fired, but the bullet was unable to penetrate the first plate, flattening out completely against it. A second shot merely duplicated the first, and it was felt that even increasing the charge significantly was unlikely to achieve very much. The muzzle velocity was a low 547fps, due mainly to its relatively short barrel length of 11.75 inches (298mm). As range time was limited it was decided to do more thorough tests with the later arquebus, which are covered in the following chapter.

The bigger **bronze gun** also had a bore of .50in and the working charge was a more potent 80 grains. Its barrel was fitted into an ash stock and reinforced with forged iron bands. A cast lead ball was loaded and rammed home, then the vent hole on the right of the breech was filled with priming powder.

The recoil was not unpleasant, although the firer certainly knew that a large piece of

*The reproduction wrought-iron hand gun which proved so ineffective in penetration tests. Its small, open touch hole was vulnerable to wind and rain, and on later guns it was moved to a more protected area on the right of the breech. Iron extensions beneath the barrel were supposedly to absorb recoil when hooked over the forward edge of a parapet, but in practice a gun of this size did not appear to need it.*

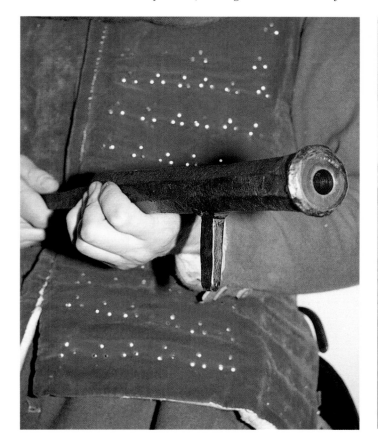

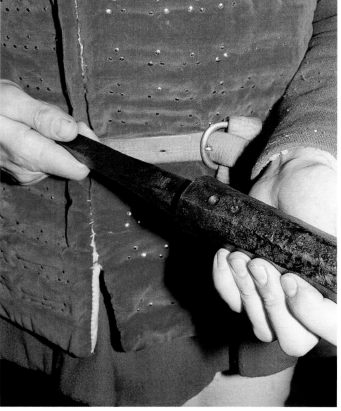

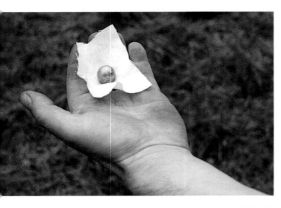

*The English hand-gunner of the Wars of the Roses rams and primes his bronze tiller-mounted weapon. For tests this replica was loaded with a patched ball. (Photographs Robert Hoare)*

lead had just left the barrel. Anyone who has fired a gun from the hip will know that it takes considerable practice to achieve any sort of accuracy, even with a relatively sophisticated rifled weapon like a modern sub-machine gun. The surprising thing was that the 25 metre target was actually hit, albeit only twice in ten shots. As with any firearm, practice brings improved accuracy; it is a moot point what time and resources late medieval soldiers would normally have enjoyed to test their hand guns, although there is documentary evidence for systematic weapons training in the best 15th century forces such as the Burgundian ducal army.

The **matchlock** we tested was slightly more civilised to use, with a similar loading procedure to the other hand guns. The simple trigger mechanism and wooden stock made it possible to bring the weapon up to the shoulder, which certainly made it more practical than the bronze gun; and it did permit some form of aim to be made, although this was not easy bearing in mind its weight (24lbs, 11kg - in World War II terms, considerably more than a BAR and not much less than a Bren gun).

The main task for the shooter in this case was to ensure that his match was exactly the correct length to reach the pan. This was something of an art, although it became quite easy to judge by eye with a little practice. Lowering it into the priming mixture, some 4ins from the eye, initially takes a slight effort of will, as the flare on ignition is considerable. There was a slight hangfire after the trigger was pulled - the fractional delay between the serpentine descending into the pan and the glowing end of the match igniting the priming charge. It was particularly noticeable on the matchlock, partly due to the distance covered by the match before it reached the pan, and partly because the glowing match end did not always manage to ignite the powder.

Most people miss the spectacular blast of flame and smoke as, like me, they have their eyes firmly shut - the instantaneous and natural reaction to an explosion in front of the face. The recoil proved moderate and nowhere near as bad as expected, the weight of the gun almost completely absorbing the force of the .60 calibre ball. Clearly, visions of bystanders having to dig the shooter out of the shrubbery behind the firing line were unfounded. Once familiar with the loading procedure it was possible to fire three shots per minute, although two were a far more comfortable rate.

When the choking smoke from the discharge had cleared the target was examined for a hit, but the whereabouts of the ball was anybody's guess. At 25 yards it missed the three-foot square target completely, and although it presumably struck the butt somewhere no one saw it. Increasing the charge from 60 to 80 grains and closing to 20 yards improved the accuracy somewhat; in ten shots the ball struck the target eight times, but in fairly random grouping. No discernible accuracy was achieved until shots were made at 15 yards, when some pattern began to emerge. Ten further balls were fired at 10 yards - about the same distance that one would use for a smoothbore pistol - and a ragged group of hits were recorded.

Purely out of a spirit of historical investigation, a small handful of spherical pebbles were

placed in a small muslin bag and rammed down. The effect was quite spectacular, the target being liberally peppered at 10 yards - at least the gun had some defensive capabilities. (This practice was still being used as late as the 1860s, and there are many references in American Civil War accounts to the use of "buck and ball" loads comprising a standard bullet and several smaller pellets.)

One interesting side effect was noticed: the tendency of the matchcord to shake itself out of the jaws of the serpentine upon firing, requiring fiddly and time-consuming replacement. In practice the gunner would presumably have held a sufficiently long piece of cord to be wrapped around his left hand, preventing it from dropping into mud or wet grass.

There were a couple of misfires when the glowing end of the match had cooled sufficiently to prevent it igniting the priming charge, and the old practice of blowing on the tip of the match before firing was obviously based on sound experience. Speed of ignition was unpredictable, varying between nothing happening at all to almost instantaneous. For the most part it was reasonably consistent, although one would not want to rely on it if ones life were at stake.

There was little doubt that the larger guns were capable of shooting out to a reasonable range, in excess of 200 yards, but there was little chance of hitting anything unless by extreme good luck. Practical considerations limited us to tests with spherical shot; I suspect that the additional stability of fletchings may well have given more accuracy with an arrow than with ball.

As to the efficiency of such weapons on the medieval battlefield, their primary impact must initially have been more psychological than tactical: the noise and smoke would have been terrifying to men and animals unused to such dramatic effects, as would the occasional strike of invisible projectiles apparently from out of nowhere.

Despite the practical limitations, however, it is simply not credible that 15th century professional soldiers would have thrown their lives away by going into battle carrying ineffective weapons, however novel. In terms of firepower a hand-gunner could easily be beaten on range, accuracy and rate of fire by a skilled archer, who on average could put six arrows into the air in the time it took to load and fire one shot. Comparisons of penetration of different defensive armours at different ranges by arrows, bolts and early bullets are a much more complex question, and it would be foolish to generalise. Nevertheless, the gun's effectiveness at battle ranges against massed foot and horse clearly made it a worthwhile addition to the inventory of a mixed-arms force. The severely practical Burgundians and Swiss did not hesitate to mix hand-gunners with the well-established crossbowmen in their light manoeuvre units well before 1500; indeed, the surviving flag of a late 15th century Bernese company bears a painted hand gun. While it clearly left much to be desired, there were already those who believed that it had a bright future.

*The shape of the stock and the need to hold the gun one-handed while applying hand-held match dictates a firing stance with the gun braced at the hip. Needless to say, aiming was a matter of luck when firing from this position, but accuracy did improve somewhat as the test progressed. Firing from the waist tends to force the shooter to take a step backwards as the whole body absorbs the recoil, rather than twisting from the shoulder as when shooting a longarm from a conventional stance. (Photographs Robert Hoare)*

**ABOVE** *A mercenary hand-gunner of c.1470 begins the long process of loading his "first generation" matchlock. He uses his powder horn to pour in a charge of coarse powder, measured by eye and experience - early flasks had no cut-off in the nozzle to isolate a predetermined charge. The simple swivel serpentine trigger bar and match holder can be seen clearly.*

**ABOVE RIGHT** *He reaches into his bullet bag for a lead ball, which he drops into the barrel. No wadding was used on this occasion.*

**RIGHT** *Ramming the ball home with his wooden ramrod. If speed were essential he would most likely have used a 'rolling ball' for the first few shots of an engagement - simply letting the ball drop into the barrel and seating it by banging the butt smartly on the ground. The gross fouling of the barrel would probably prevent this after half a dozen shots.*

Using a pricker to ensure the touch hole is clear of debris. This simple but vital tool was ideally made from a sharp piece of wire - brass, so as to avoid sparks.

The comparatively shallow priming recess is visible on top of the breech. Trying to fill it with fine powder in a high wind was a challenging experience.

Clamping the matchcord in the jaws of the serpentine; ensuring it is exactly the right length to drop into the priming takes practice. If there is a delay between this step and firing, the smouldering end of the match may accumulate ash which cools the tip and prevents it igniting the priming powder - but blowing on the tip to keep it glowing after it is clamped in place risks blowing the priming out of its open recess... This is modern matchcord, medieval cord being coarser in texture.

Ignition - the first flare of the priming is just visible against the tent in the background. The gunner would usually have the loose length of match wrapped around his left hand, because a frequent result of firing was having the match blown out of the jaws of the serpentine - as is happening in the second picture.

The alternative method of firing was simply to ignore the serpentine and hold the match to the priming powder. It seems likely that this was often done in the heat of battle.

# THE MATCHLOCK MUSKET

**A**lthough the matchlock had appeared in a primitive form by the mid-15th century, it was from the early years of the 16th that it began to develop into the arm that was to dominate the European battlefield until the start of the 18th century.

The simple serpentine lock was modified, probably around 1470, into two slightly more sophisticated forms. The first was the "snaplock", which made use of a spring action. A small stud or sear projected through the lockplate underneath the cock or upper half of the serpentine. Cocking the weapon caused this projecting button to catch in a recess in the tail of the cock, ensuring that the serpentine and its match were held away from the pan; only when pressure was applied on the trigger would the button be withdrawn, allowing the match to drop into the priming powder. The efficiency of this lock did depend on its spring being of exactly the right strength. If it were too powerful the match could descend into the pan so fast that it would knock all the priming powder out before it could ignite.

As systems go this was not exactly a quantum leap forwards, but it was the first relatively reliable safety mechanism. It must have been considered an effective enough weapon, for in 1544 Henry VIII ordered no less than 4,000 to be supplied to his army, and the remains of some of these snaplock muskets have been found on the wreck of the *Mary Rose*. However, it seems to have fallen out of use by the latter half of the 16th century.

The other, more durable form of matchlock to appear was the "searlock", which was to survive almost unmodified until the late 17th century. This relied on a simple system of levers which bore on a mainspring, all mounted inside an external lock plate. When the trigger was pulled it moved a swivelling lever, which in turn lowered the serpentine in a more or less controlled manner into the pan. As the 16th century progressed it became less common to find the serpentine simply screwed externally to the right side of the stock, and all the mechanisms soon became covered by a metal lock plate that was mounted flush with the wood. A smaller trigger enclosed by a guard gradually replaced the long lower arm, always vulnerable to damage and accident.

While the mechanical efficiency of the matchlock was improving, the same could not always be said of the ability of those equipped with them. In 1571 Sir Henry Radcliffe commented after a visit to view the Portsmouth Garrison that: *"The harquebusiers were as fare untrained and unredi, for not amonghtes three and twenty which were alowed serviceable, not fyve of them shotte within fyve foote of a marke being sette within foure score yardes of them."*

It would appear that accuracy was not a primary requirement amongst hand-gunners. Indeed, Montaigne wrote disparagingly of the gun in 1585 that as a weapon it was almost useless except for:*"... the shock caused by the report, to which one does not easily get accustomed."*

An often undervalued but centrally important feature of the matchlock was simply the match itself. The first hand guns were ignited, as we have seen, with a heated wire, but this limited their use to static positions with a constant means of reheating the wire. The ability of hand-gunners to manoeuvre offensively depended upon a reliable, portable method of ignition; and this came in the form of a length of loosely woven hemp cord which had been soaked in a solution of potassium nitrate and then dried to produce matchcord. The slow burning properties of this match proved ideal for hand-gunners, who could now carry a length that, once lit, would reliably smoulder for hours at a time.

Indeed, so vital was the match that gunners were solemnly warned in a treatise dated 1588 that they should never: *"...for any prayer or reward lend any piece of match to any other person, because it may be hurtful to him in time of service to lack the same."* Kabel, quoted earlier, also had something to say about preparing match: *"Let his match be boyled in ashes - lie and powder, that it may bothe burn well and carry a long coale, and that will not fall off with the touche of a finger."*

*Reconstruction: A musketeer of about 1600, his clothing and equipment typical of the English campaigns in Ireland but differing little from those of the English Civil War. His long-barrelled .76 calibre musket needs to be supported by a rest for anything approaching accuracy. (Photographs Jeffrey Mayton)*

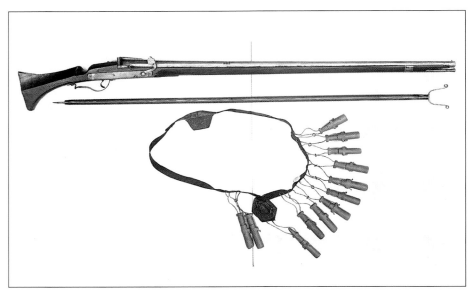

**ABOVE** *A 17th century illustration of a musketeer from the well-known series by De Gheyn. Some of the details are interesting: note the small priming flask by his right hand, his match lit at both ends, and a considerable quantity of spare match hanging on his belt.*

**ABOVE RIGHT** *Some idea of the size of this musket can be gauged from the rest and bandoleer. It weighs nearly 20lbs (8kg) and is 5ft (1.5m) long. (XII.5437; A4553/4; The Board of Trustees of the Royal Armouries)*

The match had a number of obvious drawbacks. The glow from a body of men all carrying lit matches was almost as visible at night as if they were carrying candles, and instantly betrayed their whereabouts. Once it had been placed in the jaws of the serpentine it had to be continually adjusted to the correct length as it burned down, or it would fail to reach the priming pan when the trigger was pulled. It was difficult to keep alight in bad weather, and musketeers quickly learned to keep both ends of their match smouldering - wasteful, and halving the time before it had to be replaced, but at least giving them a second chance of firing should one end be extinguished. Holding a long loop of match in the left hand while firing added the risk that falling sparks from the priming would set it alight in the middle, too. As much of the lifespan of any given piece of match was, by definition, wasted, huge amounts were required to equip an army; it was estimated that a garrison of 1,500 men would require 550lbs (250kg) of cord per day.

The carelessness of soldiers carrying lighted match was also something of a handicap when open barrels of gunpowder were lying around. One man at the battle of Edgehill in 1642 began filling his flasks from a barrel while forgetfully holding a lit match between his fingers, resulting in an impressive explosion and several deaths; such mishaps were frequent and sometimes catastrophic, involving large powder stores in wagons and buildings.

It was not only carelessness with explosives that caused problems. Some soldiers were woefully lacking in training, and were arguably more dangerous to their own side than the enemy - as Lieutenant Elias Archer graphically recounted of the Westminster Trained Band at the siege of Basing House in 1643:

*"Whether the fault were in their cheife Leader, at the present either through want of courage or discretion I know not, but their Front [rank] fired before it was possible they could doe any execution, and for want of intervals to turn away speedily the second and third wranks fired upon them, and so consequently the Reare fired upon their owne Front, and slew or wounded many of their owne men...it was told me by a Captain in that Regement, that they had seventy or eighty men slaine or hurt in that disorder."*

\*　　　\*　　　\*

Apart from mechanical improvements, the shape of the stock also began to evolve in ways which benefitted the musketeer. It had long been realised that being able to raise a gun to eye level dramatically improved the chances of hitting the target. Gradually, distinct Spanish and French styles of stock appeared in the early 16th century. The former was quite straight but with a slight curve into the butt which widened into a distinctive fish-tail shape. The latter was more sharply curved and splayed out at the end; to fire it the gunner held it close to the chest rather that to the shoulder, thus giving it its name of *petronel* - a corruption into English from the French *poitrine* or chest. While neither was exactly ergonomic, each was a clear improvement on the medieval wooden pole. That the Spanish pattern was preferred is indicated in the following passage from Sir Roger Williams's *Brief Discourse on Warre* published in 1590:

*"For the recoyling, there is no hurt if they be streight stocked after the Spanish manner; were they stocked crooked, after the French manner, to be discharged on the breaste, fewe or none could abide their recoyling; but being discharged from the shoulder, in the Spanish manner, there is neither danger nor hurte."*

Another minor but important improvement in the early 16th century was the movement of the touch hole from the top to the right hand side of the breech, where it was contained in a small concave pan. This meant that the amount of priming powder used could be increased, which was an important factor in promoting reliable ignition, and the priming had some protection from rough handling. A logical further improvement was the addition of a small metal pan cover attached by a screw next to the pan, which could be swivelled across to protect the vulnerable priming powder and touch hole from wind and rain (and also, to some degree, allowed the weapon to be carried both loaded and primed for almost instant use).

The importance of the weather throughout the long age of black powder firearms cannot be overemphasised. The vagaries of the climate could be a major factor in determining the outcome of a battle, and few commanders would knowingly risk an engagement in the face of heavy rain. A sudden downpour could render match and powder useless, and gunners became

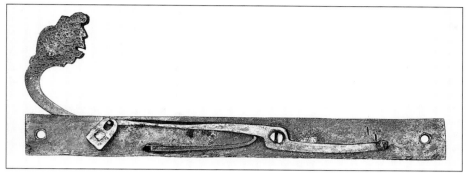

adept at coiling and packing their matches into hats, inner pockets or waterproof bags, in much the same way as their predecessors had learned to protect their longbow strings. They were then faced with the problem of relighting their match afterwards, which was not simple in the days of flint-and-steel tinderboxes and candle lanterns. Despite the amount of time and energy devoted to trying to perfect a system of ignition that was impervious to weather, no solution was forthcoming until the invention of the wheel lock in the early 16th century, and no half-way practical answer for the equipment of whole armies for nearly a century more.

Manufacturing skills for the new weapons were gradually refined during the 16th century, as more craftsmen turned away from combining blacksmithing and gunmaking to specialise solely in the art of making firearms. An important factor often overlooked in assessing the effectiveness of these early weapons was the physical difficulty of boring a barrel. All were hand-bored, and the ability to produce an accurate and true bore rested entirely with the skill of the individual gunsmith. Since levels of ability naturally varied, many of the barrels produced (especially, we may guess, once large government contracts began to be placed) were not straight, which obviously had a dramatic effect on accuracy - as anyone will know who has fired a carefully bent fairground rifle.

The simply forged or cast hollow tube did become more sophisticated, however, as barrels began to be tapered from the breech towards the muzzle. This kept the weight as light as possible while retaining the greater strength required at the breech - the point of the detonation. Gunmakers also began to add a tang attached to the rear of the breech plug - a flat metal bar with a hole in it, enabling the barrel to be secured to the stock by means of a screw. Lugs were also brazed beneath the barrel, and a hole drilled through lug and stock into which pins were tapped, snugly securing the barrel to the woodwork. This did make the barrel difficult to remove without tools, and if the pins were lost the gun was effectively rendered useless. By the late 17th century the use of metal bands which clamped the stock to the barrel was becoming more common in Europe; however, in Britain pins continued to be used almost exclusively on military weapons until the mid-19th century.

*       *       *

Anyone who has read contemporary accounts of warfare in the 16th or 17th centuries will have been left reeling by the number of terms employed for the different types of matchlock in use. These can be divided into types. The larger bore *musket*, often weighing over 20lbs (9kg), was primarily for infantry use; it seems to have been in widespread use by around 1540, and to have been adopted by all the major European powers by 1580. The English model was generally fitted with a 48in (1219mm) barrel and had a bore of between .75in and .80 inch. It was too heavy to be fired comfortably from the shoulder, so a forked rest was carried upon which the barrel was placed. This had the added advantage of steadying the gun to enable some degree of aim to be taken, although results depended entirely upon the level of skill of the shooter, as Humfrey Barwick commented:

*"...in the handes of a skilful souldier, well practiced and trained in the use thereof, [it is] a most terrible and deadly weapon but in the hands of an ignorant person... it is rather hurtfull than commodious."*

Then there was the bastard musket or caliver, which was to all appearances a scaled-down musket with a barrel of about 44ins, firing a reduced calibre ball of .70in; this became a much-used term, however, often referring to all forms of musket.

Alongside this were the *arquebus, harquebus, hagbut* or *hackbut*, which were one and the same, the names all being corruptions of the German *Hackenbüsche*. This was smaller and lighter yet, having a 30in (762mm) barrel, although generally using the same calibre ball as the caliver. It became the most popular weapon for use by cavalry, and by the early 17th century the term was used mainly for a heavy carbine.

The term carbine was actually derived from the *carabins*, mounted *harquebusiers* used in some numbers on the Continent from the late 16th century. In England it became a generic term for any gun that used a shorter barrel and fired a bullet of smaller size than the standard musket. The cavalry also had *petronels*, which were of a very similar size and weight to the arquebus but used a reduced calibre bullet of about .58 inch. If the reader thinks this

*The characteristic lines of a matchlock musket with the "fish-tailed' stock of Spanish origin. The .76in calibre barrel is 48in long, and would have required a forked rest. The simple mechanism is shown in the internal view of the lockplate and the few moving parts. The trigger works against the protruding stud on the far right of the actuating arm. The only resistance preventing the serpentine from dropping straight into the priming pan is provided by the thin spring in the centre of the lockplate. (XII.1638; A11/145, A14/188; The Board of Trustees of the Royal Armouries)*

is confusing, then perhaps it makes it easier to understand why supplying an army of this period with weapons and ball was such a logistical nightmare.

\*     \*     \*

One of the great traditions of warfare, that of individually acquired skill at arms, began to die with the introduction of the matchlock. The English longbowmen of the 14th and 15th centuries had shaken the domination of the highly skilled, expensively armoured mounted knight, but had not made him obsolete. Tactics had been adapted to exploit the different strengths of relatively small mixed armies of aristocratic horse and professional foot, assembled for a few months at a time. Though 15th and early 16th century battles were often won by the new blocks of disciplined pikemen around which longbowmen, crossbowmen and later hand-gunners manoeuvred and shot, the heavy cavalry still kept an important place in these balanced forces.

As practical man-carried firearms began to spread, however, the roles of both the armoured horseman and the skilled specialist foot soldier were called into serious question. The 16th century was the age of the revival of the Classical military manuals, and the adaption for contemporary weapons of their tactics for manoeuvring massed infantry. The nation state and its centralised government would soon invent the long-service standing army. The yeoman archer, his muscles sculpted to his weapon over half a lifetime's training, was too unpredictable a resource for this new world. Nations would soon be putting conscripted or hired infantry into the field without any weapon skills other than having been shown how to load, point and fire a musket.

The inherent inaccuracy of even the best musket dictated tactics; individually aimed precision fire was simply not achievable, and for 250 years armies would rely upon the effect of closely massed formations firing at other closely massed formations at short range. The long years of practice necessary to fit a man for fighting effectively with bow or sword rapidly became redundant. A scrawny 18-year-old, taught for a few weeks how to handle a musket and to obey commands at the same moment as a thousand other young men, could topple a lavishly equipped, patiently trained, and high-born swordsman out of his saddle at fifty paces - and probably without even seeing him.

*A close-up of the touch hole and pan of an English musket of about 1640. The pan is quite large and deep, to hold sufficient powder to guarantee reliable ignition. The swivelling pan cover was very vulnerable to damage. (XII.86)*

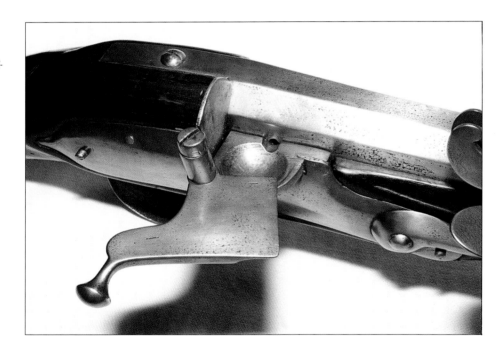

**Technical Specifications**

**Henrician arquebus:**

| | |
|---|---|
| **Overall length** | 53.25ins (1352mm) |
| **Barrel length** | 39.5ins (1005mm) |
| **Calibre** | .50in (12.7mm) |
| **Weight** | 9lbs 8oz (4.3kg) |
| **Charge** | 65 grains |
| **Ignition** | Matchcord |

**Matchlock musket:**

| | |
|---|---|
| **Overall length** | 61ins (1549mm) |
| **Barrel length** | 45.5ins (1156mm) |
| **Calibre** | .76in (20.2mm) |
| **Weight** | 10lbs 8oz (4.9kg) |
| **Charge** | 70 grains |
| **Ignition** | Matchcord |

## Firing the matchlock

The smoothbore matchlock muskets featured in this test were both good quality modern reproductions. The earlier model is a unique replica of an arquebus of about 1540 with a snap-matchlock mechanism, of a type known to have been on board the *Mary Rose*. It is comparatively delicate in both size and construction, weighing a modest 9.5lbs (4.3kg) - slightly lighter than an average World War II service rifle.

At the opposite end of the spectrum was the big musket of a type seen in its tens of thousands on the battlefields of Europe throughout the 17th century. It is typical of the pattern carried by many English Civil War re-enactors, having the later type of sear-matchlock with a separate, sprung, trigger-actuated serpentine that was soon to be superceded by the earliest of the new flintlocks. It was a robust gun, cheap to produce in large quantities, if rather on the heavy side. Our example did not use a rest; shooting it for any length of time certainly became tiring, for despite its fairly moderate weight of 11lbs (5.2 kg) it was typically muzzle-heavy.

The snap-matchlock **arquebus** was loaded in exactly the same manner as the hand guns, although a thin linen patch was placed behind the ball; initially a 50-grain charge was used for the .50in calibre ball. As with the earlier hand gun, we were interested to test its penetration capabilities - both types would have been used extensively against armoured opponents. The target was the same as that for the medieval gun: several sheets of 2mm thick steel bolted together with a gap between each pair and set up at about 30 yards.

It was easier to aim with the arquebus because of its relatively practical stock shape, and because it was comparatively sophisticated in having both a rear and a foresight. The first two shots dented the outer steel plate and the third just managed to penetrate it, the bullets achieving a creditable muzzle velocity of 1150fps. The charge was then increased to 65 grains, giving 1337fps; two successive shots penetrated both the first and second plates.

This was quite impressive, so a 90-grain charge was tried; the bullet penetrated three sheets, being defeated by the fourth. As this equated to 6mm of penetration and a muzzle velocity of 1580fps, it was felt that the arquebus had proved to be quite a potent firearm. Admittedly this was at close range, and velocities from black powder charges tend to drop very quickly, particularly beyond 100 yards; but many 16th century actions were fought at close range, so this was judged a creditable performance.

The Civil War **musket** was then tested. Powder at this period was carried either in a large wooden or horn flask, or in a bandoleer - a wide shoulder belt normally supporting eight to 12 stoppered wooden bottles each containing one measured charge. Priming powder was carried either in an extra bottle on the bandoleer or in a small flask slung separately.

A small quantity of priming powder was poured into the pan; the pan cover was swung into place, and the musketeer blew any loose powder grains away. A charger bottle was unstoppered and the contents - around 70 grains of coarse powder - were poured down the barrel. A .75in ball followed, from a small leather bullet bag worn at the waist or attached to the bandoleer. We used a very thin cotton patch, although the ball was such a close fit in the bore that this was hardly necessary; it was then rammed firmly into place.

The question of whether soldiers simply dropped a loose ball into the barrel or used some form of patch is still discussed. Certainly a sloppy ball-to-barrel fit would have meant that any musketeer who lowered his barrel risked losing the ball. (This incidentally begs the question of what cavalrymen did, since their weapons would constantly have been raised, lowered and generally mishandled whilst riding.) There seems little doubt that some form of wadding must have been used, and this may well have been in the form a pre-prepared paper cartridge. The principle had certainly been well understood for 150 years by the mid-17th century; and there exist contemporary mentions of "powder baggs for musketeers" which may possibly refer to paper cartridges, carried in cartridge boxes. A surviving contract dated January 1645 or 1646 does in fact list "1200 Cartridges, the boxes of strong plate covered with black leather".

Judging by contemporary accounts the loading of a matchlock was a long and tedious procedure; Francis Markham, writing in 1622, listed no fewer than 19 movements:

1. Open pan
2. Clear pan
3. Prime pan
4. Shut pan
5. Cast off loose corns [tip musket to shake loose powder clear]
6. Blow your pan [to blow away loose powder]
7. Cast about your musket with both your hands and trail your rest [place the butt on the ground so that the muzzle is level with the chest]
8. Open your charger [pull the cap from a charge bottle]
9. Charge your musket with powder
10. Draw out your scouring stick [i.e. ramrod]
11. Shorten your stick [grip the ramrod in the centre]
12. Ram in your powder
13. Draw out your stick
14. Charge with bullet
15. Ram in your bullet
16. Draw out your stick
17. Shorten your stick and put it up [replace ramrod in its recess under the forestock]
18. Bring your musket forward with your left hand
19. Hold your musket with your right hand and recover your rest.

(There are a further 14 commands for discharging the weapon!)

The reference in commands 10 and 11 to a scouring stick is interesting; the word ramrod is primarily an 18th century term. These sticks had a dual purpose: one end was plain, being used to ram the bullet home, while the other had a small sharp-edged collar which was used, quite literally, to scour out the fouling from the barrel. During our test the scourer for the Henrician arquebus proved very effective, and it remains a mystery why this useful fea-

*An English arquebusier of the army of Henry VIII, about 1545. His uniform has been reconstructed from surviving contemporary illustrations, and the shoes, leatherwork and sword are based on remains recovered from the wreck of the Mary Rose. His snap-matchlock is an exact replica of an existing specimen in the collection of the Royal Armouries and is of the type known to have been used at this time.*

*After powder is dispensed from a wooden and iron flask a .50 calibre ball is loaded.*

*Detail of the arquebus muzzle and foresight, and the sprung pair of scrapers at one end of the "scouring stick"/ramrod. These proved to be efficient at removing fouling from the bore, but over a period of time would undoubtedly have damaged the barrel.*

ture had been dispensed with by the end of the century.

The match was held between the fingers of the left hand as much for practicality as safety, enabling the hand still to be used but keeping it well out of the way of the powder and flasks until firing was required. That this was considered a wise precaution was reinforced by a first-hand account from one of the re-enactors present about a colleague whose lit match had been left in the jaws of the serpentine, and connected with his priming powder as he filled the pan. The resultant loss of hair and eyebrows was a small price to pay, and a salutary lesson to all present. Naturally, such fine considerations would probably have gone by the board during hard fighting when the main concern was speed of loading and firing.

One burning end of match was then transferred to the right hand, inserted into the jaws of the cock, and clamped tight. At this point a check was needed to ensure that the length of match protruding was absolutely correct to reach the centre of the priming charge, and that it was burning well. It needed a solid, glowing red end with no ash; if in doubt, blowing sharply on it was the usual procedure. Many musketeers would swing the loose end of the match in a circle, which had the effect of blowing off the loose ash and fanning a bright, hot end. We did attempt to use some hemp match, much as the original would have been; but it was too loosely braided, and splayed out so badly each time it struck the pan that it failed to ignite the charge. We reverted to firmer and more reliable sashcord.

The musket was brought up to the shoulder and, using the crude foresight as an aiming mark, lined up on the target. The pan cover was then opened, and the trigger pulled. Little happened, as the match was fractionally short and missed the pan completely. Having re-set it, squeezing the trigger and keeping one's eyes open simultaneously then proved impossible, as the flash and smoke of the priming charge automatically cause even an experienced shooter to flinch. The resultant flame, smoke and sparks were deeply impressive. The weight of the gun soaked up the recoil fairly effectively, and although it was still noticeable it was not unpleasant. There was no doubt in anyone's mind, however, that shooting without a rest for any period of time would have been very wearing. As usual a dense cloud of grey smoke blanketed out the target, but eventually we were able to see the results.

Sir John Smythe, writing in 1590, declared that a well rammed, properly loaded musket had an effective range of "twenty-four to thirty yards", so we did not expect any great accuracy at any distance - and we were not disappointed. At 25 yards it was certainly better than the medieval hand guns, producing a remarkably good group of about 12 inches from five shots. At 50 yards the story was different. Some people who fired seemed to have the ability to get their bullets to group in more or less the same area, although this did not always coincide with the actual target. Even an individual musket which had proved accurate at 25 yards became frustratingly inconsistent. It was clear that some muskets used on the range performed far better than others, many scattering shots over the target in such a random manner that it was difficult to know who was firing where. At 100 yards the effect was so random that it was decided that the safety of Yorkshire's wildlife demanded that we cease fire.

It is little wonder that massed close-range fire from a rank of musketeers produced an effect akin to that of a giant shotgun. Certainly, when a massed volley was unleashed at our target (a splendid life-sized Cavalier in fetching blue) the results were quite creditable, although the range was only 30 yards. Beyond that the number of strikes began to diminish quite rapidly. Average velocities worked out at just under 1000fps. Although no-one knew where their shot would hit, with enough bullets in the air the chances were that they would at least hit something. The big lead ball certainly packed a punch, and one that struck the upright of the target at 50 yards cut clean through a 6in oak support. Reducing the charge made little difference to accuracy at any range, although it lessened the recoil to some extent.

The matchlocks we used generally performed very reliably, but like all black powder weapons they were particularly prone to misfires and hangfires. These are essentially the same problem created by different causes. A misfire is usually the result of the priming either failing to be ignited by the match, or igniting satisfactorily but failing to set off the main charge. During our tests this was invariably due to the touch hole being blocked by fouling, preventing the spark from reaching the charge.

A hangfire is more dangerous, and may take either of two forms. Firstly, the priming may ignite suddenly after a noticeable delay, immediately setting off the main charge. Secondly, it may ignite satisfactorily but without setting off the main charge; this may be burning very slowly due to damp powder, causing the musket to fire suddenly after a delay of several seconds. The safe approach in either circumstance was to count to ten slowly, keeping the weapon pointed down range; then, if nothing happened, to clean the touch hole and reprime. Looking down the barrel is not recommended.

The matchlock musket produced one memorable misfire: despite the match dropping squarely into the pan the priming failed to ignite for no visible reason, but as the trigger was being pulled for a second attempt it suddenly detonated. Presumably a small piece of burning match lying unseen in the pan was sufficient to set off the priming charge. This served to remind all of us just how lethally unpredictable gunpowder can be.

We swabbed out the barrel of our musket after every five shots; this was primarily because of the very tight fit of the balls, and proved unnecessary on other examples with a greater bore tolerance. One quirk that it seemed to share with the 15th century matchlock was the match's tendency to fly out of the jaws of the serpentine upon firing, regardless of how tightly it was clamped in place. Having watched slow motion film of a matchlock being fired it became apparent that the reason for this lay not only in the force generated by the priming charge, but also in the back-flash which escapes through the touch hole when the main charge ignites in the breech.

At the end of our day of tests it was clear that as a weapon of mass defence the matchlock was actually quite a potent destructive force. In terms of range and accuracy (and one is of no practical use without the other) it would only be effective if used in large numbers against a massed target. One cannot help wonder if in terms of range, accuracy and penetration it was much of an improvement over the longbow; but that is an argument which was pursued to the point of tedium many centuries ago.

*Opening the pan cover. Compared to the 1640s musket shown on pages 35-37 this is quite compact; the whole design of these guns was generally more subtle than that of the larger muskets.*

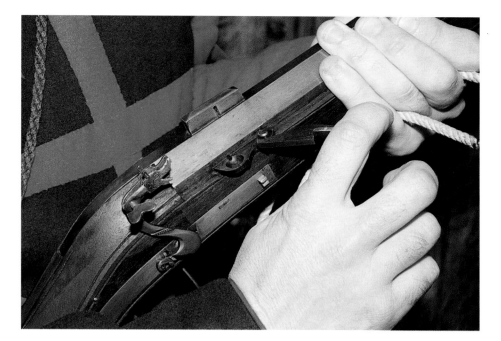

*Filling the pan with fine powder. Although the arquebus would fire with coarse powder, ignition was faster and more reliable with finer grains. The wooden and iron flask has a spring cap on the nozzle but no means of measuring.*

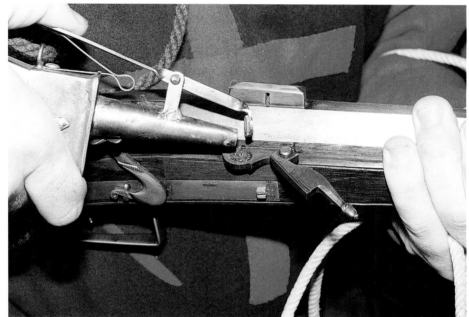

*Having shut the cover and blown off any loose powder, the arquebusier fixes one end of the match in place. It had to be kept very short, as the spring action of the serpentine was strong enough to knock the powder out of the pan. The stud which retains the serpentine in its cocked position can be seen protruding from the lockplate just above its "tail". The retaining screws on firearms of this period were typically square-headed. The unusual tunnel rearsight can be clearly seen here; with a small blade foresight as well the arquebus was very easy to sight - unfortunately, it was no more accurate than any other matchlock musket.*

*The ignition sequence on this arquebus is very rapid, the main charge igniting while the priming powder is still burning. It proved to be a surprisingly powerful weapon at short range.*

**BELOW** *The steel plate target for the 1540s arquebus. One 2mm sheet was severely dented by a 50-grain charge; two spaced sheets were penetrated when the charge was increased to 65 grains.*

**BELOW RIGHT** *Musketeer of the English Civil War period; his sword was needed for self-defence if the enemy closed in - muskets of this period did not have bayonets, though the clubbed butt could be a lethal weapon in hand-to-hand fighting. Musketeers were usually drawn up in alternate blocks with pikemen, and relied upon their thick hedge of 16- to 20-foot-long shafts for protection when unable to defend themselves.*

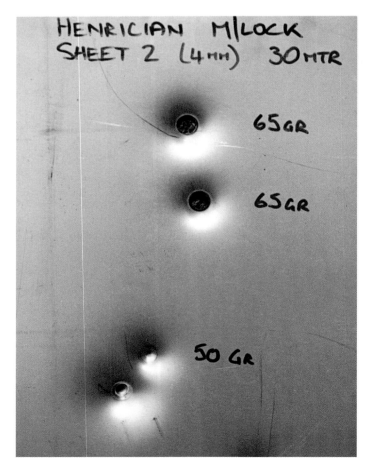

FAR LEFT *Accurately reconstructed bandoleer with wooden charge bottles; the larger bottle at the bottom holds priming powder, and has a hole in the cap so that it can be poured straight into the pan. Other accoutrements include a small powder flask, a leather pouch for bullets and wad and a tiny oil bottle.*

LEFT *The touch hole is cleaned out with a pricker. A blocked touch hole was one of the commonest cause of misfires during our tests.*

*We primed this musket from the small flask, but usually this was used only to refill the wooden priming bottle. With the match held in the left hand, well out of the way, the pan cover is opened and the pan filled.*

*The main charge is poured in from a bottle. The top and base of each bottle are suspended from the same pair of strings so that the top can be slid upwards and held safely out of the way while the powder is poured. Contemporary accounts describe grisly accidents when a whole bandoleer detonated at once.*

The bullet was often held in the mouth until the musketeer was ready to drop it into the barrel.

Ramming the bullet home. Although soldiers were well aware that failure to do this properly could lead to a breech explosion, many still preferred to seat the bullet more quickly by simply banging the butt on the ground.

Both ends of the match are kept lit, and the musketeer blows on one end to ensure it is burning well.

He then inserts it carefully into the jaws of the cock, and opens his pan.

**TOP** *A squeeze of the trigger releases the cock, and the match - this time - ignites the priming.*

**ABOVE** *As frequently happened, the match is blown out of the jaws of the cock by the explosion of the priming.*

**RIGHT** *The results of a volley fired at a man-sized target at 50 yards. This would have been about the limit for aimed fire even by a massed formation of musketeers.*

# THE WHEEL LOCK PISTOL

*There was little standardisation of firearms in the 16th and 17th centuries, and this European cavalry carbine of c.1650 is a compromise between a pistol and a musket; it has a flat, flared, squared-off butt. It is pictured with a contemporary horn flask, spanner and gloves. (XII.5475, XIII.45, XIII.313; TR1306; The Board of Trustees of the Royal Armouries)*

*A splendid reconstruction of an English Royalist officer of c.1642 carrying the wheel lock pistol used in our tests.*

The matchlock suffered, as described, from some inherent disadvantages that no amount of modification could eradicate. It was at best an unwieldy system which did not easily lend itself to any but the simplest improvements. Nor could it be made smaller; as long as a burning match was used there was little point in attempting to adapt the matchlock mechanism to produce a pistol. Relatively unsophisticated and cheap to manufacture, it would continue in large-scale use by national armies. But there were compelling reasons for gunmakers to produce something that was not only technically superior and more reliable but also considerably smaller.

At some point between the latter part of the 15th and the middle of the 16th century a weapon now commonly referred to as "The Monk's Gun" was produced. It had a small square pan which surrounded the touch hole; through the rear of the pan protruded a steel rod with a roughened upper surface and a ring at the rear. A hinged arm with jaws at the top was mounted just in front of the pan, and into these was clamped a small piece of iron pyrites. Pyrites, or "fool's gold", is a soft compound made of sulphur that has a high metal content. It sparks in the manner of flint, but does not damage metal surfaces, although it does wear away quite rapidly. Once the gun had been primed and loaded in the usual manner the hinged arm was lowered onto the rod so that the pyrites made contact with the rough surface. A finger was then inserted through the ring, which was tugged smartly backwards. This struck sparks which, all being well, ignited the priming charge.

Even the most mechanically innocent will realise that such an awkward arrangement was not only very vulnerable to damage, but also even more wildly inaccurate than the guns then in use - jerking hard on any part of a firearm as you attempt to fire it will undoubtedly send the ball in a direction at least 90 degrees from that intended. As a method of ignition it was certainly a step forward; but it was soon superceded by a less strenuous and more sophisticated system.

The actual designer of the wheel lock is believed by many historians to have been Leonardo da Vinci, who illustrated the mechanical principle in a volume entitled *Codex Atlanticus* in about 1500. (There is no firm consensus, so we follow here the convention of writing the term as two separate words - in contrast to e.g. matchlock - simply because of the awkward appearance of the double-L in "wheellock".) Da Vinci's drawings must have been made at some point late in the 15th century, and are certainly the earliest known illustrations of a wheel lock mechanism. Experiments with a working reconstruction made from these drawings showed that the lock would only work if the design were slightly modified, which indicates that the drawings were original works rather than copies made by da Vinci. Two illustrations of a wheel lock tinder lighter were published in a now lost manuscript by Martin Löffelholz of Nuremberg in 1505, but these are believed to have been copied and modified from da Vinci's original. The earliest known surviving examples of functioning wheel locks are in the Palazzo Ducale in Venice and are combination weapons, comprising a crossbow with an attached wheel lock pistol. They are believed to date from 1510-20, although there is some evidence that working examples existed ten years earlier.

The actual mechanism of the wheel lock can be likened to that of a modern cigarette lighter - an analogy which inexplicably seems to send firearms scholars into apoplectic fits. The similarities are inescapable, however, for the lighter employs a serrated wheel which, as it rotates, drags across a piece of flint to strike a spark. In the case of the wheel lock there is the addition of a backward-facing cock with jaws to hold the iron pyrites. The body of the

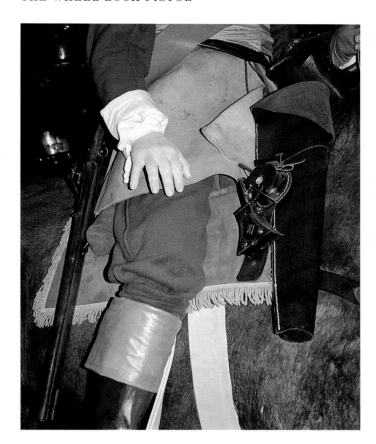

lock held a thin, grooved steel wheel which was mounted underneath the priming pan, with its top section showing through the floor of the pan adjacent to the touch hole. The whole mechanism was mounted on a steel lockplate which, on later examples, was fitted flush into the stock to protect it from dirt and damage.

Once the barrel was loaded a square key or "spanner" (hence our modern word) was placed over the square end of the spindle protruding from the centre of the wheel, and wound clockwise for about three-quarters of a turn. Once the internal spring was fully compressed ("spanned") the wheel was locked in position, and the key removed. The priming powder was then poured into the pan and a sliding cover closed to protect it. To ready the weapon for firing, the cock was swung over manually to rest on the top of the pan cover, where it was held in position by a strong V-spring. Pulling the trigger allowed the pan cover to slide forwards automatically, enabling the pyrites to make contact with the wheel, while simultaneously releasing the tightly compressed spring. The grooved wheel rotated at speed against the pyrites, causing a shower of sparks to fall into the priming.

*　　*　　*

Compared to the risks of uniting burning matchcord, black powder and careless soldiers, the wheel lock was comparatively safe - until the cock was placed on the pan cover an accidental discharge was impossible. However, it was complicated, expensive, and almost impossible to repair in the field unless there was a skilled gunsmith to hand. As a mechanism it more closely resembled a clock than anything else, and while a real advance in firearms technology it did little to simplify the ignition process. It certainly avoided many of the inherent problems of the matchlock, but its complexity and cost put it beyond the reach of the average individual, or even of a government seeking to purchase weapons on a large scale.

Naturally, improvements had been made within a few years of its introduction. One major problem with the design was the need to keep handy the special spanner or key; if the key were lost, the hapless owner was effectively left clutching a very expensive club, although in dire emergency a length of match cord could be used to touch off the priming powder manually. As a result, some "self-spanning" locks were introduced, which automatically rewound the spring when the weapon was recocked. Unfortunately they seldom proved strong enough to fully accomplish this, and most wheel lock owners simply became obsessive about the care of their spanners. Some early examples which had manually opened pan covers were also modified so that they automatically slid open when the trigger was pulled. The number of combination wheel lock/ matchlock weapons which survive shows that the complex mechanism was not entirely trusted.

Neither was the wheel lock any more accurate than the matchlock, and it says much for the accepted standards of the time that a hit anywhere on a target was regarded as valid, regardless of distance. There is an interesting account of a target match held on the estate of Archduke Ferdinand of Tyrol in the late 1560s which used a life-sized model of a rider and horse towed from one side of the range to the other, presumably by expendable servants. Any hit on the target won the shooter the same prize as the item his bullet struck; thus Emperor Rudolph won a rapier, and the Archduke won a horse. (There is no record of anyone winning a servant.)

The cost of a wheel lock ensured that they were predominantly purchased by the gentry, wealthy merchants and noblemen who regarded the possession of such weapons as conferring

**ABOVE LEFT** *Detail of reconstruction of a mounted mid-17th century trooper carrying a wheel lock carbine slung and with a pair of pistols in saddle holsters - the method of carrying cavalry pistols until well into the 19th century. His powder flask, bullet pouch and spanner are attached to the holster. At 25lbs (12kg) weight his "buff" leather ox-hide coat was thick enough to deflect a sword cut, and perhaps some pistol balls, too - but only spent shots at long range. In the Austrian test of an original wheel lock pistol mentioned at the end of this chapter a spruce wood block was penetrated to 121mm (4.7ins) by a ball fired at about 30 yards, so the more extravagant claims for the buff coat must be regarded with caution.*

**ABOVE RIGHT** *The necessary tools for using a wheel lock: a leather bullet pouch, with a wooden powder flask and the vital spanner slung beneath it. There is a simple sprung nozzle on the flask but no means of accurate measuring. By this period, however, pre-prepared cartridges were becoming more common and flasks were increasingly used simply for dispensing priming powder.*

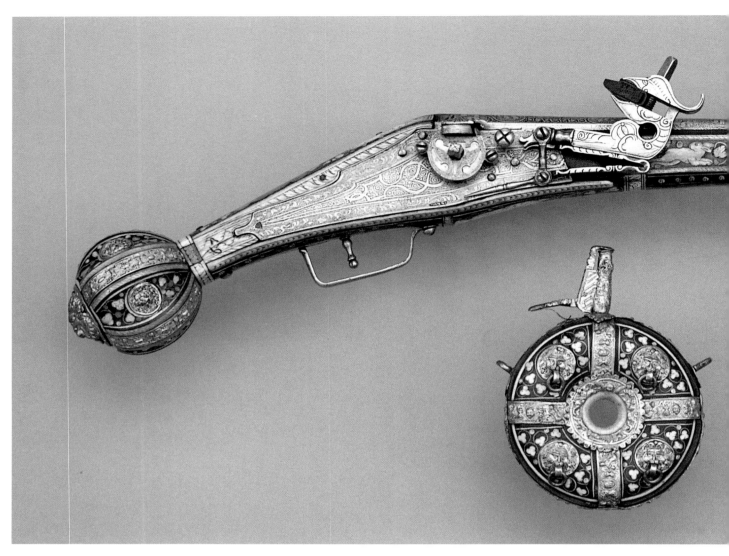

**ABOVE** *A very fine example of a German wheel lock pistol of the type commonly known as a "puffer"; this one has a matching circular powder flask, inlaid with gilt and ivory. A weapon of this quality would have been affordable only by a wealthy man. (XII.725; A2184; The Board of Trustees of the Royal Armouries)*

**RIGHT** *Winding spanners came in many shapes and sizes. Most also served a dual purpose, having screwdriver blades to dismount the locks or, as in the case of the bottom spanner, a hammer head to help remove barrel pins.*
*(XII.45, .49, .50, .52; A3/4731/7A; The Board of Trustees of the Royal Armouries)*

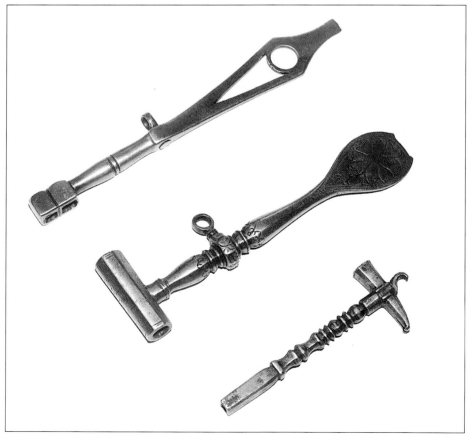

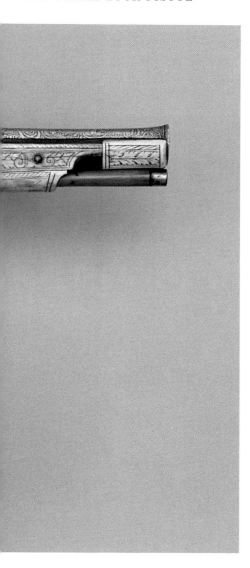

a certain degree of status, in much the same way as owning an expensive motorcar does today. This is why so many examples now in museum collections are of highly decorated type more suited for show than for the battlefield.

The main benefit of the mechanism was not so much its efficiency as its portability; for the first time it enabled a firearm to be carried loaded and ready for almost instant use - or even, concealed. It took some years for the wheel lock to develop into what was to become the now familiar pistol, and the date of the latter's appearance is not known with certainty, although it was probably much earlier than many people realise. A law was passed in 1517 by the Emperor Maximilian which declared that the use of "self-striking handguns that ignite themselves" was henceforth illegal. This was followed in 1518 by another edict forbidding people to carry "guns concealed under their clothing". Since this could hardly apply to a matchlock, the implication is that the authorities were seriously concerned by the new opportunities which the wheel lock offered to the would-be assassin.

The derivation of the word "pistol" has taxed firearm historians for many years. It was first recorded around 1540 as *pistolet*, with suggestions that it derived from the Bohemian word for a pipe or whistle. It now seems more likely that it originated from the name of the Italian town of Pistoia. In England the use of the word became more common from around 1560; before that date small guns were generally referred to *as arquebuses, dags or tags*. Why the term should have been adopted is suggested by a French document published in 1565 by Henri Estienne:

*"At Pistoia, a little town a good day away from Florence, they are wont to make little daggers, the which... were named after the place, first Pistoyers, then Pistoliers and in the end Pistolets. Some time afterwards, the invention of little harquebuses having come about, the name of these little daggers was transferred to them."*

Exactly why the term for a knife should have been transferred to a firearm is puzzling, but "dag" was to remain in common use in England until the early 17th century.

The Imperial prohibitions certainly indicate that pistols as a generic type were well known by the first quarter of the 16th century, and they were certainly plentiful enough in England by the latter part of the century to prompt a worried government to issue the following proclamation in July 1579:

*"Finally also her Majesty further chargeth all manner [of] officers in cities, towns, and other places to make search for all manner of dags, called pocket dags, as well in any man's house to be inspected for same in shops and houses of artificers that do use to make the same; and all them shall seize and take into custody, delivering a bill of their hands testifying the receipt thereof, to the intent the owners may have recompense for the same as hereafter upon certificate to her majesty's Privy Council...and herewith her majesty commandeth that no manner of person shall hereafter either make, or amend, or shall bring into this realm, any such dags, commonly called pocket dags, or such like; upon pain of imprisonment...and wheresoever there are persons that have made any shot, the same shall be bound in reasonable sums to her majesty's use by the discretion of the principle officers of the town, not to make nor put to sale, or otherwise utter any such small pieces as are commonly called pocket dags, or that may be hid or carried covertly."*

Twenty years later it appears that the term pistol was accepted into general use, as evidenced by another edict from the Queen's Council in 1594:

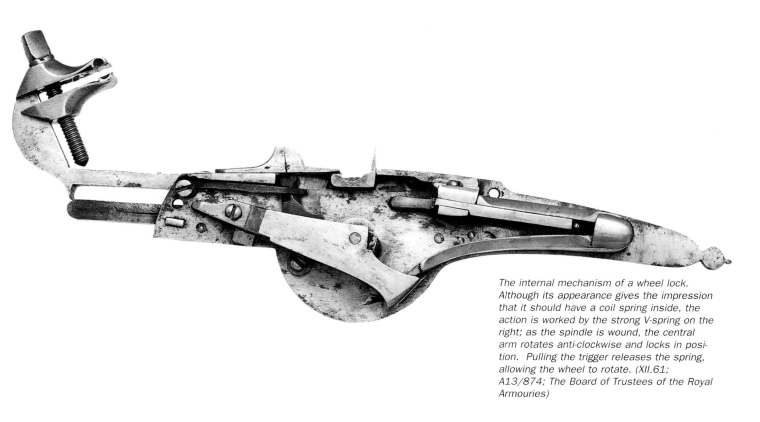

*The internal mechanism of a wheel lock. Although its appearance gives the impression that it should have a coil spring inside, the action is worked by the strong V-spring on the right; as the spindle is wound, the central arm rotates anti-clockwise and locks in position. Pulling the trigger releases the spring, allowing the wheel to rotate. (XII.61; A13/874; The Board of Trustees of the Royal Armouries)*

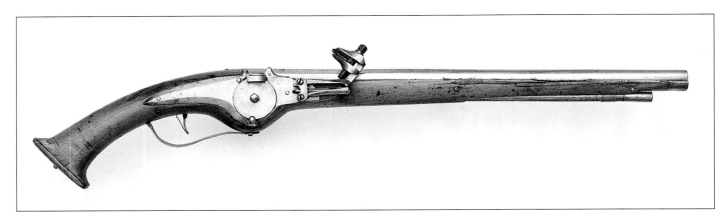

*A rare example of a munition-quality wheel lock of c.1640. This weapon, of German manufacture, was the pistol upon which our shooting reproduction was based. It has a simple form of stock with a flat butt, and the traditional three side nails to retain the lock. (XII.1815; A14/218 (9), (12); The Board of Trustees of the Royal Armouries)*

*"..there are great disorders lately grown in sundry partes of her Realme, and specially in and about her Citie of London and in the usual highwayes towards the said citie....by common carrying of Dags, otherwise called pistols to the terrour of all people..."*

To anyone still contemplating the recent legislation banning the private ownership of pistols in Great Britain, it may be a small comfort to know that history does, indeed, repeat itself.

By the time the wheel lock had gained general acceptance in Europe the drawbacks of the new mechanism were well understood, as were its benefits. Its possibilities as a light, portable sidearm were not lost on the military commanders of the day, but the problem, then as today, was simply one of economics. While many officers acquired pistols, there was little point in issuing wheel lock longarms *en masse*; they were far too expensive to justify any general military advantage they offered, given the point-blank infantry killing matches which were the basis of all warfare from the Middle Ages to the 19th century. However, there was an increasing demand among the cavalry for a lightweight, portable firearm.

Wheel lock pistols began to be more commonplace on the battlefield in the late 16th and early 17th centuries. Many contemporary battle paintings clearly show troops of mounted men in half-armour carrying saddle-holstered pistols as well as swords; and this evidence is supported by drill manuals and tactical treatises from this age of warfare, based upon a scientific combination of Classical tactics and the latest technology. German cavalry tactics early in the 1600s were devised around the *caracole*, the firing of pistols by successive ranks of troopers; and the great captain of the Thirty Years' War, Gustavus Adolphus of Sweden, co-ordinated the use of sword and pistols for maximum shock effect and exploitation. Although England was initially slow to adopt the new gun for military use, the Civil Wars of the 1640s-50s brought to the fore many influential officers with Continental experience, and consequently popularised Continental weapons and tactics.

For those who could afford one the wheel lock provided an immediate form of self-defence. However, the natural desire for a weapon that was ready to fire instantly meant that many owners kept their wheel locks spanned for long periods; this inevitably led to problems with the springs, and the wheel lock developed a dubious reputation for unreliability at moments of crisis. Over-strained springs would break, or priming powder would work its way into the serrated wheel and jam the mechanism. Sir Edmund Ludlow paid the price for such carelessness during the siege of Wardour Castle. Facing a horde of Royalists advancing through a shattered wall, he was left with only his sword for defence: *"My pistols being wheel-locks and wound up all night, I could not get to fire."*

Others suffered more serious setbacks, having forgotten that a weapon was already spanned and loaded, as Randle Holme mentioned in the 1680s: *"These kind of fire locks with their spanners to wind up the spring of the wheele were onely in use for Troopers in the Late rebellion in tyme of King Charles I, Anno 1641, but now wholly layd aside as useless and dangerous, being the sudden death of many by fireing unawares, the party thinking them not to be wound up when they have bine."*

*   *   *

Wheel locks of the 16th century did not at once take on the form of true pistols; they resembled small carbines, with flattened butts. Gradually they became more slender and the shape developed into two patterns: one had a squared and flared butt, and the other tapered down

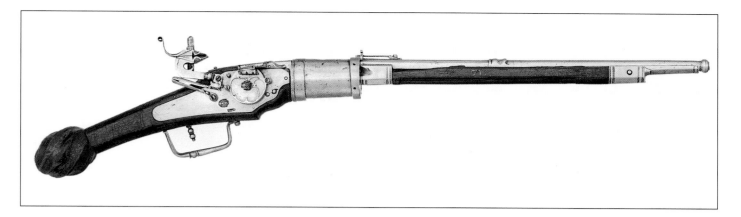

*Gunmakers were constantly looking for a means of increasing the firepower of pistols, and this German revolving wheel lock of c.1600 was a very early attempt. It has a very small bore of .30in (7.6mm) and a 14in (355mm) barrel; weighing nearly 4lbs (1.8kg), it was too big to be easily manageable. (XII.1078; A8/248; The Board of Trustees of the Royal Armouries)*

to terminate in a large, distinctive ball. This is often mistakenly claimed to have been intended for use as a club in hand-to-hand emergencies, but examining original examples reveals these pistols - generally referred to as "puffers" - to be light and often highly ornamented. Their fragile butts would shatter harmlessly if struck on a hard surface; besides, the heavy barrel would be far more effective as a club.

The real purpose of the ball was simply to provide easy grip, for these pistols would have been carried in pairs in saddle holsters by mounted men who were certainly wearing gloves. Fumbling around for a pistol while on horseback is no easy task, and the shape of the butt had to provide a good purchase for withdrawing it from the holster. Some examples also exist with small belt hooks so that they could be worn at the waist.

The wheel lock's effectiveness in combat is not well documented, but there does exist one fascinating contemporary account by Richard Atkyns, who served with Prince Maurice's Royalist regiment of horse in the English Civil War. He recounts how he attempted to prevent Sir Arthur Haslerigge, a Parliamentarian general, from fleeing after the battle of Roundway Down on 13 July 1643. Sir Arthur's own Cuirassier regiment were nicknamed "the Lobsters", being unusual for the time in still wearing almost complete plate armour:

*"Twas my fortune in a direct line to charge their general of horse, which I supposed to be so by his place; he discharged his carbine first, but at a distance not to hurt us, and afterwards one of his pistols, before I came up to him, and missed with both: I immediately struck into him, and touched him before I discharged mine; and I'm sure I hit him, for he staggered, and presently wheeled off from his party and ran...follow him I did, and in six score yards I came up to him, and discharged the other pistol at him, and I'm sure I hit his head, for I touched it before I gave fire, and it amazed him at that present, but he was too well armed all over for a pistol bullet to do him any hurt, having a coat of mail over his arms and a headpiece (I am confident) musket proof... in the nick of time came up Mr Holmes to my assistance, and went up to him with great resolution, and felt him [i.e. touched him with the muzzle] before he discharged his pistol, and though I saw him hit 'twas but a flea-biting to him... then came in Captain Buck, a gentleman of my troop, and discharged his pistol upon him also, but with the same success as before."*

When Atkyns related this story King Charles replied dryly that had Haslerigg been "well victualled as well as fortified, he might have endured a siege of seven years" - perhaps the only recorded occasion of this monarch making a joke.

Even at point-blank range the power of the bullet was thus insufficient to do more than momentarily stun a man wearing heavy plate, and we may assume that the back-and-breast armour worn by most cavalry would have given the same protection to the vital areas of the torso. However, the story also argues - as do other 17th century passages - that the use of the pistol at point-blank range was not thought unusual; and since there are many mentions of men being killed by pistols (in the hands of enemy and friend alike), it is clear that pistol bullets could penetrate with lethal effect unarmoured areas covered only by the heavy buff-leather coat of the period. As with the matchlock, when tempted to dismiss early weapons we should remember that fighting men do not burden themselves with useless contraptions: if they bought, issued, and carried wheel lock pistols, then we can be confident that those pistols were judged useful in battle.

Although the wheel lock fell from favour in England by the end of the 1680s it remained extraordinarily popular on the Continent, particularly in Germany, even into the 19th century, with some particularly fine rifled target weapons being produced. This was due to the remarkably smooth action of the wheel lock; when the trigger was pulled the only movement was of the spinning wheel, which did not cause any jerking before ignition. Prior to the modern revival of interest the last known pair of wheel lock pistols made were produced by Le Page of Paris in 1829.

**Technical Specifications**

**Wheel lock pistol:**

| | | |
|---|---|---|
| **Overall length** | 27.75ins | (705mm) |
| **Barrel length** | 18.25ins | (464mm) |
| **Calibre** | .50in | (12.7mm) |
| **Weight** | 2lbs 8oz | (1.3kg) |
| **Charge** | 45 grains | |
| **Ignition** | Pyrites | |

### Firing the wheel lock

Our example was a very good quality handmade copy of a rare, plain "munition" type (i.e. a cheap, common soldier's issue) as manufactured in Germany around 1640. The reproduction was of the correct proportions, unlike many mass-produced modern copies, which are often too long in the barrel and overly heavy. The pistol type selected was as near to a plain military pattern wheel lock as possible, conforming fairly well to the standard weapon which would have seen extensive service in Europe through to the late 17th century.

Our copy did differ in a few respects from the closest surviving originals. It is slightly heavier in overall construction, with a marginally less elegantly tapered stock. This was deliberate, as it was designed for the stresses and strains of being a much-handled and much-demonstrated weapon. It also has a reduced bore, being .50in instead of .60inch. Until comparatively recently wheel locks have not been particularly popular for shooting, but renewed interest in black powder firearms, and the greater availability of good reproductions are creating renewed interest.

*Pouring the charge, inserting the bullet, and ramming home; we used greased flannelette patches during the firing trials. The 17th century trooper must have used at least a wad of thin paper to eliminate windage and help retain the bullet - loaded pistols carried muzzle-down in saddle holsters were bounced around roughly, and would certainly have lost their load without tight wadding.*

The design of these early pistols leaves a lot to be desired in terms of handling. They are not generally made with comfort in mind, and the short, relatively straight stock found on early models forces the shooter to hold the pistol angled slightly downwards to permit the barrel to align with the target. This is not at all comfortable on the wrist, and makes a mockery of attempting to align the barrel accurately with a target. The stock on our wheel lock was slightly more comfortable, being marginally more curved.

Contemporary illustrations always show the gun canted over to the left, almost lock uppermost, for firing. There are two good reasons for this: firstly, it enables the pistol to be held with a straighter wrist, and secondly, it prevents the priming powder being ejected by the revolving wheel while the pan is open. We did try shooting the pistol at a conventional angle, and there was certainly a tendency for the action of the lock to dissipate the powder (although it must be said that only once did the pistol fail to ignite). It would be very different on horseback under battlefield conditions, so there is certainly some logic to this practice.

Loading was not quite as straightforward as with the other black powder firearms. A charge of 45 grains of medium powder was used as a starting point, and a lead ball carefully patched with greased flannelette was rammed in. There is considerable evidence that cartridges were in use from the earliest years of the 16th century, being the most convenient method of carrying a combined ball and charge. Mention is made of "patron" boxes; these were probably small cartridge boxes worn on the body, and *Patrone* has been adopted into the German language as the modern term for a cartridge. English absorbed the word "cartridge" from the French word for a large box containing musket ammunition, the *cartouche*.

The lock was spanned, then primed with fine powder, and the pan cover closed. It is significant that on the one occasion during our tests when the priming powder was accidentally poured in before the wheel was spanned, the powder grains effectively locked the mechanism solid, forcing us to empty it completely and brush it out before we could proceed.

We optimistically started firing at a range of 25 metres, with a standard man-sized target. The cock was lowered and, with the pistol held canted over to the left at about 45 degrees, the trigger was pulled. The sensation is a little odd, as the sudden whirr of the rotating wheel gives the firer the distinct impression that the weapon is about to chime. It is, however, a brief sensation as the priming charge ignited surprisingly quickly, and the main charge fired with considerable gusto. The recoil tends to twist the shooter's wrist quite noticeably, mainly because of the odd angle at which it is being held. This is not painful, but takes a little getting used to.

Accuracy was unremarkable, with eight out of ten shots hitting a man-sized target at 25 yards, but in a random way with no real grouping. At 50 yards five out of ten shots struck the target in places varying from head to toe; and in view of the increasingly wet weather it

was unanimously decided that attempting anything over that range was a waste of powder.

Interestingly, the rain made no difference to the reliability of the wheel lock until it became very heavy, at which point misfires began to occur as the priming powder became damp. It was also noticed that the pistol would occasionally fail to ignite due to the pan cover failing to move forward fast enough. We tried sliding the pan cover forward prior to lowering the cock onto the pan, which worked well enough, but had to be done swiftly if the rain was not to soak the powder. This was a peculiarity of the pistol that we were using, and had we had the means on range to slightly ease the tolerances between the cover and the tracking in which it moves this would doubtless have alleviated the problem.

On several occasions there was no visible spark from the pyrites, and it was found that washing the accumulated debris and soot from it helped considerably. Eventually we could not coax a spark from it at all, and even though there was no obvious problem it was found that turning the pyrites round in the jaws to present a new face to the wheel seemed to do the trick. Unlike a flint, whose edges become very obviously chipped, it was impossible to tell when the pyrites needed changing until it failed to spark.

Increasingly heavy rain eventually forced us to abandon the range. Since the pistol was still loaded at that point it gave us an opportunity to go through the steps to make it safe. The priming powder was brushed from the pan, the cover was slid into place, and water was poured down the barrel to help remove fouling. A threaded extractor was screwed onto a cleaning rod, inserted into the barrel and tapped with a small mallet into the face of the ball. Once the thread had started to bite the rod was screwed down. When the ball was firmly attached to the extractor it was slowly drawn from the barrel, enabling the charge to be washed out. Attempting this under fire would not be a task to be undertaken lightly.

As a short range weapon the wheel lock was doubtless quite efficient, providing the target was not wearing plate armour, which its ball was unlikely to be able to penetrate even at close range. It was too inaccurate to enable the shooter to aim specifically for an unarmoured portion of an enemy's body, particularly if either (or both) were mounted, at anything over point blank range. It was certainly a very smooth mechanism to shoot, and one can understand why it remained so popular in Europe for target use and hunting.

For comparison, it is worth mentioning published test firings at the Austrian army's Felixdorf range in December 1988 of a Nuremberg-made wheel lock pistol of c.1620. This was a smaller calibre piece - 11.8mm (roughly .45in) - and a 9.56 gram (2.96oz) ball was fired using hunter's quality powder of .3-.6mm grain size; the charge details are not immediately to hand, but the muzzle velocity was 1437 feet per second. At a range of 8.5m (27.8ft) a contemporary steel cuirass 2mm-3mm thick was pierced, but the energy was so completely dissipated that a sandbag behind the cuirass was undamaged.

**BELOW LEFT** *Spanning the lock; only a half-turn is necessary to compress the spring. The rear face of the spanner has a square aperture which fits the jaw adjustment bar at the top of the cock.*

**BOTTOM LEFT** *Priming; the sliding cover is open to reveal the pan, the touch hole, and the section of the grooved wheel protruding through the pan's bottom surface.*

**BELOW RIGHT** *A small measure of powder is poured into the pan; the cover will now be closed.*

**BOTTOM RIGHT** *The arm and jaws are lowered on top of the closed cover; a strip of lead foil or leather was wrapped around the pyrites to ensure a steady grip in the jaws. This is the state in which pistols were too often carried for prolonged periods, with disappointing or fatal results for the owner.*

The trigger has been pulled; note that the pan cover has automatically slid forward, and the blurring of the spindle shows that the spring has been released and is rotating the serrated wheel under the pyrites.

The copious smoke from the priming is blown away by a strong breeze. The wind was a usefully ally on the battlefield provided it blew - unlike here - from behind, so as to carry the blinding smoke into the faces of the enemy.

Smoke rises from the pyrites; and below the priming charge ignites. Providing the pyrites has been correctly positioned the process of ignition is remarkably quick and smooth.

The main charge fires, with burning powder leaving a trail of sparks from the muzzle. There is remarkably little recoil.

As is usual with black powder, the world is blotted out by the thick smoke of the discharge.

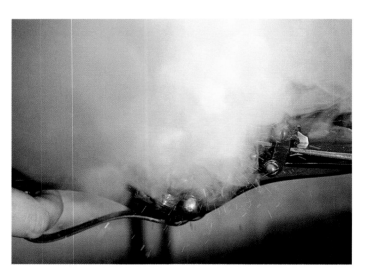

# THE FLINTLOCK MUSKET

*Reconstruction of a musketeer of the New Model Army, c.1650, with an English lock musket. Bandoleers of powder bottles, priming flasks and bullet pouches were still in common use until the early 18th century, and musketeers still wore a sword for personal protection at this date. Although the recoil of the main charge ignition lifted the barrel about 4ins (12cm) above the horizontal, at 50 yards' range this musket proved reasonably accurate, putting five shots into a target circle of about 14ins (35.6cm).*

By the middle of the 17th century the wheel lock mechanism had begun to wane in popularity and had almost vanished from military use in Europe by c.1680. The matchlock musket was to survive longer, remaining as a front line infantry weapon until about 1700. By then, however, the new flintlock had gained such popularity that it eventually relegated the matchlock and wheel lock to history.

The form of flintlock which is recognised today did not come into being immediately, being pre-dated by a similar but more complex type of lock called the "snaphaunce" or "snaplock". Because of the close similarity between the two mechanisms there has been some confusion over exactly where one type ceases and the other begins, not helped by the fact that the two locks overlapped in use for a considerable period of time.

The snaphaunce probably pre-dates the flintlock by around 70 years, being first mentioned as early as 1547, when a lock of similar type appears in a list of Florentine ordnance. The origin of the term is the Dutch *snaphaan* or "snapping hen"; this refers to the action of the cock, which makes a short, sharp, downward movement like a pecking fowl. It was something of a hybrid in mechanical terms, owing more to the common household tinder firelighter than to either the snap-matchlock or the wheel lock. It was to prove more efficient than the first and far cheaper and simpler than the second, and certainly more enduring, remaining in use in the developed form of the true flintlock until the mid-19th century.

In mechanical terms the snaphaunce works in much the same manner as all flintlock types, relying on a cock holding a specially shaped piece of flint striking a steel to produce sparks; the term is today used of weapons which have the steel mounted at the top of a swivelling arm ahead of the priming pan, rather than being combined in one angled piece with the pan cover. When the cock is pulled fully back it compresses a V-spring mounted on the lockplate, and once at full-cock a small metal arm called a sear is pushed through an aperture in the lockplate to lock the cock in position. There is no safety position in the lock mechanism, the cock either being forward or fully to the rear; but there was usually a small swivelling bar to the rear of the lockplate behind the cock, and this could be pushed into a notch to lock the sear.

To shoot a snaphaunce, the arm and its steel have to be pulled back until positioned over the pan, which has a sliding cover similar to that of the wheel lock. This cover is equipped with an internal pushrod which moves it forwards when the trigger is pulled. As the flint in the jaws of the cock strikes the face of the steel it knocks it forward, simultaneously dropping a shower of sparks onto the priming charge to ignite it and thus set off the main charge.

Whilst the origin of the name snaphaunce may be generally agreed upon, the place of its invention is not; Italy, Germany and Sweden have all been suggested. To complicate matters a number of variants of the snaphaunce developed in the Baltic, Mediterranean, and Low Countries, each of which produced their own variations on the theme. In England the first record of this new lock is in a list of equipment supplied to cavalry troopers equipped by the Dean and Chapter of St Paul's Cathedral to fight in Ireland in 1580, which included *"9 cases of snaphaunces at forty shillings the peece."* Clearly the 16th century church had not yet fully developed its theories on world pacifism.

This is an interesting entry because it underlines one of the major reasons for the failure of the wheel lock - that of cost. A snaphaunce, which was more reliable and easier to maintain, was about 30 per cent cheaper than a wheel lock: in 1631 English gunmakers were quoting £3.0s.0d for a pair of wheel lock pistols and £2.0s.0d for snaphaunces. During the Civil Wars many flint-ignited weapons were used, and their great improvement in safety over

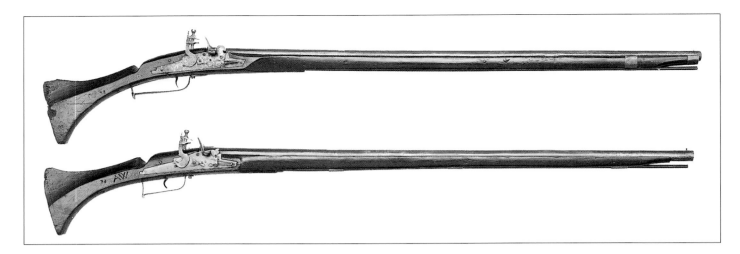

*Two interesting mid-17th century flintlock muskets. Although both have English locks fitted they are conversions from earlier matchlocks, retaining the large, simple trigger guard and characteristic butt shape. Both are of .78 calibre. (XII.5143, .5144; A3/576; The Board of Trustees of the Royal Armouries)*

*A chronological progression of types. The top musket is an Anglo-Dutch matchlock of c.1695, the last pattern matchlock used before phasing out in favour of the flintlock. The second is a William III matchlock converted to dog-lock. The third example is a James II pattern of 1685, and was the first musket to be equipped with a rather ineffectual plug bayonet. The bottom musket uses the same lock, but is a Queen Anne example made for Marine use; it has an unusual early form of flat-bladed socket bayonet. (A1596; The Board of Trustees of the Royal Armouries)*

matchlocks led to their being specifically issued to artillery guards whose duties kept them close to large quantities of stored powder. By 1685 the simplicity and reliability of the mechanism were fully appreciated by the British military authorities; in that year the Royal Regiment of Fusiliers was raised and equipped with snaphaunce muskets, which increasingly began to be referred to as *fusils*.

It is generally agreed that the form of lock now accepted as the true flintlock was first produced by a French family of gunmakers from Lisieux, the le Bourgeoys, some time between 1610 and 1620. It was, naturally, referred to as the French lock, but was to remain largely unknown outside France until the late 1630s. There has always been considerable debate about exactly when the snaphaunce was replaced by the true flintlock, and this is compounded by the habit of contemporary writers of referring to both types without differentiating between them. This is understandable, since in appearance the snaphaunce and early flintlock are very similar; the only immediate visual differences lie in the construction of the steel and pan, and the repositioning of the mainspring from outside the lockplate to inside, where it was far less vulnerable.

The fully developed flintlock differed from the snaphaunce primarily in the design of the steel. The steel of the snaphaunce existed solely to provide ignition; the flintlock's steel and pan cover were made in one simpler, cheaper, L-shaped piece. When this *frizzen* (as it became known) was snapped closed over the primed pan it gave reasonable protection from the elements, and enabled the gun to be carried loaded and ready-primed for shooting. This had never been satisfactorily achieved before, as the swivelling pan cover of the matchlock was too vulnerable to damage and had to be manually opened and closed - an easy step to overlook in time of stress, as will be understood by any game shooter today who has tried to fire at a sudden bird without disengaging his safety catch. The main advantage of the flintlock

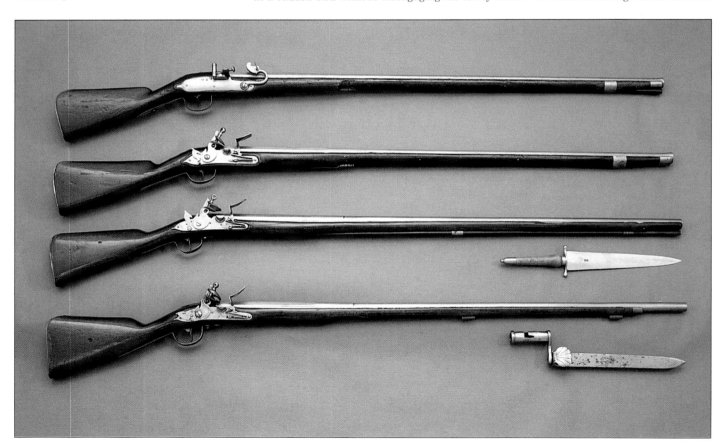

was the speed with which it could be fired without the steel first having to be positioned over the pan. Ironically, this created an inherent safety problem: the flintlock was less safe than the snaphaunce, which could not be fired accidentally as long as the steel was moved out of position.

To counter any tendency for the lock to accidentally ignite several important mechanical improvements began to appear around 1620. These mainly revolved around the internal lock mechanism. Around this time a variation appeared which has become known as the "English lock"; this copied the mechanism of the snap-matchlock, having a small steel block which acted as a safety mechanism by engaging the tail of the cock. Unlike the external safety catch of the snaphaunce the English lock had a safe or half-cock position. There were a number of different types but all used the same basic system, having their sear locked in a mid-position between full-cock and fired.

The French lock differed in having a vertically operating sear and tumbler, so that when the cock was pulled back the tumbler rotated with it, enabling the sear to engage with the first, deeper notch. This held the cock firmly in the half-cock position so that, in theory at least, the weapon could not be fired even if the trigger were pulled. Pulling back the cock still further allowed the second, shallower notch in the tumbler to engage with the sear, giving a full-cock position from which the gun could be fired.

This sear-and-tumbler arrangement distinguished the true flintlock from earlier types, and enabled a loaded and primed gun to be carried in reasonable safety (although it was not foolproof, or we would not have inherited the expression "going off at half-cock"). This occasional tendency gave rise to a feature which became known as the *doglock*. This is an inaccurate term to describe a form of additional safety catch fitted to many different forms of flintlock mechanism. It comprised a large swivelling catch attached to the rear of the lockplate behind the cock. The rear face of the cock had a notch cut into it, and in the full-cock position the hooked catch could be swung forwards to lock it firmly in place.

Although the flintlock would gradually become the premier form of gunlock the snaphaunce did not disappear entirely, remaining particularly popular in Scotland until the 18th century and in Spain, Italy and North Africa until the 19th. The true golden age of the flintlock was to begin in the last decades of the 17th century, by which time it had been mechanically refined to a point where few more improvements could be made. It was a strong design that could withstand considerable abuse, and apart from spring failure it was reasonably durable, although after long use the face of the steel would become worn away and would require refacing and rehardening. As a mechanical system this type of lock and sear mechanism was to remain in use in both flint and percussion forms until the advent of the metallic cartridge in the 1870s.

Although the perfected flintlock had become the favourite arm for sportsmen in Britain by the end of the 17th century, and its military benefits had been proven during the Civil Wars, the British army was in no hurry to re-equip *en masse* with expensive new technology. This was despite the fact that even before the Civil Wars much testing had been done by the English Council of War in an attempt to simplify and improve the types of firearm issued. In fact the first moves towards standardisation had occurred in 1630, when the Council declared that musket bore diameter would henceforth be measured at 12 balls to the pound (12 bore) which produced a lead ball with a diameter of .729 inch. This was never entirely achieved, as manufacturing tolerances could never guarantee the precise diameter of a bore. To ensure that the ball could be rammed home in a fouled barrel some allowance had to be made, so a standard calibre of .75in was settled upon. The projectile remained more or less this size for over a hundred years, although the musket underwent many other changes.

There was little doubt that the musket was too heavy, and the Council accepted a recommendation that the barrel length should be reduced from 46 to 42 inches. Additionally, the charge (usually calculated as being two-thirds the weight of the bullet) was reduced to half that of the bullet to lessen the recoil. This redesigned musket still weighed 12lbs (5.4kg), but led the way for the introduction of a lighter breed of weapon which no longer required a forked rest.

In the aftermath of the Civil War it was clear that some uniformity in weapons type was required for a British army that was for the first time to consist of professional soldiers paid for by the Crown. The old system of purchasing weapons from outside contractors had invited corruption, and a mass of guns of highly variable quality had been supplied in a bewildering variety of calibres. All this was to change from 1715, when the newly formed Board of Ordnance undertook to supply patterns of all the component parts to contract gunmakers in Birmingham and London. They in turn supplied finished parts to the Ordnance Office at the Tower of London, where they were checked by inspectors before assembly by skilled labourers called "setters-up".

Contrary to popular opinion, the muskets and pistols of the 18th and early 19th centuries were not manufactured on a production line basis. Although the component parts supplied to the Tower were supposed to be of uniform size there was considerable variation in manufacturing tolerances; skilled assembly and finishing work was necessary, resulting in every firearm having to be hand-finished. So concerned were the Board of Ordnance at how labour-intensive this process proved that in 1752 they were forced to tighten their controls over the gunmakers and raise the standard required for supply of parts, even to the extent of providing skilled men to give instructions to the makers on quality control.

The earliest Ordnance Pattern muskets weighed 11lbs, and had bores varying between .76 and .80 inch. They were ungainly weapons, with heavy, rounded stocks owing much to the design of the matchlocks that they replaced. Improvements would be made; the stock gradually lost its fishtail look in favour of a more practical shape with a slightly downwards-curving butt. It gained a longer, slimmer neck to allow a firm grip with the right hand, and a raised comb to rest the cheek against whilst aiming.

At this period the socket bayonet had yet to be invented, so these early muskets used the plug bayonet - no more than a broad-bladed knife with a tapered grip which could be inserted into the muzzle of a musket to create a rather unwieldy pike. Once in place it of course

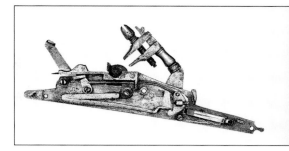

A snaphaunce lock mechanism; it is similar to that of the later flintlock, but lacks the more sophisticated tumbler that enables the half-cock position to be engaged. The thin bar running along the upper section of the lockplate operated the sliding pan cover. (XII.1785; A14/189; The Board of Trustees of the Royal Armouries)

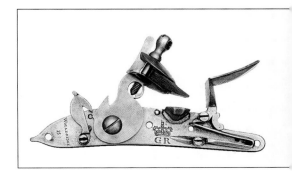

A close-up of the lockplate from a 1704 pattern English lock musketoon (a short-barrelled musket for sea service) by Wooldridge, dated 1715; note the so-called "dog" safety catch. (XII.80; The Board of Trustees of the Royal Armouries)

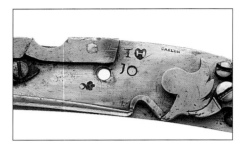

*Interior views of the 1715 English lock by Wooldridge; in the closer view the mainspring is present, in the general view it is absent. Three distinct notches can be seen cut into the tumbler. At present the sear rests in the lower one, with the cock in the forward or firing position. The other two notches are the safety or half-cock, and full-cock positions. In the close-up note the mainspring resting against the toe of the tumbler. When this became worn the spring would drop clear, rendering the lock unusable. (XII.279; A11/788, /789; The Board of Trustees of the Royal Armouries)*

*A very early pre-Land Pattern musket of George I, c.1720 - one of the earliest of the regulation type muskets adopted for military service. It is 62ins (1.57m) long and weighs almost 11lbs (5.2kg), with a 46-in (1.17m) barrel. (XII.125; A6/806; The Board of Trustees of the Royal Armouries)*

prevented the musket being fired, and could also be very difficult to remove. The British defeat by the Scots at Killikrankie in 1689 was blamed by General Hugh Mackay on the plug bayonet: *"The Highlanders are of such quick motion that if a Battalion keep up his fire till they be near, to make sure of [hitting] them, they are upon it before our men can come to the second defence, which is the bayonet in the muzzle of the musket."*

The first true flintlock musket to be uniformly adopted by the army was the Long Land Pattern, which did not appear until around 1730 when the now-familiar, rather elegant lines of what was to become universally known as the "Brown Bess" were introduced. There is, of course, considerable dissent about exactly where this name came from, for it did not appear in print until 1785. Probably the best current theory is that it is an amalgamation of terms, brown referring to the finish of the stock, and Bess being a corruption of the German word for a gun, *Büchse*. It has been said that the "brown" referred to the colour of the barrels, browning being an early form of finish applied to protect the metal from rust. In fact muskets (apart from those issued to the Light Infantry) were usually supplied with their barrels bright-finished until the end of the 18th century. It is therefore unlikely that the name Brown Bess was much used by soldiers until well into the next century, although it has now become an accepted term for all British military flintlocks up to the 1830s.

\* \* \*

Curiously enough, there is very little information available on the development and early years of service of the military musket. The first Long Land Patterns are dated to around 1725, and were 62ins long with a 46in barrel, a wooden ramrod, and a comparatively large calibre of .78 inch. Introduction was slow, and they were not issued on a large scale until several years later. Iron furniture (butt plates, escutcheons, trigger guards, etc.) was initially used, but proved impractical because of rusting and was changed to brass by about 1730. One vitally important change was the replacement of wooden ramrods by steel ones: no longer would a soldier be left helpless when a wooden ramrod snapped in the barrel.

The Long Land Musket saw the British army through many conflicts, including the Seven Years' War and the American War of Independence; but its weight and length made it awkward to use, particularly in confined spaces. Neither was it any more accurate than the old matchlocks that it replaced, for the old problem of windage and badly bored barrels still persisted. As late as 1814 Colonel George Hanger wrote:

*"A soldier's musket, if not exceedingly ill-bored and very crooked as many are, will strike the figure of a man at 80 yards; it may even at a hundred; but a soldier must be very unfortunate indeed who shall be wounded by a common musket at 150 yards, provided his antagonist aims at him; and as to firing at a man 200 yards with a common musket, you may just as well fire at the moon and have the same hopes of hitting your object. I do maintain, and I will prove, whenever called on, that no man was ever killed, at two hundred yards, by a common soldier's musket, by the person who aimed at him."*

This last qualification underlines the fact that the effectiveness of the musket lay solely in its use by massed formations delivering volley fire, which in the British army was executed by a system of three ranks. The first rank stood and fired; the second took a half-step to the right and fired between the files of those in front; and the third rank took a full step to the right before firing between the files. After firing each rank began reloading immediately, and a trained man could load and fire between two and three times a minute. Sometimes firing was done by files, with every three men shooting in turn, so that a continuous rolling fire blazed down the line. There are many accounts of its effectiveness at close quarters, one of the earliest being by George Stanhope who took part in the Battle of Culloden in April 1746:

*"...Our regiment being next to Wolfe's...had the finest opportunity imaginable which we did not let slip of giving the column of the rebels that was not forty yards distance from our regiment's right, the most infernal flanking fire that was ever given...for the rebels were soon after put to flight, and when we marched on to pursue them I never saw such dreadful slaughter we had made lying as thick as if they grounded their arms and our men gave no quarter to them; I reckon two thousand of them killed in the field besides a full thousand killed in the pursuit by the horse and dragoons with a great many of their chiefs."*

Loading by rank generally permitted two shots a minute to be fired, but in extreme circumstances a loose ball could be loaded and "firmed home" by tapping the butt on the ground. By this method - risky, as we have seen - up to five shots a minute could be fired. There is no doubt that within its limitations the musket was a very effective weapon at short ranges of up to 80 yards; an average battalion of around 350 men loading and firing would be able to project about 1,100 musket balls per minute at the enemy, or nearer 2,000 in the most desperate circumstances. At such distances there was little need to aim - in fact the command given was to "present" or "level" the musket rather than to aim it. Dirom, an English soldier of the 1st Regiment of Foot Guards, gave this account of the effect of a close volley on the French Imperial Guard at Waterloo:

*"They continued to advance until within fifty or sixty paces of our front, when the Brigade was ordered to stand up. Whether it was the sudden and unexpected appearance of a Corps so near to them...or the tremendously heavy fire we threw into them, La Garde, who had never before failed in an attack, suddenly stopped. Those who from a distance and more on the flank could see the affair, tell us that the effect of our fire seemed to force the head of the Column bodily back."*

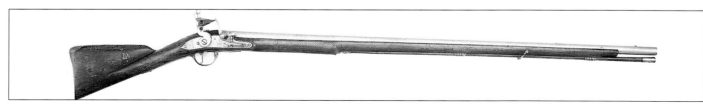

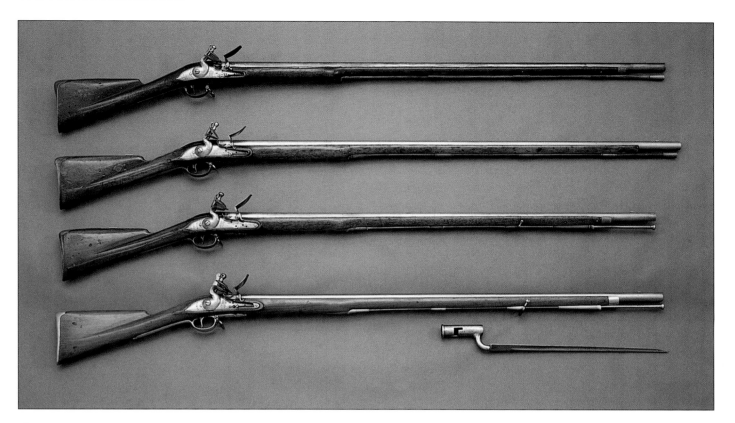

The first half of the 18th century saw the introduction of the Long Land Pattern muskets. The upper two *are dated 1731 and 1746 respectively; they have wooden ramrods and the distinctive early "banana" shape to the lockplates. The third is a militia pattern of 1762, and has a steel ramrod and a shorter, straighter lock. Both this and the bottom musket, a 1775 Short Land Pattern, have shorter barrels, and the standard triangular-section socket bayonet issued from about 1700 is also pictured. (A1618; The Board of Trustees of the Royal Armouries)*

Late 18th century illustration of a British grenadier of the type who saw service in Marlborough's army at the beginning of that century. Aside from the cast iron grenade which he is holding at a very sensible distance from the slowmatch in his left hand, he also carries a musket and bayonet as well as an infantry hanger - these short swords were a last resort weapon for close engagements.

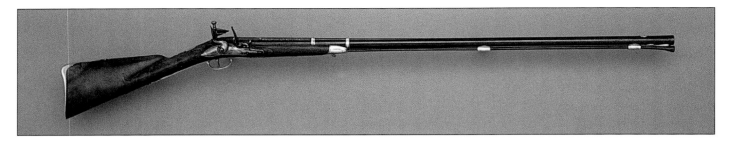

*In the 18th century military muskets were identical in shape and function to sporting guns, although of a much more plain quality. This is a typical good quality commercial gun by Mills, dated 1721, in .75in calibre. (XII.1789; A4545; The Board of Trustees of the Royal Armouries)*

The long musket was still considered too unwieldy, and in 1768 the Short Land Pattern was produced. This was almost a clone of the Long apart from a 42in barrel, and the two patterns overlapped in service until the end of the century. Minor modifications to the shape of stock and furniture continued throughout the latter part of the century, but the next major change was the introduction in 1793 of the India Pattern.

For some years the Board of Ordnance had been trying to find a cheaper, lighter replacement for the Land muskets, and this need became desperate in view of the looming spectre of renewed war with Revolutionary France. Although not regarded as ideal by the Board, the India Pattern had the advantage of having already been made in great quantities for the East India Company, so large numbers were available prior to the outbreak of war. More importantly, it could be made to pattern by established contractors who already had access to the necessary tooling, a fact of great importance to a country that suddenly found itself having to equip a huge army. Exact quantities made are difficult to establish, but were somewhere in the region of three million.

There were many within the army and Ordnance who were well aware of its shortcomings. Hans Busk, author of *The Rifle and How to Use It*, commented some years later that the British service musket was:

*"The very clumsiest and worst contrived of any firelock in the world. It required the largest charge of powder and the heaviest ball of any; yet owing to the absence of every scientific principle in its construction, its weight and windage were the greatest, its range the shortest, and its accuracy the least; at the same time it was the most costly of any similar arm in use, either in France, Belgium, Prussia or Austria."*

This was rather unfair criticism, for test results show that the India Pattern was in fact no worse than its foreign competitors and considerably better than many. It is true that it represented no giant technological step forwards - in fact, many considered it a retrograde step. But it was simpler and cheaper to make than the Land Pattern, costing an average 18 shillings and fivepence (£1.32p) each. The lock was simplified and strengthened, the barrel length reduced to 39ins and bore size reduced slightly to .76 inch. It was still a heavy and inaccurate weapon, however, and using a musket for any length of time was an exhausting ordeal for any soldier.

Infantry fire-fights at this time consisted of facing the enemy and exchanging fire with them at short or even point-blank range until casualties forced one or other side to give way. The infantryman was seldom drawn up behind cover, and as one man fell another simply stepped into his place, survival being entirely a matter of luck. Sometimes the opposing sides were so close that their bayonets nearly touched, as an anonymous soldier of the 71st Regiment of Foot recorded of his experience of fighting the French at Fuentes de Oñoro in 1811:

*"...during our first advance, a bayonet went through between my side and clothes, to my knapsack, which stopped its progress. The Frenchman to whom the bayonet belonged fell, pierced by a musket ball from my rear-rank man. Whilst freeing myself from the bayonet, a ball took off part of my right shoulder wing and killed the rear-rank man, who fell upon me. We kept up our fire until long after dark. My shoulder was as black as coal from the recoil of my musket; for this day I had fired 107 round of ball cartridge."*

As the service charge for this period was an eye-watering 165 grains it is no wonder his shoulder was tender. The quality of British gunpowder was reckoned to be the best available (due primarily to saltpetre brought from India).

Even when empty the musket could prove formidable in defence, for the introduction of the socket bayonet in England sometime after 1690 meant that the gun could be loaded and fired with its bayonet in place, and its 18in length gave the infantryman a much longer reach. The same anonymous soldier of the 71st recalled:

*"A French dragoon, who was dealing death around, forced his way up to near where I stood. Every moment I expected to be cut down. My piece was empty; there was not a moment to lose. I got a stab at him, beneath the ribs; he gave a back stroke before he fell and cut the stock of my musket in two. Thus I stood unarmed. I soon got another and fell to work again."*

Providing the rate of fire could be maintained, one side would eventually crumble under sheer weight of fire. The victorious force would then close with fixed bayonets, at which point most enemy formations would break and run rather than indulge in prolonged bayonet fighting. An officer who served with Pack's Brigade at Waterloo noted:

*"With regard to any 'bayonet conflict', I saw none. We appeared to charge, and disperse, and make a road through the [French] columns - the usual result of the British charge. The weaker body generally gives way."*

Although there were certainly many occasions when the bayonet was used with lethal effect, it was wryly regarded as having caused more injuries to its owners than it ever did to the enemy. The reason for this was simply the difficulty of reloading quickly under fire with a fixed bayonet. Sooner or later the hand holding the ramrod would connect with the point of the blade, inflicting a painful stab. Indeed, it was said that the badges of the true front line soldier were a blackened face from powder burns and a bloody bandage wrapped around the right hand.

*A mid-18th century illustration of the Long Land Pattern musket and its component parts. Interestingly, the steel (M) is referred to as the "hammer". The term "firelock" was commonly used in this period for all muskets.*

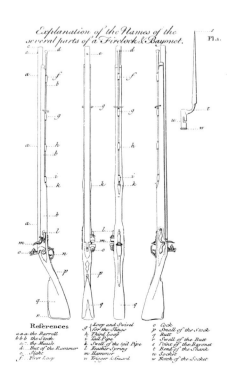

Reconstructed private soldier of the 68th Regiment, Durham Light Infantry, during the Napoleonic Wars. Over the previous century the uniform has become slightly more practical: a short-cut jacket has replaced the loose-skirted coat, a visored shako the grenadier cap and tricorn hat, and for campaign dress easy-fitting trousers are worn over short spat-type gaiters. The hanger has disappeared, but the main weapon and the other personal equipment remain essentially the same as in Marlborough's day: crossbelts supporting the cartridge box and the bayonet.

| Technical Specifications | | |
| --- | --- | --- |
| **India pattern musket:** | | |
| **Overall length** | 55ins | (1396 mm) |
| **Barrel length** | 39ins | (990 mm) |
| **Calibre** | .75in | (19mm) |
| **Weight** | 9lbs 11oz | (4.4kg) |
| **Charge** | 80 grains | |
| **Ignition** | Flint | |

The simple locking system for the socket bayonet, relying on a lug mounted on the top of the barrel engaging in a Z-slot. Using the bayonet in anger frequently resulted in it being left behind in the body of an enemy.

*Preparing to load. With musket held at waist level, he reaches into his cartridge box for a pre-prepared paper cartridge.*

## Firing the flintlock musket

Of all the firearms which we tested it was the flintlock musket which attracted the most interest from onlookers, and the most requests of "Could I possibly have a go...?" At different times a modern reproduction and an original surviving India Pattern were used; and we were able to use a chronograph, which gave some useful information with regards loads and resultant velocities.

In common with all muzzle-loading guns it was straightforward to load, particularly when a prepared cartridge was used. The soldier of the mid-18th century and the Napoleonic era was no longer laden with flasks and loose bullets, but was supplied with a cartridge which contained a charge of powder and a spherical lead bullet wrapped in stiff paper (hence "cartridge paper"). These were kept in either drilled wooden blocks, wooden boxes, or - in the case of Wellington's redcoats - open tin boxes, carried within a deep-flapped leather pouch. To shoot our musket it was decided to follow the exact procedure as laid down in Army Regulations, which involved priming the pan before loading the musket.

Firstly, the musket was raised to waist level, and put on half-cock. The cartridge was drawn from the pouch and its base, which was simply twisted closed, was torn off in the teeth. For those who have never tried chewing gunpowder, let me assure them that it will never catch on as a pastime. Not only does it taste foul, but the powder instantly dries out the saliva in the mouth, and soon causes a thirst.

The pan was opened and primed with a small quantity of powder, then snapped closed. The musket was then swung butt down to the ground, and the elbow raised square with the shoulder, while the remaining powder was poured down the barrel. The ball, still encased in paper, was then inserted into the muzzle and the ramrod drawn from its recess under the barrel. Two firm strokes were given to seat the bullet, the ramrod was replaced in its pipes, and the musket was held at the "port". The prepared charge used was a reasonably modest 80 grains of coarse powder.

The musket was cocked and raised to the shoulder, and the bayonet lug, which acts as a crude foresight, was aimed at the target. When the trigger was squeezed there was a click as the flint struck the frizzen, followed by a flash of igniting powder, but that was all: we had suffered a "flash in the pan". This was simply due to the touch hole being blocked, so a few seconds of scraping with the brass wire pricker solved the problem. The second attempt did not meet with any better success, however, due to the jaws of the cock being slightly loose and allowing the flint to slip sideways. It was at about this point that we began to be extremely grateful not to have Polish lancers bearing down on us.

Fixing the flint securely is something of an exact science; it has to be placed at the most efficient angle to ensure that its striking face hits the frizzen squarely, about one third of the way down. If the flint is poorly angled the resulting sparks can quite easily miss the pan entirely, or there may simply be no sparks at all. The flint also has to be very firmly gripped in the jaws of the cock, with a thin piece of leather or lead strip around it to ensure a good, non-slip bearing surface for the jaws. The quality of flints varied widely, with the very best coming from Brandon in Suffolk. These were completely black, but lesser quality flints could have lighter spots of grey colour in them; the poorest of all were often brown. It was generally felt that a good flint would provide about 30 reliable strikes before losing its edge. Unlike

*Biting the end off the cartridge. The recruiting parties which roamed the countryside seeking volunteers were not particularly fussy about their health, but the doctor was always supposed to check for two things before accepting a man: hernias ("bursten bellies"), and the state of his teeth - if he couldn't bite a cartridge, he couldn't use a musket.*

pyrites, flint is a comparatively brittle compound which will fail to spark once its striking edge is chipped. A bad flint may lose its edge after less then ten strikes.     As a matter of historical interest, the flint we used was one of a number of originals found quite recently on the battlefield of Waterloo; and once we had repositioned it and checked the pan, it proved more than adequate, giving a good, bright spark. At the third attempt the musket fired, giving a hefty recoil.

Using our pre-prepared paper cartridges, and ramming the bullet as carefully as we could, the results obtained were almost identical to those achieved 160 years ago. Neither was there any appreciable difference in accuracy or range between the modern replica and the original musket. Having fired ten shots at 50 yards a group of nine inches was obtained on a man-sized target, although two bullets went wide for no discernible reason. This opened out to an interesting 31 inches at 100 yards' range. This meant in practical terms that at 50 yards the shooter would *probably* hit the man he aimed at, and confirms Colonel Hanger's belief that at 100 yards a soldier could score a hit somewhere in front of him providing he was firing into a fairly densely packed mass of men.

We nevertheless rather optimistically tried shooting at 200 yards; and while the bullets were certainly reaching the vicinity of the target, they fell in such a random manner that it was not really possible to determine any measurable accuracy. At that range they seemed to have little power to them, although one or two were able to penetrate the wooden supports of the target.

The same trials were then repeated using a measured charge of loose powder and a carefully patched, lubricated ball. The patches were of a round, commercial type, and certainly resulted in more effort being required to ram the ball home even though the bore had been washed clean first. Ramming was done as gently as possible to avoid lead deformation. At 50 yards there was a marginal improvement over cartridge fire, with the bullets all striking the target and forming a seven-inch group; but at 100 yards the results remained unimpressive, the patching only reducing the group to 28 inches. While the 50-yard result was hardly sniper-like accuracy, it did prove the point that careful patching and loading could marginally improve matters at close range, although this would hardly have been practical on a Napoleonic battlefield. Of course, the huge shotgun blast of bullets produced by volley fire was quite deadly when the target was a densely packed body of men at close range, particularly as a single bullet could sometimes kill or maim more than one man before losing its lethal velocity.

The velocities were checked with the aid of the chronograph, and it was found that the musket ball varied between a low of 792fps and a high of 815fps with an 80-grain charge.

*He pours a small amount of powder from the cartridge into the pan; note its coarse texture - by this period soldiers no longer carried separate fine powder for priming. Once he has finished priming he will close the spring-loaded steel over the pan.*

*The ball and the remains of the paper cartridge are dropped down the barrel; and rammed home. The force needed to ram a bullet down a fouled bore made the early wooden ramrods vulnerable to snapping, so all service longarms were now fitted with iron ramrods.*

*The musket lock is brought to the full-cock position, having been set at half-cock throughout the loading procedure.*

With a greased patch velocities improved quite considerably, from a low of 836fps to a high of 942fps. Interestingly, using a larger charge achieved little in terms of increasing either the velocity or the accuracy, and simply increased the amount of unburned powder being blown from the muzzle (a similar result was recorded with the Pattern 1853 Enfield tested later). In view of the potency of modern powder no one felt brave enough to duplicate tests done in 1857 which used the full military charge, so we simply accepted as fact that at that date a velocity of 1500fps had been reached. The loss of velocity was quite rapid, with 627fps recorded at 100 yards and a slothlike 415fps at 200 yards. Beyond this it was impossible to determine exactly in which direction the bullet would go, so investigation ceased.

We were particularly interested in the accuracy of the weapon, for many - and often contradictory - claims have been made about the capabilities of the military musket during the Napoleonic Wars. Tests were undertaken in the early 19th century by the French using their standard 1777 pattern musket, in which one hundred shots were fired at ranges of 100, 300 and 600 paces (about 75, 230 and 340 yards). These resulted in 75, 16 and seven hits respectively. However, the term accuracy is relative here, for these shots were fired at a target six feet high and 100 feet wide, meant to represent a formed infantry unit.

In Britain more stringent tests carried out in 1830 with a New Land Pattern musket showed an appalling level of accuracy, with a mean point of aim deviation at 100 yards of nearly five feet horizontally and six feet vertically. In practical terms, at this range this would only guarantee a hit from an aimed shot if the target were a small elephant. When fired at 200 yards the deviation increased to over nine feet vertically, and could not even be measured horizontally. The maximum range for the .72in ball was recorded as 700 yards, but it had so little velocity at that range that it was not deemed capable of inflicting a wound. Indeed, the French military command believed implicitly that any infantry formation was safe from the effects of musket fire at 200 yards. Whilst our tests showed that a very carefully patched ball did have improved accuracy and power, it seems doubtful that any service musket of the period could usefully propel a ball with any effect beyond 300 yards.

The practical truth about effective ranges has little to do with the type of musket used, but lies in the distances at which the traditional infantry fire-fight took place. Studies of 19 of the best documented battles between 1750 and 1830 show that the average range for an exchange of infantry volleys was 64 yards; and that closing fire, when the lines of infantry were advancing and firing, was delivered at a mere 30 yards. By comparing the quantity of ammunition used against the rolls of dead and wounded, it has been calculated that it took 900 shots to inflict one casualty. This, oddly enough, is a statistic that did not alter much with the advent of modern firearms in the 20th century; for although accuracy has been greatly improved, modern guns fire their ammunition away much faster.

In summary, the flintlock musket provided no real surprises on the range. It was certainly tiring to load and shoot for any length of time, even with a reduced load. Although its recoil was not unacceptable at first it became quite punishing with repetition. Fouling became evident after only four shots, and it became harder to ram the bullets down as time progressed, although - providing one was not too bothered about deforming them - it never actually became impossible. Nevertheless, the flintlock's shortcomings as a military longarm had become evident even before massed frontal attacks ceased to be the normal method of waging warfare. Clearly the future lay with the rifle.

As the trigger is pulled the steel can be seen as a blur, falling backwards as it is struck by the flint. The first glow of sparks are just visible above the pan.

The copious smoke from the priming charge is blown back as the main charge ignites, and below the landscape disappears. Magnify this by between 200 and 350 for one of the two ranks of a battalion drawn up in the linear formation of the Napoleonic Wars; then add - on a still, heavy day like 18 June 1815 - the same for the second rank, before the smoke of the first volley can clear.

The substantial holes left by the .76in lead bullet from an India Pattern musket. Although this looks quite an impressive group, it should be pointed out that it was fired at 25 yards, and one shot missed totally.

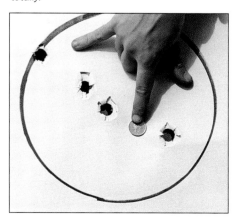

# THE FLINTLOCK RIFLE

*A so-called Pennsylvania rifle of the type which became legendary in the hands of American volunteers fighting the French and Indians in the 1750s and the British army in the 1770s. Despite its characteristic curved butt and long barrel, it in fact owed its origins to the Jäger rifles of Germany. (XII.1568; A5731; The Board of Trustees of the Royal Armouries)*

**T**he concept of the rifle had been understood for a considerable time prior to its gradual application to military firearms in the 18th century. The technique of rifling was probably introduced in Germany during the late 15th century, although most known examples date from after 1540. Rifling involves cutting a series of spiral grooves into the bore of a gun, which causes the bullet to spin as it is fired. It is not known who first realised that a spinning bullet is more accurate, but archery was probably the starting point: the triple fletchings of a medieval arrow were set on the shaft in such a way as to make it spin in flight, which gave greater stability.

Aside from air resistance and gravity, about which the science of earlier centuries could do little, the main problem with a bullet in flight was instability. Due both to windage and to the casting imperfections in the bullet, the unbalanced lead ball wobbled in flight. However, if the bullet were induced to spin on its own axis the centrifugal force thus created effectively cancelled out these negative effects. The bullet remained steady in flight, and thus travelled further and straighter than a ball from a smooth bore.

The effect, if not the theoretical cause, was certainly understood by the late 15th century; and in European shooting matches rifles were being used to great effect from the mid-16th century. It is recorded that at a contest at Mainz, Germany, in 1547 one member of the Sharpshooters' Guild fired 20 shots at 200 metres, scoring 19 hits within the bullseye and one within 18 inches of it.

The obstacle to widespread production of rifled firearms was the technical difficulty of cutting the grooves, which had to be of perfectly consistent width, depth and spacing. With the simple hand boring and reaming tools available in the pre-industrial period this was a long and physically demanding process, and naturally such work was costly. Consequently there was only a moderate demand for rifled guns in England before the mid-17th century, although they were extremely popular among hunters in Germany. There does exist a rare example of an early English patent dated 1635, which was applied for by Arnold Rotispen so that he could: *"rifle, cutt out, or screwe barrels as wyde or as close or as deep or as shallowe as shall be required and with greate ease."*

The dawn of the industrial age in the 17th century brought improvements in mechanical technology and manufacturing processes. Initially water power was harnessed to make boring and rifling less labour intensive, although it was still a highly skilled art. To make a barrel was relatively straightforward. Once a hollow tube had been formed by hammering red-hot metal around a mandrel, it was bored out with a series of increasingly larger drills

*A Ferguson pattern rifle by Hirst, with the screw breech plug removed. It had a very quick thread, enabling it to be completely opened or closed in one and a half turns of the handle on the trigger guard. However, it had to be replaced with its threads mating in exactly the right position or the breech could not be closed. (XII.257; A5638; The Board of Trustees of the Royal Armouries)*

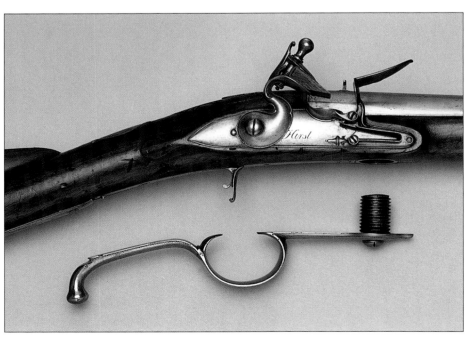

**LEFT** *Reconstruction of a rifleman of the 95th Regiment in about 1812; the uniforms of the rifle corps were unique among the British infantry in being green instead of red. All men accepted into the Rifles were expected to become above average shots, another notable innovation in an age of massed, unaimed fire.*

**ABOVE** *The lighter parts of his equipment still show up, but compared with the standard issue infantry dress the effectiveness of the green uniform for open order fighting is clearly shown here. In such surroundings the red coat and white pipe-clayed crossbelts of the "battalion regiments" stood out like a beacon. The efficiency of the Rifles lay as much in their superior tactical training as in the quality of their weapon.*

until the desired bore size was reached, finally being polished to a mirror finish. The gunsmith then checked it by eye for straightness and any surface irregularities. Blemishes caused by tiny bulges in the wall of the barrel were tapped down with a copper mallet to push them into the bore, then polished out. The barrel was then clamped steady, and a rotating reamer mounted on a complex movable carriage was introduced into the bore, where the gunsmith began to cut one spiral groove. This process was then repeated several times, depending on the number of rifling grooves required.

Although adopted by sportsmen the rifle initially had no practical military application, since the tactics of the time did not rely on individual marksmanship. However, as the advance of machine technology gradually made the process of rifling easier, faster and cheaper, rifles began to appear in military service at the end of the 17th century. Light, short-barrelled and of reasonably large calibre, they were capable of hitting a target with an aimed shot at 200 yards - well beyond the capabilities of the regulation musket. By the early 18th century a few companies of specialist soldiers equipped with rifles had been raised, principally in Germany and France; this innovation has always been credited to King Christian of Denmark, who was enthusiastic about the possibilities of introducing this new technology to the battlefield. These units were often called *Jägers* (hunters), and the term Jäger has now become synonymous with this pattern of rifle.

As usual, Britain was in no hurry to adopt new technology, and it was not until 1776 that the rifle made an appearance in limited numbers with the British army fighting in North America. The War of Independence was finally lost and won in conventional battle between musket-armed line infantry of the British, French and Continental armies; but there is too much anecdotal evidence for us to discount too lightly the degree to which British troops suffered at the hands of American riflemen whose skills had been honed through hunting for the pot. They carried long-barrelled, small calibre flintlocks capable of great accuracy. General Simon Fraser was shot dead by a rifleman named Murphy at a range of 300 yards; and Major George Hanger (whose opinions on muskets we have already heard) recounted just how capable the Americans could be:

"*Colonel, now General Tarleton and myself were standing a few yards out of a wood, observing the situation of a part of the enemy which we intended to attack. There was...a mill...to which we stood directly with our horses' heads fronting...our orderly bugler stood behind us about three yards, but with his horse's side to our horses' tails. A rifleman passed over the mill dam, evidently observing two officers, and laid himself down on his belly; for in such positions they always lie, to take a good shot at long distance. He took a deliberate and cool shot at my friend, at me and at the bugle-horn man. Colonel Tarleton's horse and mine I am certain, were not anything like two feet apart; for we were in close consultation, how we should attack with our troops which laid 300 yards in the wood...a rifle-ball passed between him and me; looking directly at the mill I observed the flash of the powder. I directly said to my friend, 'I think we had better move, or we shall shortly have two or three of these gentlemen amusing themselves at our expense.' The words were hardly out of my mouth when the bugle-horn man behind me, and directly central, jumped off his horse and said, 'Sir, my horse is shot.' Now speaking of this rifleman's shooting, nothing could be better...I have passed several times over this ground and ... I can positively assert that the distance he fired at was full 400 yards.*"

*Looking down into the opened screw breech of a decorated commercial rifle based on the Ferguson type, made in London by Durs Egg in 1782-83; although the military issue Fergusons were very plain, mechanically they were identical to this weapon. The whereabouts of the rifles issued to Ferguson's unit have never been discovered.(Royal Collection, on loan to the Royal Armouries)*

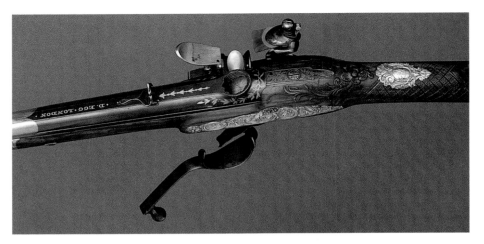

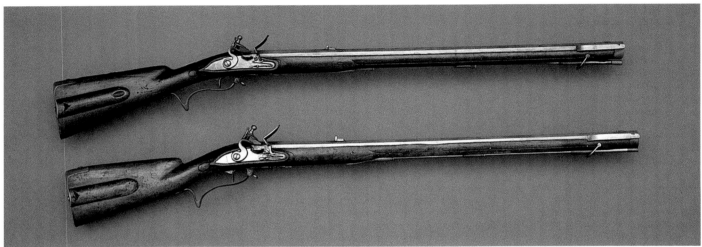

*A pair of German Jäger rifles supplied to the Dutch army; they are of very characteristic shape, with scrolled trigger guards to help provide a firm grip, and patch-boxes in the butt-stocks. Rifles similar to these were purchased by the Board of Ordnance for British army units prior to the adoption of the Baker. (XII.241/2; A5627; The Board of Trustees of the Royal Armouries)*

These Pennsylvania and Kentucky rifles were of much smaller calibre than the musket, usually between .40in and .55 inch. The barrels were also exceptionally long, from 40 to 50 inches, which gave the maximum possible velocity to the projectile. It was generally accepted that up to 150 yards these rifles had a perfectly flat trajectory, with only moderate bullet drop out to 300 yards, for which an experienced rifleman could compensate. It is little wonder that in the face of such potent weapons the British soldiers felt frustrated at their inability to reply with anything other than artillery.

The British army was obliged to review its position as regards rifles, and ordered a number of screw-breech weapons adapted from an earlier French design by Captain Patrick Ferguson of the 70th Foot. (For the impressive report on Ferguson's demonstration before the Board of Ordnance in 1776, see our later chapter on The Breech-Loading Rifle.) The guns were manufactured by a number of prominent English makers including Henry Nock and Joseph Hunt, though not all were enamoured of the breech-loading rifle as a practical weapon, as Ezekiel Baker wrote:

*"I have tried various ways of loading rifles at the breech, by means of screws placed in different positions, but after a few rounds firing, the screws have become so clogged by the filth of the powder working round them as to be very difficult to move, and will in time be eaten away with rust, which will render them dangerous to use."*

This observation is not exaggerated, as the corrosive properties of gunpowder are legendary, and the ability of the most conscientious soldier to look after his weapon under 18th century campaign conditions was limited. Still, the authorities were sufficiently impressed by the Ferguson's accuracy and rate of fire (of between four and seven shots per minute) to raise a rifle unit of 100 men. Ironically, Ferguson was himself killed by an American rifleman at King's Mountain in 1780, after which the rifle vanished for a time from British military use.

\*　　\*　　\*

Many contemporary military men cited the expertise of the American riflemen as a factor in the defeat of Britain during the War of Independence. Indeed, General Lord Howe went so far as to complain to the Government about the effectiveness of "the terrible guns of the rebels." There is little doubt, either, that the effective, individualistic style of fighting adopted by many American units had shaken the conservative military commanders, who were forced to recognise the relative success of British light infantry corps raised for the American campaigns and trained in similar tactics. Defeat in America aroused new fears about the nation's ability to defend itself, and the rising tide of turmoil in Europe towards the end of the century fuelled this concern. As a result there was a tremendous increase in the number of Militia and Fencible units raised, and the Board of Ordnance began to look more closely at the effectiveness of military firearms, particularly rifles. In 1798 some 5,000 Prussian rifled muskets of the Jäger type were ordered from Germany; but they proved to be of poor quality. Only relatively few were issued to specialist and foreign mercenary regiments such as the 5th Battalion, 60th Regiment; most saw service in the colonies.

Within the Board of Ordnance there was little agreement over which pattern of rifle should be adopted or to whom they should be issued. After exhaustive trials at Woolwich in 1799 the Board gave Ezekiel Baker an order for some trials pattern rifles in varying bore sizes, and the first of the .70in "musket bore" Bakers was produced in 1800. Production was shared between a number of makers in London and Birmingham, who produced the first batch of 800 to be issued to the newly formed 95th (Rifle) Regiment in 1802. Volunteer units also expressed great interest in the Baker, and by 1805 both infantry and cavalry variants were in production, in .70 and .62 calibres respectively.

These Bakers were based on the design of the German Jäger rifles, with shorter barrels and bores of smaller calibre than the issue musket. The barrels had seven-groove rifling with a rate of twist of one quarter turn in the length of the bore. The trigger guard was extended in a "scroll" at the rear to give a better grip for the right hand, as was traditional on the Jäger rifle. Some attention was also paid to the shape of the butt, which had a high cheek comb to help bring the eye behind the sights, and was angled slightly upwards to ensure that the recoil was taken square on the shoulder. This was important, as the service charge for the Baker was a fairly significant 101 grains - noticeably punishing for repeated shooting. Recruits who were found to have emptied out some of their powder when training to lessen the recoil were likely to be placed on a charge, since the army reasoned that teaching a rifle-man not to flinch each time he fired was more important than preventing bruised shoulders.

The capabilities of the Baker have been much exaggerated over the years, but there seems little doubt that compared to the service musket it was almost a precision weapon. As significantly novel as the weapon itself was the training; the men of the 95th and 5/60th were trained specifically as individual marksmen, and to fight in open order as pairs of skirmishers in the light infantry style. These self-consciously elite soldiers regularly held shooting competitions; and the memoirs of Rifleman William Surtees, who spent 25 years in the 95th, mention two comrades taking turns at hand-holding targets for each other at 150 yards' range. There are many well-documented accounts of the Baker's efficiency in battle in the hands of skilled shots, and the *voltigeurs* of the French light infantry were deeply frustrated by the inability of their smoothbore muskets to reply effectively, just as the redcoats had been in America.

*A Volunteer rifleman, drawn in a common stance for steadying the rifle, with the sling braced hard back by the left hand. A leather or oilcloth lock cover lies at his feet, beside a small cork to plug the muzzle against rain when not in use.*

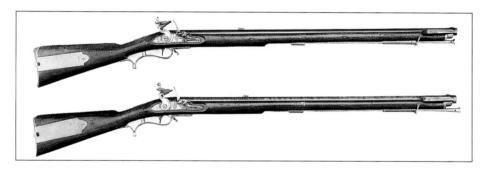

*Two patterns of Baker rifle. Although they look superficially identical, the upper example is of .62 calibre, which was generally referred to as "carbine bore", while the lower has the .70in "musket bore". Both date from between 1810 and 1820 and have seven-groove barrels; the small folding-leaf rear sight and brass patch-box lid are features which were dispensed with on later models. (XII.147/148; A6/813; The Board of Trustees of the Royal Armouries)*

Riflemen were even used on occasion to silence enemy artillery batteries; at Badajoz 40 picked men of the 95th were able to drive off a French battery by picking off the crews. An unnamed French officer whose unit suffered severely in the Peninsula at the hands of Baker-armed riflemen recalled:

*"I was sent out to skirmish against some of those in green - grasshoppers, I call them - you call them Rifle Men. They were behind every bush and stone, and soon made sad havoc amongst my men, killing all the officers in my company, and wounding myself, without [our] being able to do them any injury..."*

*Section of a Baker rifle barrel showing the lands and grooves, which make only one quarter-turn in the length of the bore. Such a "slow twist" had properties which made it particularly suitable for a black powder rifle: it collected less fouling, and gave the bullet a flatter trajectory in flight, making aiming far easier. (XII.2443)*

Despite the accounts of the prowess of riflemen at long range sniping their main everyday value lay in their ability to form strong skirmishing screens at some distance from the mass of the army: harassing and disorganising enemy units in movement by picking off NCOs and officers, blinding the enemy by holding off their own scouts, and delaying and weakening the advance of assault columns. The ranges at which they exchanged fire were often well within the reach of the musket; the important difference was that a rifle was capable of firing an aimed shot at a specific target, and the musket was not. Rifleman Harris graphically illustrated this in an account of a duel with a French infantryman during the Peninsular War. As he knelt to try on a looted pair of shoes:

*"...I was startled by the sharp report of a firelock, and at the same moment, a bullet whistled close by my head. Instantly starting up, I turned, and looked in the direction whence the shot had come...but nothing could I see. I looked to the priming of my rifle...when another shot took place, and a second ball whistled past me. This time I was ready, and turning quickly, I saw my man; he was just about to squat down behind a small mound, about twenty paces from me. I took a haphazard shot at him, and instantly knocked him over."*

Finding accounts of the use of the Baker in combat is not too difficult; the problem lies in determining the range at which these encounters occured - John Harris is unusual among contemporary writers in mentioning this.

The main drawback of using the rifle was the more difficult loading procedure as compared with the smoothbore musket. To ensure accuracy there had to be a tight fit between the bullet and the rifling of the barrel; any windage, however small, would ruin the shot. To achieve this the use of a patched bullet was vital, and early patterns of the Baker had a patch-box let into the butt which contained greased linen patches and spare flints. The problem of fouling was exacerbated in the rifle. After a few shots the barrel became choked and the tight-fitting ball could not be rammed home.

A recruiting poster printed in Hull in 1808 which underlines the crack reputation of the 95th Rifles. Its claim that recruits would be able to knock down an enemy with a rifle at 500 yards is deeply suspect, but most recruiting literature was written by shameless liars.

An original Baker rifle lock. The marks are typical for military weapons of the 18th and 19th centuries, showing this to be a government issue rifle manufactured at the Tower of London by I.Gill in about 1812. (XII.148)

The crude flip-up rear sight on a second model Baker. The browning of the barrel is original, and was applied to protect the metal from rust, although it soon wore off with use. (XII.148)

On early Bakers a patch-box was fitted in the butt. This one has round linen patches in the forward compartment and spare flints in the rear.

# RIFLE CORPS!

## *COUNTRYMEN!*

### LOOK, BEFORE YOU LEAP:

Half the Regiments in the Service are trying to persuade you to Enlist:

*But there is ONE MORE to COME YET!!!*

# The 95th; or,

## Rifle REGIMENT,

COMMANDED BY THE HONOURABLE

*Major-General Coote Manningham,*

The only Regiment of RIFLEMEN in the Service:

THINK, then, and CHOOSE, Whether you will enter into a Battalion Regiment, or prefer being a RIFLEMAN,

*The first of all Services in the British Army.*

In this distinguished Service, you will carry a Rifle no heavier than a Fowling-Piece. You will knock down your Enemy at Five Hundred Yards, instead of missing him at Fifty. Your Clothing is GREEN, and needs no cleaning but a Brush. Those men who have been in a RIFLE COMPANY, can best tell you the comfort of a GREEN JACKET.

### NO WHITE BELTS; NO PIPE CLAY!

On Service, your Post is always the Post of Honour, and your Quarters the best in the Army; for you have the first of every thing; and at Home you are sure of Respect - because a BRITISH RIFLEMAN always makes himself Respectable.

The RIFLE SERGEANTS are to be found any where, and have orders to Treat their Friends gallantly every where.

If you Enlist, and afterwards wish you had been a RIFLEMAN, do not say you were not asked, for you can BLAME NOBODY BUT YOURSELF.

### GOD SAVE the KING! *and his Rifle Regiment!*

To help force the reluctant bullet down the barrel the riflemen were provided with small mallets. There has been some disagreement over the years as to whether these were ever actually issued and used by the Rifle regiments. However, Board of Ordnance records certainly show two orders fulfilled by Ezekiel Baker to supply small mallets, at 2½ pence each, for issue directly to the Rifle regiments; and Rifleman Costello, in listing the equipment he carried in Portugal in 1809, mentions *"thirty loose balls, [and] a small wooden mallet to hammer the ball into the muzzle of our rifles."*

This raises a secondary problem, for mallet-blows on the iron ramrod would deform the soft lead bullet so that it was no longer spherical, and in flight it might become almost as wayward as a common musket ball. That the problem was well understood is illustrated by the fact that in addition to their issue cartridges with patched ball the riflemen were also issued with loose powder and musket balls which, when used unpatched, were of smaller calibre and thus easier to load. This meant that a rifleman with a fouled barrel could still use his weapon in an emergency. William Green of the 1/95th stated that during the retreat to Corunna the men carried *"fifty rounds of ball cartridge, thirty loose balls at our waist belt, and a flask, and a horn of powder and rifle and sword [bayonet], the two weighing 14 pounds."*

Nor was the rifle an easy weapon to look after, for apart from the usual working parts such as the lock mechanism its bore required regular and careful cleaning, which on campaign was all but impossible. Harris commented that at the end of the retreat to Corunna most of the 95th's rifles were unusable, being solid with rust, and that his bayonet was so corroded that it could not be withdrawn from its scabbard.

The bayonet was in fact a constant problem for the rifleman, for the original sword pattern was unwieldy, heavy, and prone to dropping off just when it was needed. Pre-1815 pattern Bakers can be recognised by the girder-like bayonet mounting bar on the right side of the muzzle. Eventually a far more sensible triangular knife pattern was adopted which, curiously, was never used on any other weapon in the British army despite its eminently practical shape.

The heavier .70 calibre (musket bore) Bakers were soon discarded in favour of the lighter and more practical .62in carbine bore. It is very difficult to estimate how many Baker rifles were manufactured, or even to whom - apart from the three battalions of the 95th, and the 5/60th - they were issued, as surviving records do not list the Baker as a specific model by name. It is believed that picked sharpshooters in the light infantry companies of a number of line units received rifles. Certainly the 65th Foot had them in India during the Napoleonic Wars, and Lawrence of the 1/40th Foot mentions rifles when serving with the light company in South America and Portugal in 1806-09. It is known that 200 Bakers were despatched to

Paris in summer 1815 to replace those destroyed in the service of the 2/95th at Waterloo. By the time the final production run of rifles was completed in 1838 something in excess of 40,000 had been made. By then the end of the flintlock era was in sight, soon to be superseded by the percussion system; so it says something for the durability of the Baker that it was still in use by line infantry in India in 1851.

Despite its success as a military weapon, the government was still not entirely convinced about the wisdom of issuing rifles to the entire army, and line regiments continued to be issued with smoothbore muskets until the gradual introduction of the Minié rifle in the 1850s.

*Original leather-patched balls for a Baker rifle. Issued to the Percy Tenantry Volunteers, these pre-patched balls solved the problem of having to carry separate greased linen patches; they were supplied in sealed tins. Although the leather has shrunk slightly they are still in remarkable condition after 180 years. (XIII.269; A8595; The Board of Trustees of the Royal Armouries)*

## Technical Specifications

| Baker rifle: | | |
|---|---|---|
| Overall length | 45.75ins | (1160mm) |
| Barrel length | 30.25ins | (768mm) |
| Calibre | 62in | (16.3mm) |
| Weight | 9lbs 2oz | (4.1kg) |
| Charge | 80 grains | |
| Ignition | Flint | |

*An original rifleman's powder horn for use with Baker-pattern weapons; this example was issued to a Volunteer rifle unit. (XIII.231; A8594; The Board of Trustees of the Royal Armouries)*

*The rifleman's cartridge box, powder flask (its green cord passing through retaining loops on the face of the cartridge box crossbelt), and waistbelt pouch for loose bullets.*

*Rust on the face of the steel might cause a misfire which could cost a soldier his life. Many riflemen fashioned for themselves leather covers to protect the frizzen from damp.*

The nozzle of the flask has a removable measure held by a spring catch. It holds 106 grains of coarse powder, which was poured directly into the barrel.

A patched ball is removed from the pouch and rammed down the barrel, with some effort. As a last resort a small mallet could be used to ensure that the bullet was sent securely home down the rifling, eliminating any air space which might cause a breech explosion.

## Firing the Baker rifle

The question that everyone was keen to answer on the day of this trial was, of course, exactly how accurate was the Baker? Can the feats recounted in Sharpe's fictional adventures be believed, or did the Baker get its reputation simply because everything else available at the time was so awful?

The first impression one gains when picking up a Baker is one of solidity. It is a very well constructed gun, similar in style to the German Jäger rifles, with a typically excellent wood-to-metal component fit, and the comfortable barrel length of 30.25ins does not render it too muzzle heavy. Were it not for the massive bayonet bar on the right side of the muzzle it would actually resemble in form a good quality early sporting gun. The example we used was one of a small number of copies modelled on a first pattern Baker held in the collection of The Royal Armouries.

It sits very well in the shoulder, and there is a prominent two-position flip-up rear sight set well forward of the breech, with a short blade front. By modern standards these sights are crude, and trying to obtain any sort of reasonable sight picture is difficult, the more so at longer ranges; this would certainly limit the shooter's marksmanship unless he was very familiar with his particular rifle. The muzzle is "relieved", being slightly countersunk at the end to permit easier loading of the ball, and a steel ramrod is fitted underneath the barrel.

As with all muzzle-loading rifled longarms, the secret of accurate shooting lies in the quality of ammunition and the care given to loading. In the case of the Baker this seems especially important, as poor loading practice dramatically affects the range and accuracy. It became clear that trying to shoot a Baker with pre-prepared paper cartridge and ball did not enable it to function particularly satisfactorily as a rifle (although it worked well enough if used as a musket, this was rather defeating the point).

Another problem was speed of loading. To patch and load a bullet takes about one minute, giving a rifleman a comparatively slow rate of fire compared to a line infantryman. Accepted practice appears to have been to carry a large powder horn as a magazine, refilling a smaller flask from it for the business of loading and priming. For optimum accuracy the best loading method for the Baker was found to be to charge directly from the powder flask, and to use a pre-prepared, lubricated linen patch. A charge of 80 grains was used as a starting point, and a measured charge of powder was poured into the barrel from the flask nozzle.

The next step was to place the greased patch over the muzzle and centre a ball on it. The lubricated patch was important for ensuring a tight fit, but it also helped with ramming home the bullet and with keeping the bore clear of fouling. These patches would originally have been kept in the butt-trap of the rifle and must have been pre-cut to size, although there seem to be no documentary references to this practice. As they were greased they must have been extremely awkward to handle, and after any length of time in the butt-trap they probably stuck together like a bag of warm toffees. Whether soldiers would have bothered to try to separate them under battle conditions is a moot point. Given the ability of soldiers to improvise they doubtless found a means of keeping them usable - unless, of course, they dispensed with them entirely.

The production of later pattern Bakers without provision for a patch-box in the butt would seem to indicate use of pre-prepared cartridges incorporating balls which did not require separate patching. We illustrate on page 63 surviving examples of Baker bullets issued to a Volunteer rifle unit which are pre-patched with thin greased leather glued into place. This was a practice not unknown in sporting circles, and would have been a reasonable compromise for the rifleman who found separate greased patches impractical to use in the field.

Ramming the ball home when the bore was clean was not too difficult, but if the rifle were to be used effectively it was vital that the barrel be kept as clean as possible. Our rifle had its bore lightly cleaned after every ten shots and we had no serious problems loading; but it did become progressively harder to ram the bullet home after the sixth or seventh shot. As was our usual practice, the pan was primed last, using the measure from the main flask with the same coarse powder as used for the main charge. With the rifle raised to port, and the hammer brought back to full-cock, the weapon was ready to fire.

The trigger pull is firm but not too heavy at about 6lbs, and the recoil quite hard, but not painfully so - the design of the stock helps to absorb it. As usual, the target vanished in a thick cloud of grey smoke, bringing to mind Rifleman Harris's comment that during most of a battle the smoke from the discharge of their rifles meant that he could see nothing at all in front of him *"save the red flash of my own piece amongst the white vapour clinging to my very clothes"*.

One of the few reliable tests performed at the time was by Ezekiel Baker himself, who stated that he had found: *"...200 yards the greatest range I could fire with certainty. I have fired very well at over 300 when the wind was very calm. At 400 and 500, I have sometimes struck the object, though I have found it to vary much."*

This was pretty much confirmed by our experience on the range. In modern terms the performance of the Baker was not brilliant. At 50 yards, shooting without a rest, we achieved

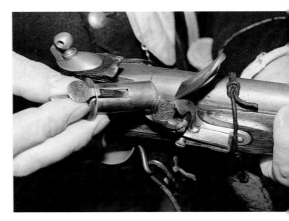

*Some riflemen carried a small separate flask for priming. In this instance a small amount is poured from the measure of the main flask into the pan. After the pan is closed the rifleman will blow any loose grains away; if this were neglected for a few shots powder worked its way along the stock, and would burn the left hand when the priming was ignited.*

*Firing the Baker: we may assume that most riflemen had singed peaks on their caps. Below It should be borne in mind that the most accurate weapon loses its advantage if its user is unsighted, and that many actions were fought by the Rifles within normal musket range. Harris of the 2/95th wrote that "...on a calm day, until some friendly breeze of wind clears the space around, a soldier knows no more of his position and what is about to happen in his front...than the very dead lying around."*

*Constant careful maintenance of the rifle was absolutely central to its continued effectiveness. Like their musket-armed comrades, riflemen carried a brush and a pricker kept handy on chains or thongs fastened to a buttonhole, to clean their pans of the residue of burnt powder and the touch hole of the debris which could quickly block it.*

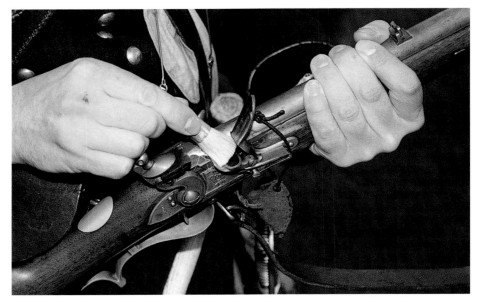

*At longer ranges the Baker was best fired with a rest. Riflemen developed their own methods of supporting their weapons, including resting the barrel on a shako when firing prone. Here a ramrod braced between left hand and hip steadies the barrel for a kneeling shot.*

good four-inch groups, and at 100 yards this opened out to ten inches. With a rest the rifle was capable of an eight-inch group at 100 yards, opening out to 18 inches at 200 yards. Despite plaintive requests for a volunteer no one seemed prepared to assist with recreating Surtees's account of shooting a square of card from a comrade's hand at 150 yards, although qualified assurances were given about the value of such a unique scientific experiment.

A common army saying of the period was "if you can't see the face, you can't hit the heart", and at 300 yards the Baker proved this to be true, achieving six hits out of ten on a man-sized target. This also seemed to confirm Baker's claimed trial results of a certain hit at 200 yards, a good chance at 300, and occasional hits at 400 yards. It must be borne in mind that a "certain hit" meant that the bullet would strike the body of a man-sized target; it was not a claim to be able to place each shot in the heart. At 500 yards firing the Baker proved to be a waste of powder; increasing the charge to 90 grains did not seem to produce any worthwhile gain, the fall of the shot being very scattered (although the recoil increased noticeably). In practical terms this would have enabled a skilled rifleman to seriously disconcert a field gun team from perhaps as far away as 400 yards, providing he were able to use a rest and sufficient shots could be fired. To achieve this, however, the barrel had to be kept reasonably clean, which would have been easier said than done while on campaign.

As an illustration of how difficult it can be to produce accurate comparative data, another reproduction rifle was used which produced an unimpressive five-inch group at 50 yards and a 14-inch group at 100 yards. At 200 yards it just about managed to place its bullets in an area roughly the size of a man's torso six shots out of ten; but at 300 yards its accuracy was very poor indeed. So which of the two rifles was the most representative?

Given the fighting conditions under which Bakers were used, and allowing for the time the average soldier would have been able to spend on maintenance, the second weapon was probably the more typical of performance in the midst of battle. As with any firearm, the skill of the shooter counted for much, regardless of how well an individual weapon had been put together. Comparing the Baker with modern firearms is neither valid nor interesting; it should obviously be judged in the context of the other weapons in use during the early 19th century. The Baker was about three times as accurate as the contemporary infantry musket - which must, in the eyes of the common soldier, have made it a very desirable weapon indeed.

*The back prone position, of which several variations were taught for long range firing. This soldier braces the rifle with a foot through the sling; it is uncomfortable to hold this position for any length of time, though the pack can give some support. It was from a back prone position, with the right leg crossed over the left and the barrel rested on the right calf, that one of the most famous shots of the Peninsular War was fired when Rifleman Tom Plunkett of the 95th killed Général Colbert at Villafranca at a range of about 300 yards.*

*The awkward Baker sword-bayonet. Long, heavy and prone to snapping, it was heartily disliked by the soldiers, and eventually abandoned in favour of a knife pattern. A long reach with cold steel was less important to skirmishers than to line troops massed to receive enemy attacks.*

# THE FLINTLOCK PISTOL

The demand for a simple, reliable military pistol of plain "munition" type increased in Europe during and after the Thirty Years' War (1608-1648). Whatever refinements were made to the wheel lock its mechanism would always remain too complex for mass purchase and use by cavalry troopers; and from the end of the 16th century examples of pistols fitted with the new snaphaunce and early flintlock mechanisms began to appear.

From about 1640 clear differences in taste and style between Continental and English pistols were emerging. In Germany and the Low Countries there was still a strong demand for the wheel lock, whilst in Italy and Spain the snaphaunce was becoming extremely popular. In France and England there tended to be more interest in the new flintlock, and by the latter half of the century both the snaphaunce and "English" lock were seen more widely throughout Europe.

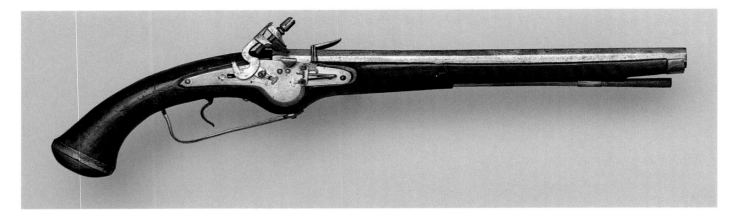

A fine early English lock pistol from the Littlecote House collection. This particularly handsome example shows the unusual lines echoing the shape of the earlier wheel lock pistols, with a rounded lockplate even though this was no longer dictated by its function. These early flintlocks were manufactured as such, and show no signs of having been converted. (XII.5430; TR1300; The Board of Trustees of the Royal Armouries)

As with the musket, gunmakers had attempted to improve the performance of the pistol, and there had been early attempts to add rifled barrels. In 1594 Sir Hugh Platte published a paper describing the form and effectiveness of a rifled pistol:

*"How to make a Pistol whose barrell is two foote in length deliver a bullet point blank at eight skore [paces]. A Pistoll of the aforesaid length and beeing of Petronel bore, or a bore higher, hauing eight guttres somewhat deepe in the inside of the barrell, and the bullet a thought bigger than the bore, and so rammed in at the first three or four inches at the least, and after driuen downe with the skowring stick, will deliuer his bullet at such distance."*

The argument against rifled pistols was not simply their cost, but also their cost-effectiveness: was it actually worthwhile fitting an expensive rifled barrel to a weapon designed purely for close range self-defence? By the end of the 17th century several distinct types of pistol had emerged, which in 1680 Randle Holmes very thoughtfully defined for posterity as follows:

*"...a pistall...this is a small gun discharged with one hand of which there are seuerall sorts, whose names are according to the bigness of them, as:*

*The pocket pistall, is the least of fire Armes, the Barrell of such peeces being from 4 to 6 Inches long.*

*The Girdle, or belt pistall, is a degree longer in the barrel then the former; and is generally hung by the side by a long peece of Iron screwed on the contrary side of the stock, to the lock. The barrells of such are from 7 to 9 or 10 inches long.*

*The Troupe, or Holster pistall, this is longer than the foresaid by as much againe, the barrells of these being generall some 16, 18 or 20 Inches; all troupers haue two of these put into holsters fixed to their sadles, and brest plates of the horse on each side."*

This description seems to be borne out by the regulations of the Council of War, who in 1639 stated that a cavalry pistol should have *"a barrell length of 18 inches, and bore of twenty four bullets to the pound."*

This gave a calibre of about .57ins, which was quite substantial. However, the authorities had modified their thinking somewhat by the turn of the century, reducing the barrel length to a modest 14 inches. There is little doubt that by this date even the pistol was being loaded with pre-prepared cartridges, the practice of using a loose ball and powder having virtually died out by the end of the Civil War. John Vernon, in a book printed in 1644, gives details of the manufacture of cartridges for cavalrymen (and reminds us that consistent spelling was not held to be a particular virtue in the 17th century):

*"Now if you use Cartages, you shall finde in your Crattreg case a turned wooden pin which you must take, having cut lengths of white paper something broader than the pin in length, and rowle the paper on the pin, then twist one end of the paper, and file it almost full of powder, then put the bullet on top of the powder, twisting that end also, then put it into your Cartreg case, now when you come to lade your carbine or Pistols with these Cartreges, you must bite off that end of the paper where the powder is, powring it into your Carbine or Pistol, then put in that bullet and some of that paper will serve for a wad after it and Ram home..."*

Pistols were being issued to British cavalry units from quite early in the century. Later, there is mention of 198 pairs of "Pistols for Dragoons" being supplied to Prince Rupert's Regiment of Dragoons in 1672. A list of the weapons supplied by the Master General of the

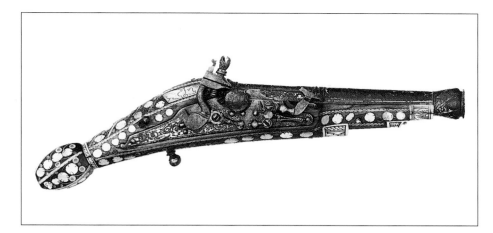

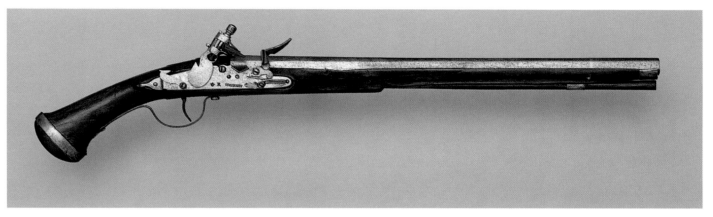

Ordnance some twenty years later includes "Ordinary Pistols with Brasse Caps", which were a plain flintlock type with brass reinforcement on the butts, not dissimilar to those available for civilian use. During the reign of Queen Anne in the first decade of the 18th century pistols became far more popular as a means of self-defence; small examples were made for pocket or purse, some with "turn-off" barrels, which unscrewed to permit easier reloading and did away with the need for a ramrod.

Of more interest to the military was the gradual development from the mid-17th century of the heavy "troop or holster pistol" described by Holmes, which was to evolve into the basic design for the 18th and 19th century cavalryman. Although this evolution paralleled that of the heavier type of civilian pistol, by the early 1700s it had begun to develop a form of its own.

Instead of having a length of barrel protruding from the stock military pistols were almost always stocked up to the muzzle, usually with a brass end cap. This not only strengthened the barrel against damage, but protected it from the corrosive effects of horse sweat, which could turn polished metal to rust in a couple of hours. The furniture on the pistol stocks was usually of brass or steel, although on the more elaborate examples purchased by officers it could be gilded or silver.

One major weakness was the short ramrod - easily lost, and rendering the weapon instantly useless when this happened. The early cavalry pistols were fitted with flimsy wooden rods which were only retained in their slots under the barrel by friction, and naturally loosened with use. Some heavy cavalry pistols were not even equipped with a fitted ramrod, a separate one being carried in the holster. This problem was recognised by the Board of Ordnance, and from the end of the 18th century an effective "stirrup ramrod" was fitted. This featured an S-shaped double-swivel link under the muzzle, which held the steel ramrod permanently attached but allowed it to be withdrawn from its recess and reversed for use.

The shape of the pistol was also changing, from the straight- stocked wheel locks of the late 15th/early 16th centuries to the far more curved and elegant style found in the 18th century. It was during the late 1640s that the popularity of the large, spherical "puffer" pommel began to fade, this gradually giving way to a far more serviceable rounded and flared butt, frequently with an inset metal butt-cap. This not only protected the wood, but also served as a useful club in emergencies. Pistols also began to appear with a more squared butt, sometimes cut straight across and reinforced with a metal band. In some instances the old wheel lock style of stock was retained, resulting in a curious form of flintlock whose shape mimicked the curves of the earlier mechanism. Many people believe these actually to be converted wheel locks, but this is hardly ever the case. Several examples survived in the Civil War armoury of Littlecote Manor, now held at the Royal Armouries Museum, which show this curious transition very clearly.

The 18th century saw a host of changes to the design and function of the pistol, many of which were simply copied from the improvements made to sporting and military muskets. One particularly useful modification copied from the musket was the introduction in about 1700 of a "bridle" to the interior of the lockplate. This was a simple metal bridge on the inside of the lock between the tumbler and sear, reinforcing the pivot points, which was an area notorious for stress fractures. Within a few years another similar bridle began to appear on

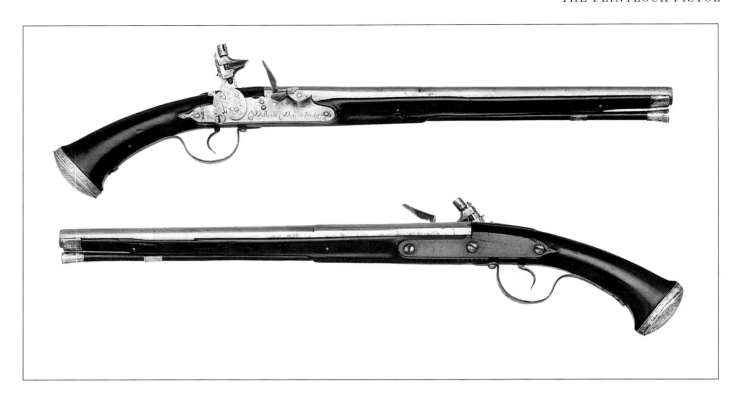

the exterior of the lock, performing the same reinforcing function between the steel and pan cover.

Gunmakers and shooters were always concerned with speeding up the action of the lock to minimise the lag between pulling the trigger and firing the main charge. At some point in the mid-18th century an unknown gunmaker found a solution in the form of a tiny roller fitted on the bearing point between the steel and its spring. This drastically reduced friction and speeded up the ignition, and within twenty years it was a common feature on all of the better quality civilian flintlocks.

Another persistent problem was the tendency of the heavy mainspring inside the lock to slip off the tumbler. This was sometimes caused by poor hardening of the spring, but more often simply by wear. Once it happened it rendered the gun inoperable without professional fitting of a new spring. The solution, which seemed to originate in England, was to fit a small link or hook to the end of the spring which prevented it slipping.

The waterproof pan cover also made its appearance, having a raised lip around the pan which located into a channel cut in the underside of the steel. It was not truly waterproof, of course, but did at least prevent rainwater from running directly off the steel and into the pan.

If the mechanical improvements did little to influence military thinking, there is little doubt that civilian fashion did affect the style of the pistol. Both lockplate and cock changed in shape dramatically from the introduction of the earliest English locks. The traditionally long, rather curved lockplate with a pointed tail became shorter, straighter and more blunt, and these changes can be seen on the military pistols of the late 18th and early 19th centuries. The cock also changed, the squat, flat style of the English Civil War period gradually giving way to a far more elegant swan-neck cock.

Safety mechanisms also began to appear. Despite the later flintlocks being equipped with a half-cock position, careless handling could still cause accidental discharges. This was far more easily done with a short pistol than a long, cumbersome musket; in addition, the users of pistols were often relatively untrained in handling them. Accidents were common; a surgeon's account dated 1742 mentions tending to "*...the wound to a trouper of his Majesty's dragouns, having by accident discharged his pistol into his bodie with the resulte of a most serious injurie to his legge...*"

The back- or dog-catch adopted on muskets in the 17th century had also appeared on pistols; it was clumsy but reasonably foolproof, being clearly visible. Another safety catch which began to appear in the late 17th century was a simple oscillating catch which locked into place on the lower edge of the cock when it was pulled back to the half-cock position; fully cocking it allowed the catch to drop away. A more sophisticated sliding bar catch was introduced some time before 1750; mounted behind the cock, this slid forward to lock the tumbler. Unusually, this little device was actually re-adopted on a number of 19th century government issue pistols.

There were other, structural weaknesses in the design of the cavalry pistol. The first was in the stock itself, where it was at its narrowest just behind the lockplate. If the barrel or butt were struck hard the stock could snap at this point; to counteract this the stock was always cut so that the grain of the wood ran at an angle of about 55 degrees to the barrel, giving the longest and strongest possible grain. Another weak point was the side of the stock opposite the point where the lock was inset into the wood. As a considerable amount of wood had to be cut away to enable the lock to be inserted, a reinforcing bar or plate was inset into the stock engaging with the lock securing screws (traditionally called "side-nails"). Improvements in metallurgy and mass production techniques allowed the number of side-nails to be reduced from the traditional three found on the wheel locks to two.

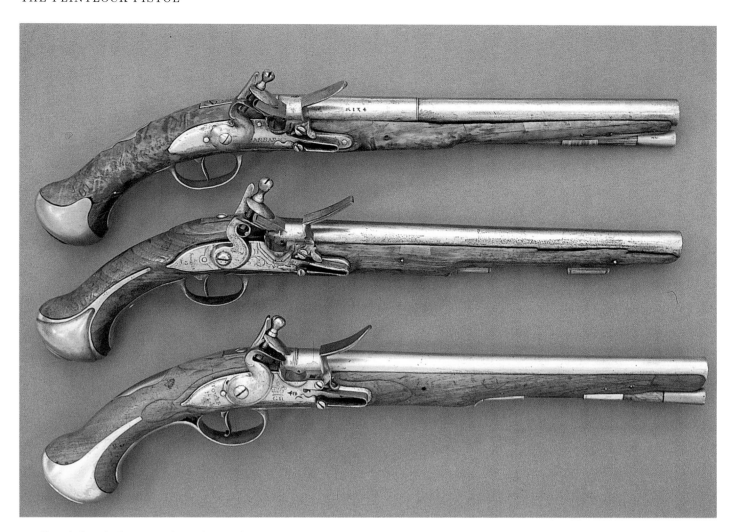

Exactly how little practical use the pistol was to a cavalryman in action is probably best illustrated by the following quotation. During the 18th century few common soldiers were educated enough to record their experiences in writing; but a notable exception was Trooper Edward Stilman, whose letter to his brother describing an English cavalry attack during the Battle of Dettingen in 1743 is of unique interest. Stilman's original manuscript is in a confusing phonetic English almost innocent of punctuation; I have reproduced this delightful document at the end of the chapter, but for the sake of the reader's sanity the passage is here translated into something closer to modern grammar and syntax:

*"I send you these lines to let you know that I am in good health, and can now with pleasure send you the happy news of our success in the battle which happened on the 15th of this month; the particulars were as follows:*

*"On Thursday, at 5 o'clock in the morning, the French... turned tail and ran to the waterside in the hope of getting over the bridge... so then our left wing came into play, and our regiment pushed in upon the Gendarmes (which are the French Life Guards) and a regiment of dragoons. During the first push we made Mr Vizard was at my right hand. We had our swords slung from our wrists and our pistols in our hands, but before Mr Vizard could draw his trigger his horse was shot dead upon the spot and his leg lay under the horse's belly. I dropped my pistol and held out my sword with a stiff arm and caught the blows, and never wavered until I saw Mr Vizard's leg clear of his horse.*

*"... It was as mortal battle as ever was seen in this century, as I have heard officers say since. God knows I thought every minute to be my last, for I thought that all of them were aiming at me, and the whirling of the balls made me almost deaf; but God Almighty heard my prayers and brought me clear without any wound.*

*"... The most shocking thing was to hear the cries of the wounded French as we rode over them when we pursued them, but we could not help it... Four men of "A' Troop were ordered to go back... and I was one of them, and then my heart was shocked most of all; for almost a mile... we could not step for dead men and horses... and I though it hard work, but nothing is so hard as killing of men."*

The significance here is obviously that Stilman preferred to rely upon his training in swordsmanship in a crisis; when fighting off the French while his comrade freed himself from the fallen horse he flung away his pistol without even bothering to use it.

It is difficult to identify precisely what was issued to the mounted units of the British army before 1770, as records are frustratingly vague; but after that date specific types appeared which were issued, and recorded, in considerable numbers. Britain had adopted a number of different types of flintlock pistols, including Heavy Dragoon with 12in barrels, Light Dragoon with 9in, and Life Guards and Blues pistols with ten-inch barrels. To complicate matters both for us and for contemporary quartermasters, some of these were manufactured in carbine bore and some in smaller pistol bore. *(continued on page 74)*

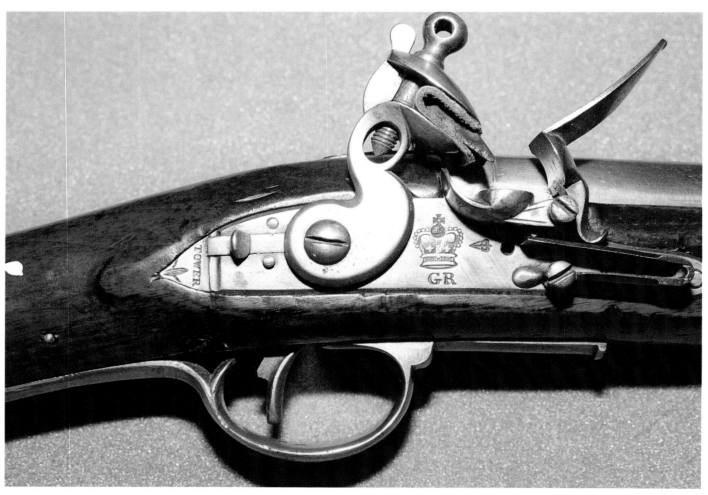

**OPPOSITE PAGE** *Two forms of safety catch found on flintlock weapons were the oscillating catch, which was more often seen on sporting guns than military ones, and the sliding bar. The bar safety mechanism was fitted to a number of late 18th century service pistols and muskets.*

**RIGHT** *A nice example of a "turn-off" barrel pistol by W.Parker, showing the tiny chamber and concave seat for the bullet. In .45 calibre, it has a 1.5in barrel, but would have been sufficiently powerful to kill at twenty paces. (XII.1695)*

**BELOW** *Officers' pistols were frequently good quality commercial weapons purchased from one of the better London or provincial retailers. This brass-furnished pair in .65 calibre are by Heylin, and date from c.1777. (XII.1699/1700; A5614; The Board of Trustees of the Royal Armouries)*

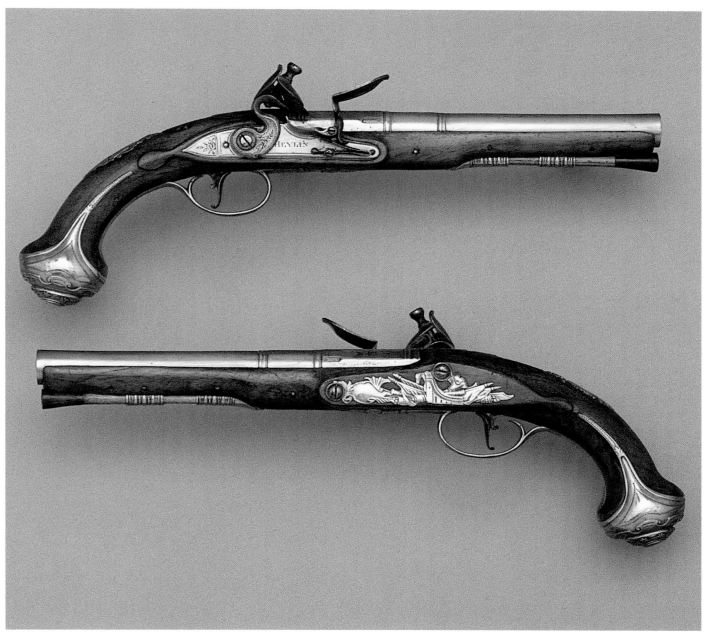

*A great deal less elegant than the Heylin pistols, but probably not much less accurate in practice, is this issue Heavy Cavalry pattern of 1797 with Henry Nock's screwless lock. Its 9in barrel, in a massive .75 calibre, had no provision for a ramrod, which had to be kept separately in the holster - where it was easy to lose. (XII.1754)*

By the end of the 18th century the cavalrymen of most European nations were equipped with at least one smoothbore saddle pistol, although many regarded it as a useless encumbrance. Once fired it had no further practical use, as it was virtually impossible to reload while attempting to control a horse in the midst of battle. Tactical doctrine still reflected its practical limitations, acknowledging that the only sure way to hit your opponent was from short enough range for the muzzle to actually touch him - seldom a practical plan if he were wielding a sharp sabre. Rifleman Harris described a close encounter with a French dragoon during the march to Benavente in the Peninsular campaign:

*"At length he stopped so near me that I saw it was almost impossible he could avoid discovering that the Rifles were in such close proximity to his person. He gazed cautiously along the ridge, took off his helmet, and wiped his face, as he appeared to meditate upon the propriety of crossing the ditch in which we lay; when suddenly our eyes met, and in an instant he plucked a pistol from his holster, fired it in my face, and wheeling his horse, plunged down the hillside. For the moment I thought I was hit, as the ball grazed my neck, and stuck fast in my knapsack, where I found it, when many days afterwards, I unpacked my kit on shipboard."*

From Harris's description it would appear that the pistol was fired from a distance of no more than perhaps ten feet, and it well illustrates the difficulty of shooting accurately with a smoothbore weapon from horseback. Primarily because Marlborough's cavalry tactics of the early 18th century were so successful, virtually no time was given to pistol shooting practice; almost all cavalry weapons training was devoted to developing skills with the *arme blanche*, the sword or sabre. Then as now, few men can have possessed a natural talent for handgun shooting, and the average cavalryman would have been incapable of hitting a barn door from the inside when mounted on the unpredictably moving platform that was his horse.

When using a pistol against other cavalrymen the problem was compounded by its limited penetration; although heavy leather buff coats had largely disappeared early in the 18th century some cavalry troopers still wore vestigial armour in the form of breast and back plates, which were proof against all but a very close range pistol ball.

Exactly to what use the cavalryman was expected to put his pistol is a mystery, as he typically went into action with sword in hand and secured by its wrist strap, and always needed the other hand to control his mount; and a high proportion of troopers of the Napoleonic period were also issued with a carbine, which typically hung down by their right leg. In the event of losing or breaking his sword the pistol theoretically provided an emergency means of defence - always given that he had the time to pull aside the front of the sad-

*Two Tower-made Light Cavalry pistols dating from c.1810, the upper with a plain lock and cock, the lower with the engraved edge decoration commonly found on these military patterns. They both have the very effective stirrup ramrod. This could be pulled out of its recess until the swivelling link held the small end; the double swivel allowed the rod to be reversed over the muzzle, and the large end inserted for ramming. (XII.3906/3907; A10/87; The Board of Trustees of the Royal Armouries)*

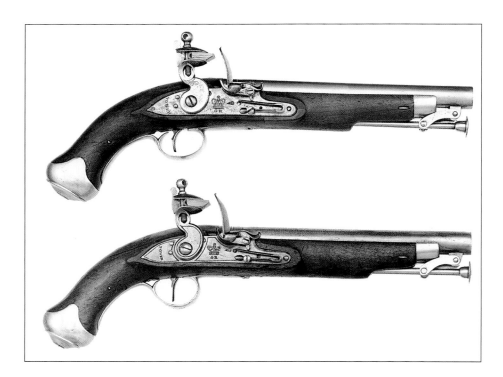

dle cloth which covered the pistol holsters at his pommel, and the rolled cloak which was often strapped over them. He then had to draw and cock, an action for which two hands were needed. By the time he could aim and fire his sabre-armed opponents must often have begun to sever important working parts from his body. If he were issued with a carbine it would normally be carried slung handily muzzle-down on his right side, and must surely have been the preferred weapon of emergency defence?

Even if he went into action pistol in hand with his sword hanging from the wrist strap (a rare practice by 1800), as described by Stilman, when things became desperate the trooper's instinct was to rely not upon his pistol but his sword. He was, after all, well trained in its use both for defence and attack.

The cavalryman also faced the problem of ammunition supply, for even though the calibre of his pistol was often (though not always) the same as that of the carbine which he (sometimes) carried, the powder charge was not. Common practice was to use a standard carbine cartridge and empty out between one third and half of the charge before loading the pistol. Should he forget this precaution, which was easily done in the heat of battle, the trooper who fired a full carbine charge stood a good chance of seeing his pistol disintegrate in his hand - with ugly consequences.

The alternative was to carry a separate supply of smaller paper cartridges for the pistol; but since he had only one pouch, and that very inconveniently slung high behind his back, it must have been extremely awkward to draw the correct type of cartridge by feel alone during a mounted action, if not actually impossible.

Soldiers on campaign always tended to keep their weapons loaded, but leaving a gun charged with black powder for any length of time was a recipe for trouble, as Thomas Hasker wrote in 1816:

*"As many accidents have happened by the improper loading of firearms... that for the pistols two thirds of such a charge (as fills the top of a powder horn) is proper. That they must be particular to ram the charge well that air may not be confined between or beyond the charge, and that they keep their arms clean and never loaded above a week."* The reasons for this last were not only black powder's remarkable ability for absorbing moisture, which would render a charge unusable, but also the likelihood of the ball becoming dislodged through rough handling and creating a dangerous air gap.

So poorly was the military pistol regarded that in the early 19th century it was being issued in many British regiments only to trumpeters and senior NCOs. The Duke of Wellington scathingly dismissed it as "an ineffectual weapon" and ordered it to be discarded. Little wonder, therefore, that its use was generally relegated to dispatching wounded horses or lighting campfires.

\* \* \*

While essentially no more effective than their troopers' weapons, the pistols carried by officers could at least be selected by personal choice and at greater expense. Most officers' pistols were of a lighter and more elegant design than the issue weapons, and by the 1770s there was a fashion among British officers for acquiring pairs of good quality sporting or duelling pistols from makers such as Egg, Manton or Nock. These had the unmilitary refinements of set triggers, sights and cased accessories, and were very costly. For the most part true duelling pistols were more for show than practical use in the field, as the rigours of campaigning would soon have ruined their exquisite workmanship; but there was a thriving trade in officers' pistols, which were often very well made. With iron or brass barrels, they followed the style of similar civilian pistols and were usually sold in pairs. For the most part, however, officers still relied on the sword, and it was not until the advent of the revolver in the mid-19th century that the pistol became synonymous with officer status.

*Reconstruction of a trooper of the Lifeguards, c.1815, with an original Lifeguards pattern pistol of 1780. It has a 10in barrel and is of .65 (carbine) calibre, firing about half of the charge of a standard musket cartridge. (XII.5141)*

**Technical Specifications**

**Light Cavalry flintlock pistol:**

| | | |
|---|---|---|
| Overall length | 15.5ins | (394mm) |
| Barrel length | 9ins | (228mm) |
| Calibre | .65in | (16.9mm) |
| Weight | 2lbs 9 oz | (1.3kg) |
| Charge | 40 grains | |
| Ignition | Flint | |

*He holds the pistol in a leather saddle holster of the early 19th century. Two holsters connected by leather straps were hung on either side of the saddle pommel, often with leather flaps to protect the pistols from horse-sweat, dirt and rain. Note the cartridge pouch attached by a second length of strap inside his carbine crossbelt. Here it is pulled round to bring the pouch conveniently to hand; during a mounted action it would be in the small of his back, making it even more difficult to reload his firearms.*

## Firing the flintlock pistol

The model chosen was a good, original British Light Cavalry (or Light Dragoon) pattern of the type used during the Napoleonic Wars. It had a crisp lock, and the barrel appeared to be almost unworn internally. Exactly what charge to use was the subject of some debate, bearing in mind the age of the piece. Initially it was decided to use 40 grains of medium powder in the 9-inch barrel, and a commercially produced .623in ball in a pre-prepared cartridge. Loading was done in exactly the same manner as all previous flintlocks, with the priming charge being loaded last for safety. The stirrup-mounted ramrod proved to be a neat and practical design, with a large mushroom-shaped end which enabled a good, firm thrust to be given to the ball.

With powder and ball loaded and the priming powder in place, we tried to see if it were actually possible to cock the pistol single-handed; but it was found that even a man with very large hands was unable to both retain his grip on the trigger guard and reach the cock as well. The best method was found to be to hold the pistol in a loose shooting position in the right hand and then to reach over with the left hand to pull the cock back to the fully-cocked position.

A man-sized target had been set up at 25 yards, and after taking careful aim the trigger was pulled. When the smoke cleared the target was revealed in its pristine state. A second try put a small nick in the shoulder of the figure. Using the bench as a rest produced the same result; so, having observed where the shots were landing on the backstop, the point of aim was adjusted to slightly left of the target's right knee…. This improved matters no end, with balls striking in roughly the central chest area, although in a very random manner.

The target was moved to 15 yards, and this time the first ball struck in the top right shoulder, which was pretty much where it was expected to strike. A second shot at the same point of aim hit the opposite shoulder. A series of ten shots produced solid body hits and a

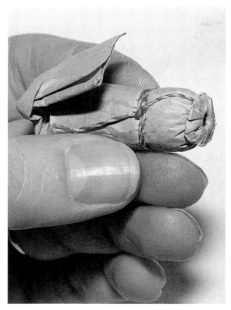

*Our Lifeguard undoes the cover of his cartridge pouch, and lifts the lid of the inner flap - a necessity for a cavalryman, as the constant bouncing and pounding his equipment received on horseback made it all too easy to lose small items such as cartridges. Hanging from the crossbelt is the spring hook and security chain for attaching his carbine.*

*An original early 19th century carbine cartridge, of similar type to that normally used with these saddle pistols, part of the charge being tipped away before loading.*

*Removing a prepared cartridge, he bites the end off and pours sufficient into the pan for priming; the large touch hole can just be seen inside the pan.*

pattern that covered about 18 inches; and it began to look as though the advice given to cavalrymen to wait until the muzzle was touching their opponent might not have been unduly pessimistic.

Undaunted, we loaded the pistol with 60 grains and repeated the tests. Dispensing with the paper cartridge and using careful patching of the ball did improve matters, giving some semblance of grouping at 25 yards - five shots out of five landed within the approximate chest area of the target, although point of aim was still low and to the left. The recoil was certainly more noticeable, and was uncomfortable without actually being painful (but it should be borne in mind that these were pistols designed for single-shot use, not continual target firing). If the accuracy remained unimpressive, the power of the bullet could not be ignored, as it punched half way through a six-inch oak support. The muzzle velocity using the paper cartridge and 40 grain charge had averaged out at a fairly low 520fps, but remember this is a big, heavy bullet. With the 60 grain charge and patching this improved dramatically, achieving in one instance 743fps, which is quite impressive for a smoothbore pistol.

Loading time was actually quicker compared to other flintlocks, due mainly to the stirrup ramrod; this made three shots a minute easily possible. Having used normal detachable and easily-dropped ramrods it was easy to see why such a system was adopted. In other respects the Light Cavalry pistol provided no surprises. It was very solidly built, with a heavy trigger action and a very strong mainspring which made cocking tiresome; a duelling pistol it certainly was not.

For practical purposes the pistol really had to be regarded as a last ditch weapon to be used when all other options - like running away - had failed. It would probably have been able to penetrate a breastplate at perhaps 20 yards, but beyond that its bullet velocity began to drop sharply. It is little wonder that it became the least used and least liked weapon on European battlefields in the 18th and 19th centuries.

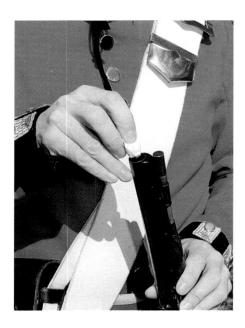

**FAR LEFT & LEFT** *Closing the steel over the pan, he pours the contents of the cartridge down the barrel, followed by the ball and cartridge paper, and rams the load home. The ramrod was both short and flimsy, and once the bore was fouled it would be very easy to snap, leaving the trooper with no means of reloading his weapon.*

**BOTTOM LEFT** *Bringing the pistol to full-cock. The mainspring was too strong to enable this to be done one handed, which made it a tricky manoeuvre on horseback. Cavalrymen would ensure that their pistols were primed and cocked before going into action.*
*(As this particular pistol was too valuable to risk shooting, at this point we substituted a more common Light Cavalry pattern for test firing.)*

Original of letter from Trooper Edward Stilman after the battle of Dettingen, 1743: *"To Mr Thos Stilman. In Froom in Somersethir in England. Thus: Dear Brother, I send you thes Lins to Let you know that i am in good helth and now i can with plether send you the happy nus of ouer Suckses in the Batel that hapened on the 15 of this Month and now i shal proceed with the perteklers which was a folos thursday in the morning a 5 a Clock the french ...tunred tail and run to the water side in hop of getting ouer thar brige...so then ouer Lift wing cam into play and ouer regmont pusht in upon the gandarins which is the french Life gards and a regmont of Dragguns and the first pus we mad Mr Vizard was at my rite hand so we had ouer Sords upon ouer rists and ouer pistols in ouer hand, and before Mr Vizard could droy his triger his hors was shot ded upon the Spot and Mr vizard's legg laid under one horses belly i dropt my pistol and i hold out my Sord with a stif arm and cot the blos and neuer waged tel i so Mr Viz Leg clear of his hors...it was a mortel batel as euer was seain in this aeige as i haf heard ofescers say since God knos i thoye euery minute to be my last for i thote that all of them presented at me and the whirling of the bols mad me all most dif butt god almighty heard my prars and brot me clear without anny woond...wel the most shocking thing is to hear the cris of the wooned french as we rid over them when we prsud them but we could not help it...and 4 Men of a trop was ordered to goe back... and i was one of them and then my hart was shoked mos of all for mos a mile...we could not step for ded men and horses...and i though it hard work but no thing is so hard as kiling of Men."*

**BELOW, TOP TO BOTTOM** *The pistol is at full-cock and the steel (frizzen) is in the lowered position over the priming pan.*
*The trigger is squeezed; the flint strikes the frizzen, simultaneously knocking it forward to expose the pan and striking a shower of sparks which drop onto the priming powder; the frizzen is still moving forward.*
*The sparks ignite the priming; some are now passing through the touch hole to the main charge in the breech.*

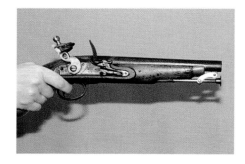

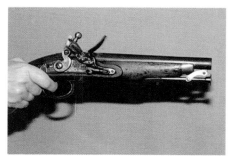

**TOP TO BOTTOM, LEFT** *With the priming still burning, the main charge ignites; sparks from the priming are being blown away from the pan by the back-blast of gases through the touch hole.*

*As the burning gases from the main charge exit the barrel, sparks from the primary ignition still shower down. The large quantity of smoke generated is clearly visible.*

*The ball is well on its way down range, and the main charge is almost spent; but sparks from the priming still rain down, having been blown in all directions for a distance of over 12 inches (30cm) from the pan.*

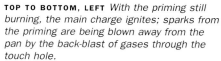

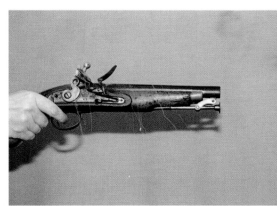

**ABOVE** *The pistol has now finished its firing cycle, after approximately 1.25 seconds. Note that as the cloud of smoke drifts upwards stray sparks from the priming powder are still drifting down. Throughout the period when loose powder was present on the battlefield historical accounts frequently mention accidents - always dangerous, often fatal, and sometimes catastrophic.*

# THE PERCUSSION RIFLED MUSKET

An 1853-dated Pattern 1853 Enfield rifle, with its cartridge and percussion caps. Its simple design and solid construction earned it an excellent reputation as both a military and a sporting rifle.

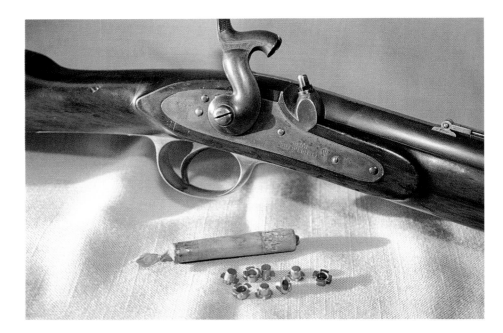

**B**y the early decades of the 19th century the rifled musket was not, by any standards, new technology; and steam power would soon be harnessed to enable barrels to be bored and rifled and other components to be manufactured faster and more efficiently. The Baker rifle had shown in a small way what could be accomplished by a military rifle; but once again, it was the commercial pressure to improve sporting weapons that was to provide the biggest technological improvement seen since the Middle Ages.

The use of fulminate of mercury, or a similar compound called "fulminating gold", dates back to the early 17th century. Gunmakers and chemists had long sought a propellant more powerful than gunpowder, and in 1625 Guiliano Bossi had written in his book *Breve Trattato d'Alcune Inventione* of a powder with astonishing properties:

*"… Two or three grains of powdered gold precipitated with Aqua Fortis adulterated with sal ammoniac and congealed with oil of tartar… if you take ten grains of that powder and put them on a wooden table… then set fire to it as you would ordinary powder it will make more noise than a well charged musket when it is fired, and have an effect that runs against nature, in so much that fire… flies upwards and seeks the air, but this fire strikes downwards… and breaks the table. The gun barrels that are fired with this gold must be strong and if you put in more than three grains there is a risk that they will burst."*

In England we find Samuel Pepys noting in his diary on 11 November 1663 that a German doctor had demonstrated *"…something made of gold which they call in Chymistry Aurum Fulminans a grain I think he said of it put into a silver spoon and fired, will blow like a musket and strike a hole through the spoon downward."*

The problem with all fulminates is that they are an unpleasant combination of power and instability. Many who dabbled with them paid the ultimate price through failing to understand the very different chemical properties of fulminate and gunpowder. Persistent attempts were made to use fulminate as a replacement for powder, particularly in the wake of a paper published on the subject by a Fellow of the Royal Society in London, Edward Howard. Howard managed to severely injure himself during his experiments, and thereafter abandoned fulminates, commenting that he felt *"more disposed to prosecute other chemical subjects."*

It was an unknown Scottish minister and amateur chemist, Alexander John Forsyth, who realised that the tendency of fulminates to detonate violently when struck made them extremely useful for priming. Hunting was his passion, and like all hunters with flintlocks he suffered from the frustrating delay between the ignition of priming and main charge; this time lag, and the tell-tale plume of priming smoke, were often sufficient to scare off any bird or animal. Forsyth reasoned that producing a smokeless and instantaneous form of ignition would dramatically improve the sportsman's chances of hitting a wary target.

After much experimentation Forsyth produced, in 1805, a percussion lock that could be fitted to any flintlock gun. He used a small, flask-shaped steel container (generally called the "scent bottle", from its shape) which was filled with fulminate, and rotated before each shot to dispense a few grains into a cavity above which was a striker. A solid-nosed hammer was fitted in place of the old screw-jawed cock; when this was released it hit the striker, firing the fulminate into the touch hole. Ignition was almost instantaneous, virtually impervious to the weather, and produced no smoke. The scent-bottle system was, however, expensive and vulnerable to damage; and although it interested the British army a series of tests conducted by Forsyth at the Tower of London did not convince them of its worth as a military

*Reconstruction: a Union infantryman of the American Civil War prepares to load his Enfield, reaching into his pouch for a cartridge and biting off the twisted end. Nearly half a million Enfields were purchased for the Union and Conferate armies.*

weapon. The sporting fraternity certainly had no such qualms, and Forsyth Patent guns sold well.

From around 1810 all manner of similar percussion locks began to appear, using small pre-prepared fulminate charges packed into a variety of patches, tubes, pellets and pills. The inventor of the now-familiar copper cap, which became the most successful form of percussion primer, may never be known. The most likely claimant was an English artist named Joshua Shaw; in 1814 he reputedly invented a steel cap holding a small charge of fulminate, and later modified the design to use first pewter and then copper. He emigrated to America in 1817, where he received a patent for his percussion cap in 1822; but it is a moot point whether Shaw actually invented it. The idea of using a cap which fitted over a hollow nipple screwed directly into the breech of the gun was generally known by 1822, and in common use by sportsmen by 1825.

Although percussion ignition had initially been dismissed by the Board of Ordnance it soon became apparent that other European countries were taking a great interest in the new system. By the 1830s it had become clear to even the most wooden-headed military conservative that the days of the smoothbore flintlock musket were numbered; but a number of obstacles stood in the way of any large scale re-equipment of the British army with percussion weapons. Firstly, the cost of re-arming with new models would be prohibitive, as the numbers involved would be colossal. Secondly, whatever was supplied to the army had to be of a sufficiently familiar and simple type to ensure that proficiency could be attained with the minimum of retraining. As importantly, the selected system had to be able to stand up to the abuse notoriously meted out by the average infantryman; Thomas Atkins was not renowned for his mechanical sensitivity.

A number of enlightening tests were carried out at Woolwich in 1834 to compare the reliability of these new percussion guns with their flintlock predecessors. It was found that the flintlocks misfired once every seven shots, whereas the percussion muskets failed only once every 166 shots. It was also noted that the percussion muskets were marginally more accurate: in 6,000 shots the flintlock struck the target 3,680 times, and the percussion 4,047 times. Why this should be so was not explained, though the removal of the "flintlock flinch factor" seems likely to have been one cause.

The advantages in terms of reliability and speed of ignition seemed clear, but the percussion smoothbores had no significant advantage in terms of accuracy or range over the flintlock. As was usual in such cases, the Board of Ordnance sensibly looked first at converting existing stocks of old weapons, appointing George Lovell, Controller of the Board of Ordnance Stores, to oversee the adoption of a percussion system for military use. These early guns were called either Pattern 1838, which were newly manufactured muskets, or Pattern 1839, which were modified late-model .76in flintlocks. The P38 proved to be expensive to produce, so the P39 was introduced; this solution was not only cheaper, but solved the immediate problem of shortage of arms. In 1839 the first 2,000 P39 muskets were issued to the Foot Guards.

Plans to convert the remaining stocks of smoothbores to percussion were thwarted by a disastrous fire in 1841 which destroyed most of the weapons stored in the Tower. As a result a new series of muskets was ordered: the Pattern 1842 differed little from the P39 except in having a rudimentary rear sight, and an improved side-action lock. (This had its mainspring mounted inside the lockplate but forward of the hammer, rather than behind as with the back-action type briefly fitted to the P38 muskets.) Unfortunately, tests by the Royal Engineers at Chatham in 1846 proved it to be no more accurate. Although its maximum range was 650 yards, the report noted that of ten shots fired at 150 yards only five hit the target - which was 11ft 6ins wide by 5ft 6ins high... . At 250 yards the target remained untouched.

The Board had also looked at replacing the ageing Baker, and after a number of trials selected the Brunswick rifle to be issued to the Rifle Regiments. It was not a marked improvement over the Baker, being quite heavy at 9.5lbs, and as slow to reload. Its two-groove rifling relied on a very tight-fitting "belted" bullet, so called because it had two raised ribs cast into it. These had to be fitted exactly into the grooves in the bore, which was not only time-consuming but proved impossible if the bullet was deformed - as often happened

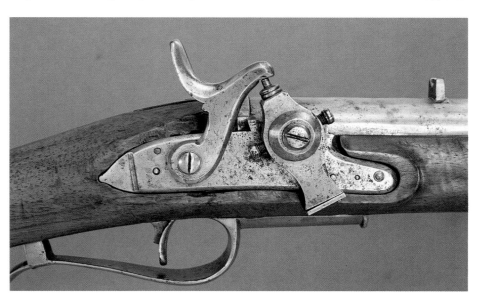

*A Baker cavalry carbine converted to the Forsyth "scent bottle" percussion system for trials purposes. It is dated about 1807. (XVI.51; A1630; The Board of Trustees of the Royal Armouries)*

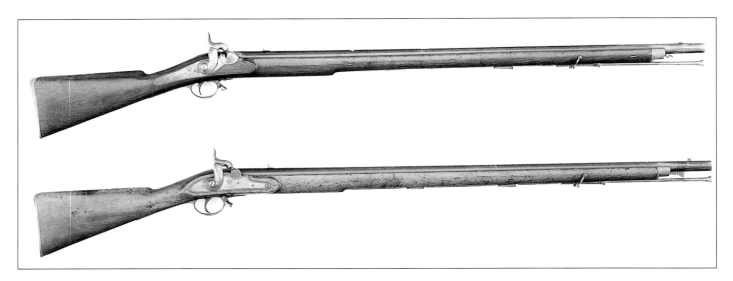

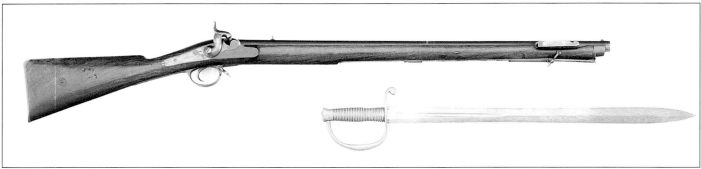

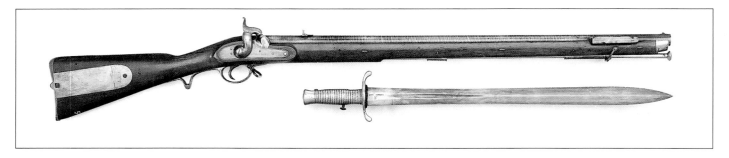

**TOP** *New-manufactured British Pattern 1838 musket, top, and Pattern 1839 converted from a flintlock. There are few external differences apart from details of the locks, though the sharp-eyed reader will notice that two different patterns of bayonet catch are fitted beneath the muzzles. (XII.303/304; A6/859; The Board of Trustees of the Royal Armouries)*

**MIDDLE & BOTTOM** *An early Brunswick rifle, top, with back-action lock and plain, rounded trigger guard, above a second pattern Brunswick dated 1844. The Brunswick bore more than a passing resemblance to the Baker which it replaced, as did its massive and unpopular bayonets.*
*(XII.311/2999; A6/861, A7/421; The Board of Trustees of the Royal Armouries)*

when carried for a long time - or once the barrel became fouled. The Select Committee on Small Arms agreed after firing tests in 1852 that the resultant velocity was insufficient for consistent accuracy:

*"At all distances above 400 yards the shooting was so wild as to be unrecorded. The Brunswick rifle has shown itself to be much inferior in point of range to every other arm... the loading of this rifle is so difficult that it is a wonder how the Rifle Regiments have continued to use it so long - the force required to ram down the bore being so great as to render any man's hand unsteady for accurate shooting. Further comment is unnecessary."*

Although some units had few problems with their Brunswicks, others were loud in their complaints; but for the time being it was all that was available. It was subsequently found that the Brunswick was faster to load and shot much better if the belted bullet was abandoned and the new Minié bullet substituted. Despite its shortcomings it was still a great improvement on the service musket, and was to remain in service for over 20 years.

A solution to the Board's problems dawned in France in 1844, when Colonel Louis de Thouvenin created the "pillar breech". This was a metal rod screwed into the base of the breech and projecting a short distance up the barrel. When a conical bullet was rammed home the rod forced its base to flare out, preventing windage and enabling it to grip the rifling without distorting its symmetry. It was left to yet another French officer, Claude-Étienne Minié, to come up with the ultimate expanding conical bullet which was to revolutionise the performance of the rifled musket. (Unsurprisingly, Leonardo da Vinci had illustrated a hollow conical bullet centuries before, although it is unlikely that it was ever put to the test.)

Minié's invention was to insert an iron cup into the hollow base of a conical lead bullet which was deliberately cast slightly smaller than the bore, enabling it to be rammed easily down the barrel. On firing, the blast of propellant gas pushed the cup firmly up into the softer lead bullet, causing its skirt to expand into the grooves of the rifling, ensuring consistent accuracy and no loss of velocity through windage. (In fact the cup initially proved to be too efficient, having a disturbing habit of propelling itself right through the bullet and exiting at high speed from the muzzle while leaving the shredded remains of the bullet behind it in the breech.)

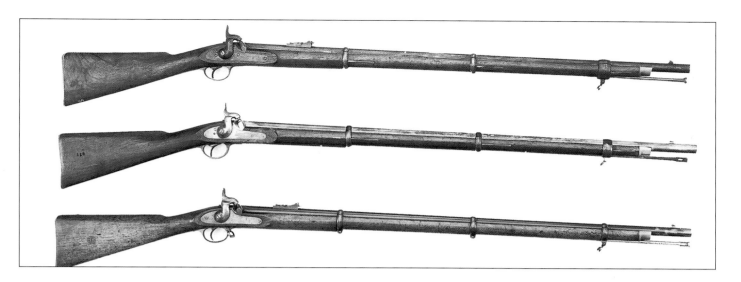

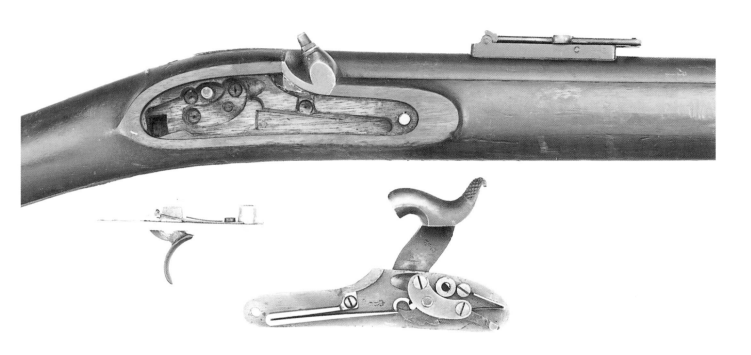

**ABOVE** *A detached lock from a P51 rifle. The internal mechanism is almost identical to that of the earlier flintlock, the major difference being the replacement of the cock and flint with a solid hammer. The simple trigger mechanism is beside it. Remarkable care has been taken to cut out of the stock precisely the correct amount of wood needed to allow exact fitting of the lockplate. (A7/427)*

**TOP OF PAGE** *Variations on a theme: although these muskets appear identical they are all different. The top example is a smoothbore P39 of .76in bore; centre is one of the early rifled P38s issued to the Foot Guards, with .70in rifled barrel. At bottom is a .577 calibre Pattern 1853 rifle, Enfield-manufactured from new parts. (XII.320/1898/1914; A7/439; The Board of Trustees of the Royal Armouries)*

**LEFT** *A Brunswick belted bullet - the raised ribs can be seen to the left and right of the lower half. It was a frustratingly intricate task to fit these into the two rifling grooves at the muzzle when loading in battle.*

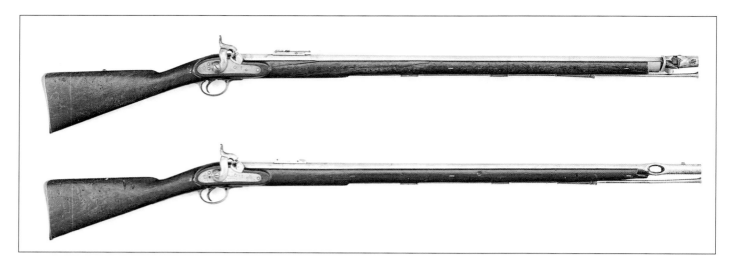

*Two casualties of war: both of these P51 rifles saw service in the Crimea and were returned as unserviceable - see muzzles. (XII.373/373; A6/874; The Board of Trustees of the Royal Armouries)*

Tests with the new Minié rifle nevertheless proved very encouraging, its .70in bullet providing terrific power at ranges hitherto impossible to reach except with artillery. The Minié was quite capable of hitting a man-sized target two shots out of five at 600 yards. The Board of Ordnance were so impressed that they sanctioned production of the new Pattern 1851 rifled musket, a small number of which were issued during the Cape Border Wars in South Africa (1846-52) on the basis of six per company, to the best shots. The results were encouraging, with regular hits being obtained at 500 yards; one Private Wickens claimed that *"When the enemy began to show themselves... we opened fire on them... we made them move at a distance of 1,200 yards."*

The Board settled on the P51 as standard issue, though the troops affectionately referred to it as the "Minnie" rifle. At a casual glance it looks almost identical to the P39, but has a leaf rear sight graduated to 900 yards, a four-groove barrel, slightly lighter weight woodwork, and a calibre of .702 inches. Approved in October 1851, the first 500 were issued in February 1852 divided between the Foot Guards, the 1st Battalion of the Royals, and seven line regiments. The first soldiers to receive it now had the novel experience (for line infantry) of being trained to pick their target and shoot at it. Teaching soldiers to estimate range was difficult, and Guardsmen were given the following advice:

*"Each Captain sent out men to the front and placed them at intervals, so that the soldier may form a tolerably accurate conclusion as to the proper adjustment of the stadium [rearsight] in actual service. Thus it is pointed out to them that at fifty yards, the features of the man, the buttons of his jacket, the band and star on his foraging cap, can be plainly recognised; while at 100 yards the lineaments can no longer be discerned, the buttons seem to form a continuous line; the star is scarcely separable from the band; and at 150 yards the buttons are quite invisible, and the face looks like a whitish ball under the line of the cap."*

Of the 35,000 "Minnies" manufactured between 1852 and 1855, 34,000 were issued to line regiments; and over half of those went out to the Crimea. First used during the battle for Sevastopol, they proved devastating against the massed infantry attacks of the Russian troops, as *The Times'* correspondent Charles Russell witnessed:

*"As the Russians come within six hundred yards, down goes that line of steel in front, and out rings a rolling volley of Mini_ musketry. The distance is too great; the Russians are not checked, but still sweep onward through the smoke... but ere they come within one hundred and fifty yards, another deadly volley flashes from the levelled rifles, and carries death and terror into the Russians. They wheel about... and fly back faster than they came."*

The Russian soldiers were baffled by the strange bullets landing in their midst, believing that they must be a new form of artillery shrapnel. Naum Gorbunov, whose Vladimir Regiment came under fire from the Miniés, wrote:

*"... We dismounted from our horses and watched with curiosity these strange things... even the artillerymen could not name them, suggesting that these bullets... were aimed at our artillery's cartridge boxes but were in no way meant for us... we looked death right in the eyes. But after a few seconds we learnt from experience the significance of these 'thimbles'."*

Armed predominantly with smoothbore muskets which had nowhere near the range of the British rifle bullets, the Russians were unable to reply. The P51 as delivered in quantity did have its shortcomings, however: with its bayonet and 60 rounds of cartridges the whole equipment weighed nearly 18lbs, which was far too heavy at a time when the Board of Ordnance was seeking to reduce the weight of the soldiers' load. In addition, the accuracy of the P51 proved unsatisfactory, the new rifle totally missing a six-foot square target at 500 yards. Nevertheless, 20,000 were still ordered from commercial contractors.

*   *   *

This experience prompted the Board to look once again at the rifled musket; and for the first time in British military history it was decided that a new bore size would be introduced that was determined by projectile weight rather than by calibre. As a result a series of public tests were held in 1852, to which any manufacturer was invited if they had a suitable rifle to demonstrate. Some of Britain's more prominent gunmakers were represented, including Purdey, Whitworth and Greener; but it was a design which owed much to George Lovell's original modified muskets that was selected. With an improved barrel and rifling, it was to become the Pattern 1853.

Britain's longarms had traditionally used a ball of .70in diameter or greater, with a weight of about 485 grains. In a smoothbore this gave tremendous smashing power at close

*An early .76 calibre Minié pattern bullet, left, compared to the later .577in projectile, centre; at right is the wooden plug which forced the skirt of the bullet into the rifling.*

range - hence the serious injuries which resulted from comparatively light arm or leg wounds - but the projectile lost velocity very quickly. However, the rifled musket, with comparatively little loss of propulsive pressure through windage, could maintain not only its accuracy but also much of its velocity. Even at 1,000 yards a bullet with a 65-grain service charge behind it could penetrate four inches of pine. As a result, the Small Arms Committee settled on a cylindro-conoidal bullet of Minié type, but using a boxwood plug in the base instead of a steel cup. It was designed by R.Pritchett, who achieved the rare distinction of receiving £1,000 from the Board of Ordnance for his efforts. His bullet was in .577in calibre, smaller than ever adopted before; its service charge weight was between 62 and 68 grains.

The new rifle was to use a 39in, three-groove barrel; and in a wild break with tradition this was secured into the stock with iron bands instead of transverse keys. The Crimean War had ended before the new P53 could be supplied, so production at the Royal Small Arms Factory at Enfield north of London was increased to enable the rifle to be supplied to all British land forces. Manufacture was on a radical new American-based production line system, pioneered by Colt and others.

For the first time in British manufacturing history each part was made to very close tolerances and checked against a set of master gauges to ensure that it was truly interchangeable. This was a radical departure from the traditional methods of hand fitting historically practised at the Tower and by commercial manufacturers. Before the new rifle entered service a "sealed pattern" was made. Every component of this rifle was manufactured exactly to a rigidly specified tolerance by skilled engineers, each stage of its assembly being checked meticulously by inspectors before it was finally approved by the Master of the Ordnance. The rifle then had the wax seals of the Board of Ordnance applied, and became the pattern from whose dimensions all others would be made.

At the factory each inspector was provided with a set of gauges which enabled him to check every part for which his assembly line was responsible - locks, barrels, triggers - all were produced to within rigidly specified tolerances. Should a component fail to fit the gauge the entire batch could be removed for checking, and immediately replaced with a new batch. Even gunstocks, always time-consuming to shape, were made on a lathe six at a time using a single metal blank as a master. Unremarkable today, in the 1850s this was a truly revolutionary process which not only produced very high quality weapons but, more importantly, allowed immediate field repairs by simply replacing a damaged component with a spare.

There were eventually a bewildering number of variations of the Pattern 1853 rifle, with three artillery carbines, three cavalry carbines, four short rifles and a smooth-bore musket being produced. It was probably the best weapon of its type ever developed for military use, over 323,000 being made between 1858 and 1864.

*    *    *

It was not perfect, of course: ironically, its muzzle velocity was so great that at short ranges the bullet frequently passed straight through its target without exerting the brute stopping power which was often desirable in Colonial campaigns. The rank and file serving in India sometimes took to cutting the nose off the lead cone, or carving a deep X into it, to shorten its range and improve the expanding effect when it struck a solid object. Such mutilated bullets eventually became known as "dum-dums" after the arsenal near Calcutta which produced much of the army's ammunition. This trick was, as one soldier bleakly commented, "only to give them an idea of the advantages of civilisation"; but the use of such rounds was outlawed by the Hague Convention as early as 1899.

The .577in Minié bullet in its final and most sophisticated form; this example is from a Snider cartridge of 1866. It incorporates both a hollow base with a wooden plug to expand the skirt of the bullet, and a hollow point with a boxwood plug to aid expansion on impact. This was not a missile to be treated lightly.

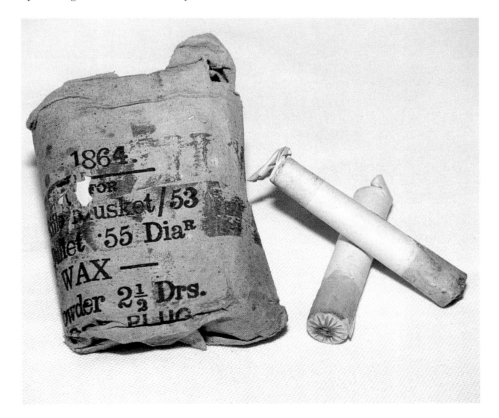

An original pack of ten .577in cartridges for the P53 Enfield rifle, as issued in their millions during the British Colonial wars and the American Civil War.

An original box of Joyce percussion caps, c.1860. Unlike the more modern "top hat" shape pictured on page 80 these were ribbed and straight, making them more difficult to handle and remove.

The new .577in bullet was still quite a tight fit even in a clean barrel; and after firing a dozen or so shots, or in very hot weather, a combination of fouling and expansion could make it impossible to ram a bullet down the bore. In 1858 soldiers fighting in the Indian Mutiny found their rifles rendered useless by temperatures of 100 degrees Fahrenheit: not only had the steel of the barrels expanded, but so too had the lead bullets.

The rifle proved very popular with sporting and trade customers, and huge numbers were manufactured commercially for export. Target shooters were particularly impressed with the Pattern 1853 and its variants, in particular the expensive but very accurate Whitworth rifles with their hexagonal .45in bores, which proved unbeatable on the target ranges.

On average, the P53 was ten times more accurate than the smoothbore musket that it replaced. True, it was still slow to load - two rounds per minute was usual - and it still produced vast clouds of smoke; but it was consistently capable of killing at long range. In fact, the rifle rendered obsolete one of the most devastating arms of the old battlefield, the horse artillery. Galloping up to between 300 and 400 yards from an enemy line, the "flying artillery" had been able to bring their guns into action to rake the enemy with roundshot, shell, or canister (tightly packed loads of musket calibre lead shot). The hapless infantry armed with smoothbore muskets had been able to do nothing but stand and endure; now the rifled musket changed all that.

Surprisingly, in tactical terms that was about all it did change. Given the accuracy of the new rifle it would seem reasonable to assume that battlefield tactics from the Crimea onwards changed radically; but they did not. Commanders refused to accept any change in tactical doctrine, and accepted the higher casualties inflicted by aimed fire as an inevitable part of the progress of warfare.

\* \* \*

Such was the demand for the new rifles that many thousands were also made under contract in Belgium and the United States, as well as by commercial producers such as the London Armoury. These were purchased in great quantities during the American Civil War, with the Federal government buying over 428,000 and the Confederacy nearly 90,000. Far from revolutionising tactics, however, the War Between the States saw combat sink back almost to Napoleonic levels. In a study undertaken by John Keegan into 113 battles where the ranges of combat are known, some 85% are shown to have been fought at less than 250 yards. Generals still ordered massed infantry to attack static lines of defenders, often in well-protected positions, and the outcome was as predictable as it had been during Napoleon's campaigns: both sides faced each other, frantically loading and firing until one gave way after suffering unsustainable casualties.

In fairness, it must also be said that the efficiency of the troops using the new weapon was not all that it might have been. Tales of abandoned rifles found with multiple unfired charges rammed in one on top of another are well documented. After the battle of Gettysburg 27,500 discarded muskets were collected and examined. Of these 24,000 proved to be loaded; half of them had a double charge in the breech; another 6,000 had multiple loads of between three and six charges; and one even had 17 charges in the barrel, which must be a record. This may seem incredible; but it was easy, in the panic of battle, to load a charge but forget to put on a percussion cap, or to check that the nipple was clear. A flustered soldier pulls the trigger, and perhaps the cap goes off but the main charge misfires; deafened by the blast of regimental volleys, it is easy for an individual to think he has fired when he has not. It would be interesting to know how many rifles left on the field of Gettysburg had been burst by breech explosions.

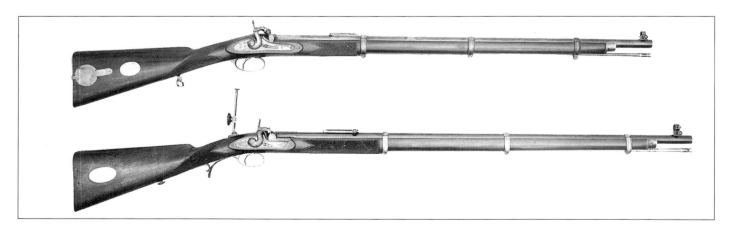

The extraordinarily accurate Whitworth rifles. Manufactured in a variety of barrel lengths, their .45 calibre hexagonal bores made them virtually unbeatable as long-range target rifles. They were particularly prized by sharpshooters during the American Civil War, although each cost $500 - a small fortune in the 1860s.
(XII.1425/1992; A6443; The Board of Trustees of the Royal Armouries)

**Technical Specifications**

**Enfield Pattern 1853 rifle:**

| | | |
|---|---|---|
| **Overall length** | 53.5ins | (1358mm) |
| **Barrel length** | 39.5in | (1003mm) |
| **Calibre** | .577in | (14.6mm) |
| **Weight** | 8lbs 8oz | (4kg) |
| **Charge** | 80 grains | |
| **Ignition** | Percussion cap | |

### Firing the Enfield Pattern 1853

The P53 enjoys a reputation as "the shooter's rifle"; and the number of original P53s still in use on ranges in Europe and America gives an indication of the standard of marksmanship still achievable with rifles that are now well over 140 years old. Loading is a simple process, which differs hardly at all from the flintlock musket. The body of the cartridge consists of a stiff tube of paper with a greased bullet at one end. The twist of paper at the bottom of the cartridge is torn off with the teeth and the charge poured down the barrel, followed by the bullet and the remains of the cartridge paper. The steel rammer seats the bullet quite easily, and it is the work of seconds to place a percussion cap on the nipple. The hammer is pulled back to full-cock, and the rifle is ready to fire.

Charge weight for the cartridges was set initially at 65 grains of coarse powder, but a number of different charges were tried to see what effect they had on accuracy. We also had use of a chronograph, which was to prove interesting. The Enfield managed consistent six-inch groups at 100 yards, and 14 inches at 200. At 400 yards its grouping was ragged, but 14 out of 15 shots struck a six-foot square target.

At 100 yards the bullet would easily punch through a railway sleeper, leaving an exit hole three inches across. Penetration tests during the American Civil War showed that the Minié bullet was still capable of passing through four inches of pine at 1,000 yards. This power is a grim reminder of why so many wounded became amputees, since any bone mass splintered if struck by the heavy lead bullet. The wound would also be contaminated not only with particles of the bullet's heavy grease lubrication mixed with bore-scrapings, but also with pieces of uniform, and even unburned powder embedded in the base of the bullet. Little wonder that amputation was considered the only relatively safe treatment for most limb wounds.

The velocities obtained were certainly instructive, being predictably higher than those recorded for an India Pattern musket which we fired for comparison using the same charge. Loading each with 65 grains of powder, the P53 recorded between 940 and 1020fps compared to 820fps for the musket. However, the standard charge for the musket was higher than that of the Enfield at 80 grains, which one would expect to have given marginally better velocities, windage notwithstanding; and it did improve with careful patching, pushing the musket ball up to 942fps on one heady occasion. However, it was striking to note the distance over which the P53's .577 bullet maintained its velocity compared to the larger .76 ball. At 800 yards the Minié bullet had lost about half of its initial velocity, while the musket ball had lost half of its power by the 200 yards marker.

*The detail shows a sectioned P53 Minié cartridge. Once the paper tail was torn off the coarse powder was poured into the barrel, and the cartridge turned over so that the bullet entered the muzzle base first. This seated it firmly on the charge, and the paper rammed down on top of it ensured that the bullet remained in place. A few shots caked the barrel and ramrod with slippery powder residue, and reloading became a filthy job.*

Even more impressive was the rifle's performance at 900 yards: it placed ten shots consistently around a six-foot square target, and although in fairness only one struck it, that was not lacking in velocity, passing completely through a 4x2in post support. Bear in mind that these shots were fired over open sights, at high trajectory, and with a fairly strong crosswind blowing. Heavy-barrelled rifles such as Whitworths, fitted with long-range target sights, would achieve far greater accuracy, particularly with their smaller .45in bullet. Our experience does, however, give some credibility to the 1,000-yard sights fitted to our P53 rifle, although in military terms attempting to hit a specific target at that range would be fairly pointless. The P53 has a mean point of aim deviation of over 11 feet at 1,200 yards, and few soldiers were trained sufficiently to understand the complexities of long-range shooting. Nevertheless, it was certainly possible to lay down harassing fire on area targets at 900-1,000 yards.

Also impressive was the P53's ability to be loaded and fired without fouling. There is a published record of reliability tests in which a single rifle was loaded and fired 16,000 times without cleaning over a period from August 1863 to September 1866. I have long regarded this claim with suspicion; but on the range our second pattern rifle was shot over 100 times without any hint of a problem, so perhaps such a feat may indeed be possible. The design of the bullet is largely responsible for this, as the expanded skirt scrapes accumulated debris from the rifling as it exits. The animal-fat grease which covered every cartridge (notoriously, a catalyst in sparking off the 1857 Indian Mutiny) also helped to ensure that the fouling remained soft. It certainly did become progressively harder to load as more shots were fired, but it was never impossible. The recoil got worse as the rifling became progressively dirtier - and it was certainly noticeable to start with. The only slight problem encountered while shooting was blockage of the nipple by debris from the percussion caps, but this was cleared in seconds using the pricker supplied with the combination tool.

We also tried different loads to see what difference they made to accuracy; as with earlier experiments, the answer seemed to be "not much". Measures of 70 and 80 grains were used at 500 yards; there was no appreciable change in point of impact, and the rifle also become noticeably more uncomfortable to shoot as the recoil really made itself felt. In common with tests of the flintlock musket, an amount of unburned powder was visible on the ground when a charge of 80 grains was used, which would indicate that using so much powder did not achieve much except a bruised shoulder. The reason for this may have been that the Minié bullet does not allow sufficient pressure build-up to efficiently burn the larger charge, and as a result grains remain behind the bullet to be blown out as it exits from the muzzle. Certainly 80 grains seemed to be the maximum practical load, producing 1040fps at the muzzle and 932fps at 100 yards, and giving consistent accuracy. It is not surprising that the rifled percussion musket of the 1850s generation became the standard by which infantry rifles were judged for nearly two decades.

**RIGHT & OPPOSITE** *Placing the hammer on half-cock, Billy Yank reaches into the cap-pouch to find a percussion cap. The tiny caps were easily fumbled and lost, and to help prevent them spilling out the pouch was lined with lambswool around the top, which worked very effectively.*

**THIS PAGE** *With a cap placed on the nipple, the hammer is brought back to full-cock and the rifle is raised into the firing position. Compared to the spectacle provided by earlier forms of ignition with exposed priming, the enclosed system of the percussion rifle was rather undramatic. A secondary advantage of the percussion cap was that it reduced the number of facial injuries from careless priming.*

**OPPOSITE TOP** *However, when fired in any numbers percussion weapons still generated large clouds of powder smoke, as demonstrated by this reconstructed Confederate unit firing a volley. After the second volley the rear rank men were barely able to see the front rank, let alone a target.*

**OPPOSITE BOTTOM LEFT** *The effective rear sight on a P53 Enfield, graduated in 100 yard increments up to 900 yards. While this was beyond extreme range for aimed fire at individual targets, area harassing fire was still effective at such distances.*

**OPPOSITE BOTTOM RIGHT** *The P53 bullet did not lack power. This six-inch oak post bears witness to its impact at 100 yards, giving some idea of its effect on a human body.*

# THE PERCUSSION REVOLVER

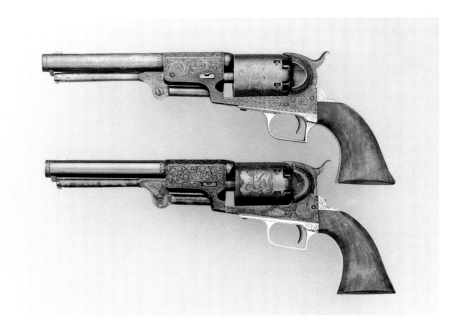

Since the invention of the firearm, gunmakers and shooters alike had been united in a common purpose: to create a firearm with the capacity for discharging more than one shot. The single-shot muzzle-loading pistol was acceptable as a last-ditch self-defence weapon provided it was used within its very narrow limitations. With its lack of accuracy, limited range, and lengthy reloading process it was just about adequate for deterring footpads or highway robbers; but in warfare only the suicidal would rely upon it.

The concept of repeating firearms had been in the minds of gunmakers since the 16th century, but there were only two possible means of achieving this end. The first was superimposed loads, where a number of charges were rammed down a barrel one on top of the other and then ignited in reverse order, so that the last charge loaded fired first. This posed a number of technical problems, not least the tendency of such systems to ignite all the loads simultaneously, with results that were invariably gruesome. The second and infinitely preferable method involved adding some form of revolving cylinder with a number of chambers each containing an individual charge. This did have some disadvantages, primarily weight and bulk, since the more chambers that were added the heavier the weapon would become.

There had, of course, been many attempts to increase the rate of fire from hand guns, some of which date back to the first half of the 16th century. There is a three-barrelled matchlock pistol in the museum of the Palazzo Ducale in Venice which is recorded in an inventory dated 1548, although it is doubtless of earlier manufacture; and the Tojhusmuseum in Copenhagen has a six-chambered wheel lock petronel dated to around 1597. As we have seen, it had been the introduction of the wheel lock which enabled the pistol to come of age as a practical firearm in the 17th century.

An example of one of the more workable designs of revolving pistol is held in the Royal Armouries; this is an elegant six- chambered wheel lock pistol made in Germany in about 1610. It is an unusual piece, for it is one of the earliest known pistols with a mechanism providing a positive means of locking a chamber in place behind the barrel prior to firing. This was obviously a major problem of designs marrying a revolving cylinder with a single barrel. The German pistol has a simple spring-latch mechanism which locates the cylinder in position for each shot, although this is not mechanically activated and has to be engaged by hand each time. Aside from barrel alignment, the main disadvantage with all early designs of revolving pistol was the need for priming powder to be added to each cylinder before it could be fired.

There exist several patterns of revolver from the early decades of the 16th century employing either snaphaunce or flintlock mechanisms. Most took a form similar to the brass English snaphaunce which we illustrate, but relied on hand-rotated cylinders; this particular example was somewhat ahead of its time in being fitted with a mechanically operated arm which rotated the cylinder as the cock was pulled back. This system was not successfully repeated until an expatriate German gunmaker from Suhl, J.G.Kolbe, produced a workable flintlock example some time between 1730 and 1737. This used a rather neater internal gear train to rotate the cylinder automatically as the pistol was cocked.

As with the snaphaunce, these early revolving pistols were generally too large and heavy to be very practical, and manufacture was both complicated and expensive. Nevertheless, as the 18th century progressed the increasingly widespread use of the perfected flintlock mechanism gave a new impetus to such experiments; and from the 1730s onwards a plethora of revolving-cylinder pistols began to appear. Amongst others, some fine examples were made

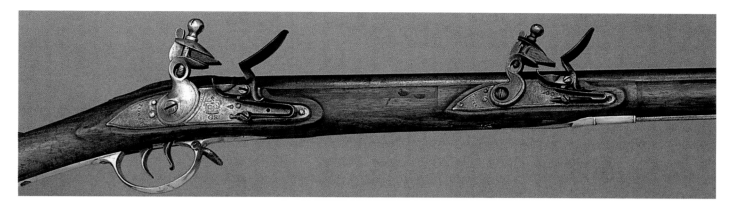

by English gunmakers such as Deane, Dafte and Gorgo, and many excellent multi-barrelled pistols were also manufactured; but most suffered from the same three basic design problems.

First was the difficulty of creating a strong, enclosed mechanism to both rotate and lock the cylinder before each shot; shooting a hand gun with the chamber misaligned would, at the very least, blow off the barrel, and probably injure the firer into the bargain. Second was the problem of retaining the priming charge, which was nearly impossible on an open rotating cylinder. It could be done by fitting sliding pan covers, but this was at best awkward, as each cover had to be opened before shooting, and spilling any of the small quantity of priming powder also made the early revolvers prone to misfires. Last was the challenge of keeping the weight and size of the pistol down to manageable proportions.

As is usually the case with mechanical inventions, no one person achieved all three goals at once; but Artemis Wheeler of Concord, Massachusetts, manufactured a revolving rifle in 1818 which almost succeeded. With the assistance of Elisha Collier he refined his original design to produce an eminently workable five-cylinder flintlock revolving pistol in 1825, which was subsequently patented as Collier's design. It had an ingenious self-priming magazine attached to the steel, as well as a locking mechanism for the cylinder operated by the action of the cock. Cocking the pistol pulled back a locking-bar which freed the cylinder. This then had to be manually pulled backward against a strong spring, and rotated. Once released, the mouth of the chamber, which was slightly rebated, was pushed forwards onto the rear of the barrel, which was tapered to give a positive and reasonably efficient gas seal. Finally, the locking bar slid forwards to ensure the cylinder could not move out of alignment. It was not perfect, but it was a great improvement on previous attempts; and whilst it was not exactly pocket-sized it was certainly portable, with a six-inch (150mm) .44 calibre barrel and weighing a modest 2lbs 2oz (1 kilogram).

This design even aroused the interest of Britain's notoriously conservative Board of Ordnance, who tested a seven-shot example with a mechanically-rotated cylinder at Woolwich in 1818. This was, rather predictably, rejected as being *"by far too complicated and expensive to be applicable to the Public Service."*

In view of the Duke of Wellington's feelings about pistols this is not surprising, since he was Master General of the Ordnance at the time.

Many other multi-shot designs proliferated, in particular the "pepperbox", which was simply a cluster of between five and seven barrels grouped around either a central barrel or a solid spindle. The barrel cluster had to be rotated by hand, and the early flintlock variants were prone to misfires as well as being overly heavy and, of course, massively unbalanced. The most successful revolvers in America had been pepperbox types; there was far less interest in them in England, with sales recorded of only about 250 per year from 1830 to 1850. Because of physical necessity most pepperboxes were of small calibre, but they proved very enduring, surviving until well into the era of the percussion revolver.

*       *       *

It was the invention of the percussion cap in the early 1800s which was to stimulate the creation of the true revolver. At a stroke it solved the problems of keeping a pistol loaded and primed ready for instant use. As the most effective revolving pistols available were the pepperboxes, many were manufactured using the new percussion system and a number were converted from flintlock - it took little modification to drill the chambers to accept a nipple and replace the old cock with a bar-type hammer. By the mid-19th century the barrel cluster was being machined from a solid bar of steel rather than using the old and expensive method of soldering separate barrels together. The percussion caps were placed on steel nipples screwed into the rear of each barrel and surrounded by a small protective shield. The method of rotating the barrels was refined and simplified by using a "hand" or "pawl", a long pivoting lever which locked into one of a number of teeth cut into the rear of the cylinder. This lever was actuated by the trigger and - assuming the pistol had six barrels - turned them through one sixth of a full rotation to line up each in turn with the hammer. It was a sound and reliable system, even if the pepperbox did have an amusing habit of "chain firing" its barrels. This was usually caused by the concussion of the first shot setting off the primer of the second, and so on. It was not actually dangerous to the shooter, but it was extremely

*Superimposed loads were one method used in the search for greater firepower; generally their bulk and weight made them unsuitable for use in handguns. With one charge and ball inserted on top of a second, the lock furthest from the shooter was fired. This theoretically left the second charge in place, to be ignited by the other lock, but in practice simultaneous detonation was not uncommon, with destructive results. (XII.4540; A5646; The Board of Trustees of the Royal Armouries)*

*An early brass-barrelled English snaphaunce revolver of c.1600. It was not the most compact design, and was slow to fire despite its mechanical cylinder rotation, as each chamber had to be primed separately before shooting. (II.1780; A4547; The Board of Trustees of the Royal Armouries)*

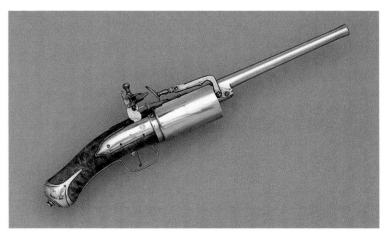

The Collier Patent revolving flintlock of c.1825; the metal box on the steel is a self-priming mechanism. Sam Colt examined this particular pistol during a visit to England in the early 1850s. (XII.4000; A10/738/739; The Board of Trustees of the Royal Armouries)

spectacular, as one Chaplain White found out when accompanying the 18th US Infantry in July 1866. His detachment were surprised in a ravine by a Sioux war party, and as the warriors sprang from hiding White fired his seven-shot pepperbox. All seven chambers ignited at once, killing two Indians and frightening the others so badly that they fled without realising that he was now defenceless.

The invention of the first completely mechanically operated percussion revolver has long been attributed to Samuel Colt, who was born in 1813 in Hartford, Connecticut. Many firearms historians have argued against this, and it must be said that no single individual was responsible for inventing all of the mechanical refinements that were required to produce the revolver. Certainly Colt had examined all of the available designs during a number of visits to England, including the early snaphaunce revolvers and Collier's design. However, Colt's genius lay in combining all their best features into a single serviceable firearm, whose internal design was subsequently incorporated into almost every other make of revolver.

He had produced a workmanlike revolver by 1837 which employed a fixed barrel and revolving cylinder. These first Paterson models were produced from 1837 to 1841 in a number of calibres. They were five-chambered, with an unusual folding trigger and a single-action mechanism - this simply meant that the hammer had to be cocked by hand each time a shot was to be fired. The most notable feature was the ratchet mechanism, rather similar to that of the pepperbox, which used a pawl to rotate the cylinder each time the hammer was cocked. In addition there was a small sprung lug, the bolt, set inside the lower frame and connected by a linkage to the hammer. Each time the hammer was cocked to fire this rose up to engage into a machined slot in the cylinder, locking it solidly in place for each shot.

The Paterson was used in earnest for the first time in 1844, when a party of 15 Texas Rangers led by Colonel J.C.Hays were attacked by a large number of Comanche Indians. The Indians were accustomed to running into Rangers armed with single-shot percussion pistols; on this occasion they continued to close in after the Rangers fired a first fusillade of shots, only to be met with a continuous and withering hail of fire which laid 40 of them dead by the end of the engagement.

Despite this operational success the Paterson was, surprisingly, a commercial failure; but Colt had astutely transferred the patent rights to a new company, and in 1847 he began to make a new revolver, the Walker or Dragoon model. This massive .44 calibre pistol weighed nearly 5lbs loaded and fired a 57-grain charge, which gave it muzzle energy almost comparable to a modern .44 revolver. It had initially been produced in response to a plea from the US Dragoons and Mounted Rifles for a revolver that was guaranteed to be powerful enough to knock down a man with a single bullet.

The American use of cavalry as scouts and skirmishers was very different from the "cavalry as battering ram" tactics seen on the battlefields of Europe. On the expanding frontier of the USA dispersed mounted units, usually outnumbered, were typically involved in fast, hit-and-run fighting. Until the Civil War single-shot carbines and pistols were carried by both officers and men; the benefits of repeating weapons in patrol encounters and ambushes far from support were well appreciated, and the new pistol became an essential part of field equipment rather than a useless encumbrance.

The Walker/Dragoon Colts were still often carried in pairs in leather holsters attached to the saddle; they were simply too large and heavy to be worn comfortably on the hip (although the Rangers are recorded as carrying them holstered or thrust into sashes during the Mexican War, 1846-48). Increasingly soldiers found that a holster slung on a waistbelt was a more practical

One of the many types of pepperbox produced; this fine example from c.1845 is by John Edge of Manchester. The percussion lock pepperbox was quite a practical design from the viewpoint of ignition; its major drawback was its weight and gross imbalance due to the barrel configuration. (XII.1188; A10/791; The Board of Trustees of the Royal Armouries)

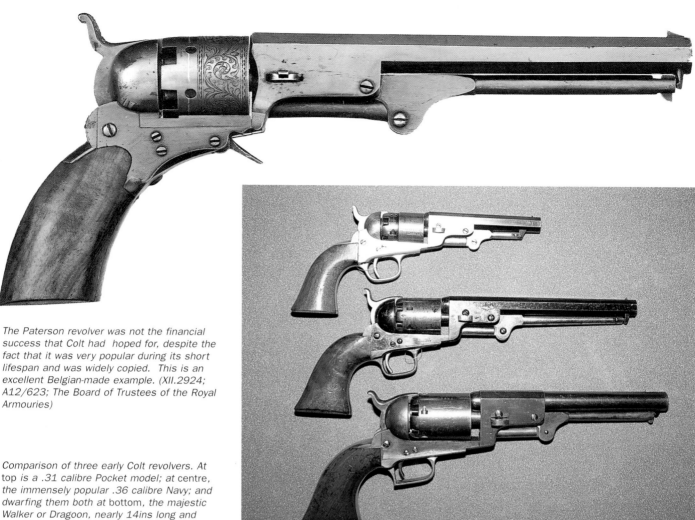

*The Paterson revolver was not the financial success that Colt had hoped for, despite the fact that it was very popular during its short lifespan and was widely copied. This is an excellent Belgian-made example. (XII.2924; A12/623; The Board of Trustees of the Royal Armouries)*

*Comparison of three early Colt revolvers. At top is a .31 calibre Pocket model; at centre, the immensely popular .36 calibre Navy; and dwarfing them both at bottom, the majestic Walker or Dragoon, nearly 14ins long and weighing more than 4lbs empty. (XII.3783/5490/908; A123; The Board of Trustees of the Royal Armouries)*

method of carrying a revolver ready for use.

Colt and other American manufacturers were caught out by a sudden demand for pistols created by the California Gold Rush of 1849. Among the miners and prospectors out West the perceived need for weapons of self-defence became so great that a good quality revolver could fetch five times its original purchase price. J.D.Borthwick, an English gentleman who travelled widely in the West between 1849 and 1851, commented on this new American obsession with the revolver, as he watched men being searched before entering a saloon in San Francisco:

*"... Most men drew a pistol from behind their backs... demure, pious-looking men, in white neck cloths, lifted up the bottom of their waistcoats, and revealed the butt of a revolver... and there were men, terrible fellows no doubt but who were more likely to frighten themselves than any one else, who produced a revolver from each trouser pocket, and a bowie knife from their belt."*

It was clear to Colt that there was a good market for a more compact revolver, and he scaled down the Dragoon to produce first the 1849 Pocket model in .31 calibre, and then the larger Model 1851 Navy. This .36 calibre pistol was to prove hugely successful for Colt, the more so in the wake of the publicity he received at the Great Exhibition of London in 1851.

\*     \*     \*

Although Europe was flooded with small calibre pistols, many of Belgian manufacture, British gunmakers had been extraordinarily slow to appreciate the level of public and military interest in the new revolvers. The Birmingham gun trade did have a number of capable manufacturers, such as Adams and Tranter, who had been manufacturing on a modest scale since the late 1840s. However, the interest in the new revolver prompted Adams to look very closely at the Colts, and in 1851 he produced a similar five-chambered pistol. It was actually an improvement on the Colt in that it was self-cocking - the mechanism did not have to be hand-cocked prior to each shot, as simply pulling the trigger would fire it. It was also a stronger design. The Colt relied on a weak sliding bar to hold the barrel to the frame assembly. In practical terms this meant that if it were dropped heavily or used as a club the barrel would almost certainly be bent out of alignment, to the point where the cylinder could not be rotated. Adams and most other British manufacturers used a solid frame design; a flat bar over the top of the cylinder joined the barrel and frame, making the revolver much stronger and preventing accidental movement of the barrel. American manufacturers such as Remington and Smith and Wesson also preferred the solid frame design, and Colt eventu-

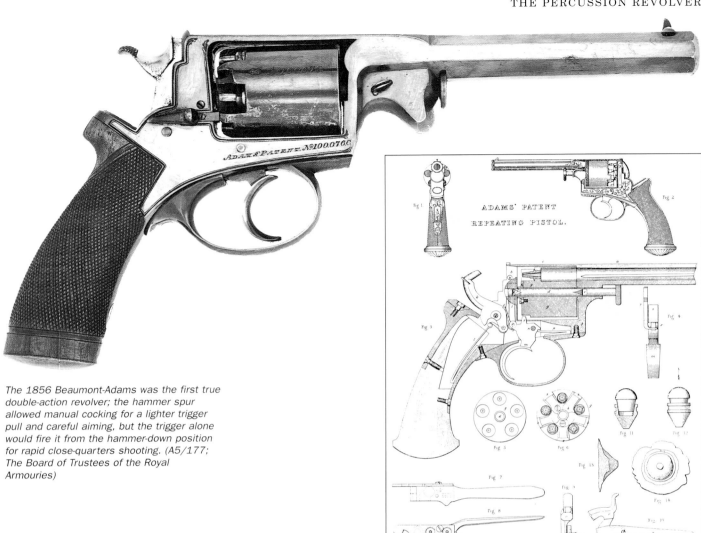

The 1856 Beaumont-Adams was the first true double-action revolver; the hammer spur allowed manual cocking for a lighter trigger pull and careful aiming, but the trigger alone would fire it from the hammer-down position for rapid close-quarters shooting. (A5/177; The Board of Trustees of the Royal Armouries)

**ABOVE RIGHT** *The patent drawing for Robert Adams' self-cocking revolver of 1851. Its large calibre of .50in only permitted five chambers to be machined into the cylinder. Also illustrated are a bullet mould, bottom left; and life-size illustrations of the expanding Adams bullets, beneath which is an example of a bullet which had expanded on impact - Figs.11 & 12, 13 & 14, lower right. The classical elegance of the butt shape, recalling fine flintlock and percussion weapons, was also practical: it gave an excellent grip.*

ally abandoned the open frame with the introduction of a new range of revolvers in 1873.

In September 1851, amid much publicity, a public test was held at Woolwich between a .44 calibre Dragoon and a .50 calibre Adams. A report stated that the Adams was faster to load at 38 seconds compared to the Colt's 58 seconds. Penetration tests on one-inch elm board were inconclusive, the bullets of both revolvers passing through; unfortunately the reporter does not mention the range. What was at once apparent was the greater reliability of the Adams, which did not misfire once, whereas the Colt misfired ten times in 42 shots. Immersion tests in which the loaded chambers were soaked before firing posed no problem to the Adams, whereas the Colt failed to fire four of its six chambers.

In almost every respect the Adams was superior to the Colt, but it did have a couple of significant weaknesses. Whereas the Colt used a strong lever-action rammer mounted beneath the barrel for loading the ball, the Adams relied on a pre-prepared cartridge very similar to that of a musket. Once this was torn open and inserted into the chamber the bullet had to be pressed home with the finger. As a certain amount of fouling built up this became harder to accomplish, and doubtless painful. The problem was remedied on later models of the Adams fitted with a side-mounted rammer.

The other problem lay in the heavy self-cocking mechanism, which made the pistol difficult to shoot accurately without considerable practice. This was solved in 1855 by a Lt.F.Beaumont, who patented the first true double-action mechanism; this enabled the revolver either to be hand-cocked like the Colt, or cocked and fired just by pulling the trigger. It was a system immediately adopted by the company of Deane, Adams & Deane, who produced revolvers with great success. Unable to copy it because of the patent, the William Tranter company took a different route; they produced pistols with double triggers - squeezing one rotated the cylinder and cocked the hammer, and squeezing the second fired it. The complex internal mechanics and a series of manufacturing problems led to the Beaumont-Adams ceasing production in the late 1860s, but the basic double-action design lived on in many other revolvers and is still in use today.

So great was the demand for his .36in Navy revolver in Britain that Colt had opened a London factory in Pimlico in 1852, the success of which was noted with interest by the Board of Ordnance. After the outbreak of the Crimean War they had been moved to form a Select Committee to undertake tests on available revolvers, with a view to meeting the sudden demand from both the Royal Navy and the army. The rivalry between Adams and Colt was fuelled by the Board of Ordnance; in 1854, in spite of the Select Committee's recommending the purchase of the Adams, the Board decided instead to order Navy Colts, in order to "*supply 3000 revolving pistols immediately for the use of the Army… either by the Cavalry, or by a storming party or by Colour Sergeants, or in any other way... "*

They were certainly needed. The savage trench fighting in the Crimea had found officers especially vulnerable, for a sword or single-shot pistol were hopelessly inadequate. Many officers ordered pistols to be sent from England, and found them of great value in hand-to-hand fighting. Lt.Crosse of the 88th Regiment wrote a letter of appreciation to the Adams factory:

*"I had one of your largest-size revolver pistols at the bloody battle of Inkerman, and by some chance got surrounded by Russians. I then found the advantages of your pistol over that of Colonel Colt's, for had I to cock each shot I should have lost my life. I should not have had time to cock, as they were too close to me... so close that I was bayoneted through the thigh immediately after shooting the fourth man."*

After forty years in the military wilderness the revolver was finally beginning to make a mark for itself in the British army through its unequalled value as a close-quarter weapon. All the new revolvers were rifled, which increased the chance of hitting a target about ten-fold. Indeed, officers proved themselves very keen to practice, setting up target ranges wherever there was the time and space.

All revolvers, and Colts in particular, were known for having very varied points of aim, and in practice this meant that even though two identical pistols were being fired at the same target their shots would group in different places. Thus at 25 yards, to ensure a hit in the chest area, one pistol might simply have to be aimed at the centre of the torso while another might have to be aimed at the right hip. The cause of this was to be found in fractional differences in machining tolerances and assembly methods. To become proficient a shooter had to practice until he knew exactly where his pistol would place a bullet, and then alter his aim accordingly.

One problem with revolvers lay in their comparatively small calibres. The old single-shot pistols might have been inaccurate, but no enemy struck by one of their slow-moving .60 to .70 calibre balls felt well enough to persist in his original course of action. The new revolvers' accuracy made them deadly in capable hands at quite considerable ranges, but only a tiny proportion of revolver owners were accomplished shots. Most embraced the theory that if enough bullets were fired at a target at least one of them would probably do some damage. Although capable of accurate shooting at 50 yards or beyond, the .36 and .44 calibre bullets were comparatively light; they had relatively high velocity but not a great deal of stopping power, which is one of the ballistic anomalies of the revolver. Lt.Col.G.Fosbery recalled after an incident during the Indian Mutiny:

*"An officer, who especially prided himself on his pistol shooting, was attacked by a stalwart mutineer with a heavy sword. The officer, unfortunately for himself, carried a Colt's Navy pistol, which... was of small calibre [.36] and fired a sharp pointed bullet. This he proceeded to empty into the Sepoy as he advanced but, having done so, he waited just one second too long to see the effect of his shooting, and was cloven to the teeth by his antagonist, who then dropped down and died beside him... five out of the six bullets had struck the Sepoy close together in the chest, and all had passed through him and out of his back."*

What was needed was a combination of a very large calibre bullet and a reasonably high velocity, but due of the very nature of the revolver this was impractical because of size and weight limitations, as can be seen from the demise of the Colt Dragoon. The laws of physics being fixed, the larger the bullet, the greater the charge required to propel it, leading to a consequently heavier recoil. It was not really until the advent of the centrefire cartridge in the early 1870s that the combination of higher velocities and large calibre was successfully achieved.

*The Tranter revolver of 1865, here a highly decorated example for a wealthy civilian buyer. The lower trigger rotated the cylinder and cocked the hammer, the upper one fired it. The external bar following the edge of the frame and barrel is the ramming lever. (XII.4671; A13/444; The Board of Trustees of the Roysal Armouries)*

**Technical Specifications**

**Colt Walker/Dragoon revolver:**

| | | |
|---|---|---|
| Overall length | 13.75ins | (349mm) |
| Barrel length | 7.5ins | (190mm) |
| Calibre | .44in | (11.2mm) |
| Weight | 4lbs 2oz | (1.9kg) |
| Charge | 53 grains | |
| Ignition | Percussion cap | |

**Adams revolver:**

| | | |
|---|---|---|
| Overall length | 13.25ins | (337mm) |
| Barrel length | 7.5ins | (190mm) |
| Calibre | .50in | (12.7mm) |
| Weight | 2lbs 6oz | (1.2kg) |
| Charge | 30 grains | |
| Ignition | Percussion cap | |

**Firing the Colt Walker/Dragoon & Adams revolvers**

It was felt that re-creating the test between the Dragoon and Adams revolvers would prove interesting, and a reasonably good Adams of 1852 vintage was available. Unfortunately, the owners of two original Dragoons inexplicably resisted all efforts to persuade them to let their extraordinarily rare and valuable pistols be used. The alternative was to employ one of a number of reproductions now available from Italian or American manufacturers.

The example finally used for the test is unusual on several counts. It has no maker's name, and the only clue to its origin is a set of Italian proofmarks. It is a fairly old reproduction, fitted with large nipples for a size of percussion cap that is no longer commercially available. It is a beautifully finished piece, both internally and externally; when it was passed to a skilled gunsmith for fitting with smaller nipples that would accept modern caps, he declared it to be the best-made reproduction that he had ever seen. It shows no signs of ever having been blued, and bears a very low four-digit serial number. Though its age and manufacturer are a mystery, it was felt to be as good a copy as was likely to be found.

There are few percussion revolvers as physically impressive as the Dragoon, and even by the standards of today's Magnum revolvers it is a great big pistol. Weighing 4lbs 9oz (2.2kg) and measuring 13.75ins (349mm) in length, it gives one the reassuring feeling that even when empty it was probably solid enough to beat a buffalo senseless. It does suffer from the design faults common to the early Colts, however. The first is the inherent weakness in the method of joining the barrel and cylinder to the frame, which is particularly noticeable in a revolver as big as the Dragoon. The second is the balance: when loaded it became extremely muzzle-heavy, and very tiring to hold single-handed.

Additionally, the back strap of the butt and the small, plain wooden grips have a smooth contour which prevented a firm grip when shooting. This resulted in the pistol twisting upwards under recoil, making it very difficult to maintain a consistent aim at the target. A firm grip is needed, as this is a powerful pistol producing an impressive 455 ft/lbs of muzzle energy. To put this into context, the .50 calibre Adams managed 255 ft/lbs; a .36 Colt Navy recorded a paltry 148 ft/lbs; and a modern nitrocellulose–loaded 44 Special cartridge has a muzzle energy of 616 ft/lbs.

There is a lot of published loading data available for these pistols, so working up an optimum load was not difficult. For the Dragoon we started with 45 grains of medium powder,

*Before loading the Colt Dragoon the hammer has to be pulled back to the half-cock position. This frees off the mechanism, allowing the cylinder to be rotated by hand.*

*Pouring a measured charge of medium powder into the first chamber. The flask has a spring-loaded cut-off which ensures that a fixed amount of powder is dispensed; all six chambers must be loaded before the bullets are inserted, with the revolver held upright throughout to prevent the powder spilling out again. Three hands would be welcome during this lengthy process.*

for the Adams with 30 grains. The cylinders were loaded, the spherical balls rammed home in the Colt, and the conical bullets pushed into the Adams' chambers with a short piece of wooden dowel. The mouth of each chamber was sealed with a mix of tallow and beeswax, which serves the dual purpose of helping to lubricate the ball and preventing chain-ignition.

This can occur when the flash from the first cylinder jumps across the mouth of the other cylinders and ignites their charges. While this may be an exciting spectacle for onlookers it is absolutely terrifying for the shooter, who suddenly finds himself clutching a small, slow-firing machine gun which he can't turn off. It was a common problem with percussion revolvers, and one that eventually led to the demise of the revolving rifle - on which the natural position for the left hand to support the weight of the rifle was holding the frame immediately in front of the cylinder...

Given its poor sights - a bead front, and a simple V-notch cut in the nose of the hammer - the accuracy of the **Dragoon** was quite impressive. When fired at 25 yards using a two-handed grip (almost a necessity in view of its weight) groups of four inches were possible, and this opened out to 12 inches at 50 yards. Given slight modification to the grips, which were a little too small and slim for the size of pistol, the big .44 Colt would even compare well against modern revolvers. Shooting at 100 yards proved less successful; although the bullet would reach quite happily, the trajectory was high, with the point of aim being about two feet above the target, and hits registered all over it without any discernible grouping. Nevertheless, all struck a board which was slightly larger than a man, which was an impressive performance for a black powder revolver at this distance.

The balls were then swapped for conical lead bullets, which performed with fractionally improved accuracy at 25 and 50 yards, but were far less satisfactory at 100 yards, several missing the target altogether. The reason for this could be that the conical bullets were less stable than the balls at the extreme edge of their range, and as their velocity dropped they began to wander in flight more than the spherical balls.

We tried again using the optimum recommended load of 57 grains, which certainly improved matters. The recoil was quite heavy but not unpleasantly so, which was to be expected in view of the weight of the pistol, and was nowhere near as punishing as a modern .44 revolver using a standard factory cartridge.

The **Adams** was certainly more pleasant to shoot, having a more comfortable grip shape which offered better support on recoil, and at a shade under 3lbs was lighter and more compact. The 30-grain charge seemed to be about right for ranges up to 50 yards, but accuracy was very variable until one became used to the heavy pull of the trigger. The "double action only" mechanism tends to pull the point of aim off to the right, and even attempting to compensate by aiming to the left gave mixed results, depending on who was shooting and what sort of grip they had.

The Adams was certainly capable of placing all of its five bullets into a man-sized target at 25 yards, with grouping of about six inches. At 50 yards it took considerable care to hit the target; using a rest improved matters considerably, and five shots then covered an area of around 14 inches. As the revolver we were using was not in the first flush of youth, and the trigger action was heavy, this could doubtless be improved upon.

With a heavier charge of 40 grains we were able to shoot the Adams out to 100 yards, and despite there being a distinct lag between the gunshot and the sound of the bullet striking the board it proved capable of placing all five shots into a man-sized target, given still weather conditions. The point of aim was even higher than the Colt's - unsurprising in view of the larger calibre bullet and smaller charge - but once this was allowed for it proved fairly consistent. With its heavier weight and lighter charge the Adams bullet was generally considered to be at the limit of its performance at 100 yards, but could still penetrate a 2x2in support.

If these revolvers had one failing it was the percussion caps, which dropped with malicious glee behind the recoil shield or between the cylinder and hammer, locking the mechanism up completely. On a couple of occasions one or other pistol had to be dismantled to clear the obstruction, and one has to wonder how many lives were lost as a result of this failing. In fairness it must be stressed that this was a problem common to all percussion revolvers, not just the two on test.

It was when trying to reload these pistols that one appreciated why many soldiers preferred to carry several. On average, it took us 58 seconds to load the Adams and 1.5 minutes for the Colt *under perfect conditions*. These included having steady hands, a bench to rest the gun on, not dropping any balls, powder or percussion caps, and not having anyone trying to shoot or eviscerate you meanwhile. Under close quarter combat conditions pausing for that length of time to reload would be suicidal, so spare pistols - or failing that, at least one spare loaded cylinder - must have been essential. Swapping cylinders took about 45 seconds, and could certainly have been accomplished on horseback by a reasonably dextrous and experienced man, albeit with a certain amount of luck.

The Dragoon proved more susceptible to misfires than the Adams, and tended to be more affected by the problem of insecurely seated percussion caps. The big Colt never failed to draw a crowd, probably because the noise and smoke generated made spectators think a small cannon was being fired; but despite the Dragoon's seductive and folklorique lines, the Adams was generally felt to be better constructed and finished. It was a pity that we did not have a chance to try a later Beaumont with a true double-action mechanism, as it would doubtless have proved even steadier and more accurate. As it was, the majority of those who fired it believed that notwithstanding its heavy trigger, its lighter weight, better balance and reliability made the Adams the more practical weapon - which was pretty much the conclusion reached in 1851.

Our tests did seem to confirm the theory that single-action mechanisms were better for accuracy while the double-action was more suited to close-quarter fighting because of the speed with which the cylinder could be emptied – 11 seconds for the Colt, and four for the Adams, which was identical to the results achieved in 1851. In their day there can have been few other handguns quite as impressive or potent.

The shooter places a spherical ball at the mouth of the first cylinder, and unlatches the loading lever to push it down onto the powder charge. When the lever meets firm resistance the bullet is properly seated. For target shooting a filler such as corn meal was often placed between the bullet and powder to ensure it was well compressed and protected from chain-ignition, but battle conditions would not permit such an indulgence. Failure to fully ram home can lead to a ruptured cylinder.

A percussion cap is removed from the pouch and placed on the nipple. This is a particularly fiddly operation, as the caps are smaller than those for a musket and easily dropped. If they are not a tight fit on the nipples there is a high probability that one or more will come loose during firing and jam the hammer or cylinder.

The hammer is pulled back to full-cock position, and the Colt is levelled. This profile view suggests why most men would need a two-handed grip for any kind of sustained aimed shooting - not because of the recoil, which is largely absorbed by the Dragoon's massive weight, but because of the muzzle-heavy balance.

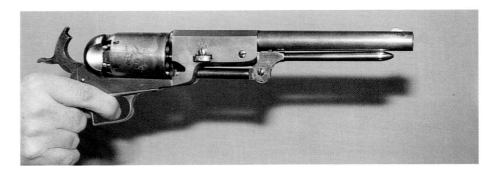

The first chamber fires. Note the spray of particles radiating out from the cylinder, and the trail of flame from the nipple, as tiny fragments of the copper percussion cap are blown away by the back-pressure through the nipple. (The author is totally unable to explain the reason for the hammer apparently being caught by the camera shutter in the cocked position at this moment in the cycle...)

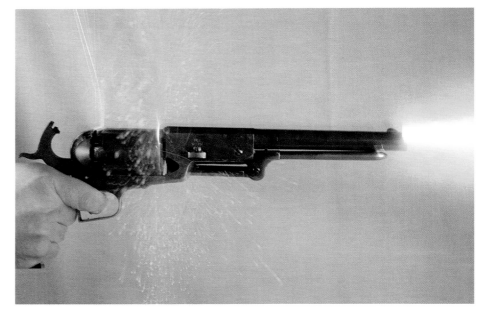

As the gases from the chamber exit down the barrel, smoke and sparks still fly out from the gap between the cylinder and barrel.

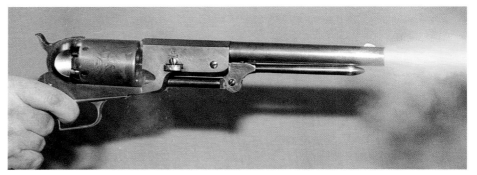

Chain-ignition: a flash-over to the mouths of the other cylinders causes a multiple discharge. Although partially obscured here by the pyrotechnics, four of the six chambers have in fact ignited, generating a startling quantity of smoke and flame.

The penetration of a spherical ball from the Colt into an oak post six inches thick, at 50 yards' range. (Photograph Jeffrey Mayton)

The big **Adams** 38 bore revolver. Its actual calibre is .497in; with a 7.5in (162mm) barrel and weighing nearly 3lbs (1.3kg) it was one of the largest British percussion revolvers ever produced. Officers would have purchased their own revolvers privately, complete with a suitable holster for field use. (XII.900)

The Adams hammer lacks a spur; since the pistol was designed purely for double-action use a spur was unnecessary, and was anyway prone to getting snagged in clothing and equipment. The cylinder shows the typical mottled blue and grey marks of case hardening. Squeezing the trigger gently to allow the hammer to move back enables the vertical bar behind the cylinder on the left to be pushed into a recess, which locks the pawl and frees the cylinder to be rotated by hand for loading.

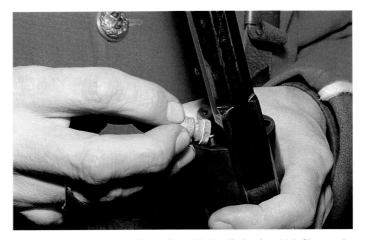

*The Adams has to be turned upside-down for loading, as the machined recess in the frame for access to the cylinder is on the right side. This gives just sufficient room for the chamber to be loaded.*

**BELOW** *Taking a pre-prepared cartridge from his pouch, our redcoat pulls on a thin black ribbon to tear the paper open and expose the powder. The charge is poured into the chamber, and the paper casing is discarded. (Several eyewitness descriptions of battlefields over the past two centuries have mentioned the immediate impression made by the extraordinary amounts of scrap paper left lying around.)*

*The bullet, with its distinctive thick fibre wad, is placed on top of the powder and firmly pushed down with the thumb. On a clean revolver this was easy and quick, but once the chambers became fouled it proved to be hard work, and we resorted to ramming with a short length of wooden dowel.*

*A loaded chamber with the bullet properly seated. If the bullet could not be pushed down far enough then it would prevent the cylinder from rotating, effectively rendering the revolver useless.*

**BELOW** *A 12-inch circle, showing the ten hits registered by the Adams at 100 yards. This was quite impressive for a pistol made before the Indian Mutiny.*

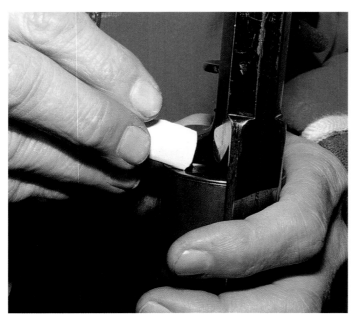

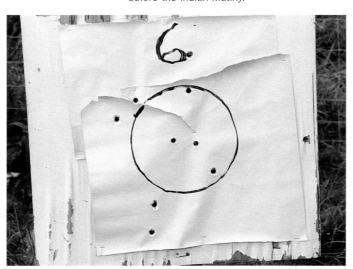

# THE PERCUSSION BREECH LOADING RIFLE

*Reconstruction: US Cavalry patrol, c.1863. The corporal still carries a sabre, but this was giving way to the carbine and the revolver as the cavalryman's primary weapons. He carries one Colt holstered on his hip and two more on his saddle, with a Sharps carbine hanging from a crossbelt.*

*Reconstruction: a sergeant of the Union army's 42nd Pennsylvania "Bucktails" takes aim with his 1859 Sharps New Model rifle; the .52 calibre barrel was about 10ins longer than that of the carbine, giving much greater accuracy. The US government bought about 2,000 of these rifles and issued them to three complete regiments: the 1st and 2nd US Sharpshooters and the 42nd Pennsylvania, who later received seven-shot Spencer repeaters.*

The history of breech-loading guns stretches back to at least the 14th century and possibly even earlier. In 1342 a French gun was recorded as having a separate chamber for powder; and there is mention of "guns with pots" in 1372 in an inventory of weapons held by Edward III. The "pots" were almost certainly removable iron breech chambers fitted with a large handle, which thus resembled a household pot or tankard. Many examples of these cannon and their breech chambers survive, in various sizes, in artillery museums around Europe. They were commonplace on 15th century battlefields, and tests with modern replicas have established that a rate of up to three shots per minute is consistently achievable, depending solely on the number of breeches provided and the size of the reloading crew.

This design offered the quickest and safest means of loading a gun. Reloading any muzzle-loading firearm involved an inherent element of risk. Powder had to be poured down a barrel that was already hot, and a worn or hastily sponged-out bore could easily conceal tiny glowing particles which could ignite the charge without warning. With a removable chamber the barrel was open at both ends, allowing much more thorough swabbing, and the chamber containing the next charge could be tightly wadded before bringing it into contact with the hot barrel.

Muzzle-loading is also a slow process, which for a hunter could mean watching his quarry vanish, and in a military context left gunners vulnerable to attack once their weapons had been fired - and usually obliged them to stand upright in full view of the enemy. The gradual introduction of the military rifle in the early 19th century increased this danger, as it became possible to take aimed shots at specific targets at ranges considerably beyond that attainable by a musket.

Any technical improvement that speeded up the process was welcomed by both civilian and soldier alike, and it will not surprise the reader to know that one of the earliest detailed descriptions of a breech-loading gun was illustrated in Leonardo da Vinci's *Codex Atlanticus*. This showed an open-ended breech and a tapered iron chamber drilled with a touch hole. Once this was positioned inside the breech a small metal wedge was tapped into a slot behind the chamber to hold it tightly in place; it could then be fired, removed, and replaced by another - essentially the system used on breech-loading artillery pieces.

It was not long before neater methods of breech-loading were being tried. Henry VIII was always interested in new firearms technology, and there exist in the Royal Armouries two breech-loading guns (one dated to 1537) which are rare survivors of the 139 breech-loading weapons he held in his personal collection. Also recorded were "thirty five targetts steilde with gonnes" - circular metal shields, each with a small breech-loading matchlock pistol mounted in the centre.

As a history of the development of these breech-loading guns would demand more space than this chapter allows, it is fair to summarise the technology of the period from 1600 to the end of the flintlock era simply as "complicated": there were dozens of attempts to produce efficient breech-loading designs using a bewildering number of systems. These can be broken down roughly into four basic types: guns with removable barrels, with removable breech plugs, with removable chambers or with hinged chambers. They made use of every kind of ignition system then available; but it was not until the latter part of the 18th century that designs began to appear which showed some real promise.

Apart from increasing the speed of loading there were other, less obvious benefits to breech-loading, one of which was improved accuracy. As we have seen, because of fouling muzzle-loaders had to be loaded with bullets of smaller size than the bore, which led to windage and poor accuracy. If the bullet could be introduced from the breech end then it could be cast to the correct calibre, since it no longer had to be rammed down a fouled barrel. Some gunmakers capitalised on this by making the chambers of their guns slightly tapered; when the gun was fired the coning effect of the chamber slightly squeezed the bullet into exactly the right calibre to ensure a perfect fit in the bore. As a useful byproduct, this also helped to reduce the level of fouling. It was also much easier to reload a breech-loading longarm while lying or crouching behind cover.

A number of tolerably successful breech-loading guns were produced in the mid- to late 17th century, and there is an early English patent dated 1664 taken out by Abraham Hill for a *"Gun that is charged and primed in like Manner at a hole belowe the sight or Visier, which is shutt with a screw smaller below then above."* This was an early screw-plug mechanism, which enabled the gun to be loaded when the plug was removed by means of a key from the top of the breech. It was a crude system, and it took the genius of a French engineer, Isaac de la Chaumette, to perfect it. This obsessive and brilliant inventor was unable to resist improving the mechanical function of almost anything he encountered. Intrigued by the theory of breech-loading, he devised in 1704 a mechanism which unscrewed a breech plug using a threaded, swivelling trigger guard which lowered the breech plug until the chamber became accessible.

Chaumette emigrated to England, where his gun attracted a great deal of interest, particularly after a public exhibition in London in 1721. In fact, so great was the interest that the London Gunmakers Company issued a formal protest about the efficiency of the new system (for which they obviously did not have the manufacturing rights), complaining about *"...the sole making of a new invented hand-gun of which a considerable Quantitye had been made and more bespoke to the great prejudice of the Trade."*

Although efficient by the standards of the 18th century it was an expensive system requiring a high level of manufacturing skill. It was never a commercial success, and within 20 years had almost, but not quite, faded into history. In 1776 Captain Patrick Ferguson revived Chaumette's design in an attempt to have the rifle adopted for British service, and he also made a number of small but important improvements. He demonstrated his breech-loading rifle before the Board of Ordnance, whose report of the trial stated that the weapon:

*"... performed the following four things, none of which had ever been accomplished with any other small arms; First he fired during four or five minutes at a target, at 200 yards distant, at the rate of four shots a minute. Secondly he fired six shots in one minute. Thirdly he fired four times per minute, advancing at the same time at the rate of four miles in the hour. Fourthly, he poured a bottle of water into the pan and barrel of the piece when loaded so as to wet every grain of the powder, and in less than half a minute fired with her as well as ever, without extracting the ball. He also hit the bull's eye at 100 yards lying with his back on the ground; and, notwithstanding the unequalness of the wind and wetness of the weather he only missed the target three times during the course of the experiments."*

*     *     *

Not only in Europe did the search to perfect a breech-loading design continue. In America John Hall and William Thornton took out a patent in 1811 for a gun which used a removable breech block, complete with its flintlock mechanism. It was quite a clever arrangement, and usefully enabled a soldier to carry the loaded chamber and lock in his pocket for emergencies. In the 1830s the Hall was redesigned to accept percussion ignition, and was re-adopted for use by mounted troops. One US Dragoon, Sam Chamberlain, described how a Hall breech saved his life during the Mexican War; caught in a local saloon by guerrillas, he:

*"... sprang behind a large table used for a bar, drew the chamber of my Halls Carbine*

*An Italian gun-shield of c.1520, a number of which were purchased by King Henry VIII. It has a removable breech block, and was ignited by means of the swivelling serpentine visible in the top right of the inside face of the shield. Although doubtless of more use as a novelty than a practical battlefield weapon, it does reflect the king's great interest in firearms. (V.39; A12/305, A13/100; The Board of Trustees of the Royal Armouries)*

**BELOW** *Two of the earliest breech-loading guns surviving in Britain. The upper one dates from c.1540 and is shown with its removable breech block. Originally made as a wheel lock, it weighs 18lbs (8.1kg), with a .71 calibre barrel 43.5ins (1105mm) long. The carbine-length matchlock below it dates from 1531, and has a 25.5in (647mm) barrel of .54 calibre; it weighs a more modest 9.5lbs (4.3 kg). (XII.1/2; A1745; The Board of Trustees of the Royal Armouries)*

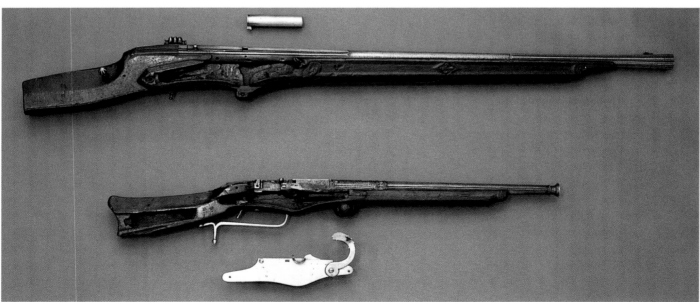

*(that I always carried in my pocket), said a short prayer, and stood cool and collected, at bay before those human Tigers, guerrillars. There was one grizzly old fellow who seem'd more ferocious than the others, he had but one eye… he rushed for the table as if he would spring over, when the sight of the little iron tube pointing straight for his solitary optic, caused him to pause… twenty brigands were held at bay by the strange weapon I held, they seemed to know it was sure death to one, and none seemed willing to be that one."*

In Britain the military authorities began to look more closely at the benefits of breech-loading, and in 1839 they examined an unusual system invented by a Danish gunmaker named Nikolai Løbnitz: the barrel unlocked and was slid forwards to expose the breech. Cautious as ever, the Ordnance rejected it, but were sufficiently impressed to keep an eye on future developments. In 1859 a similar rifle invented by Frederick Prince was demonstrated at the musketry proving ground at Hythe. This employed a breech locking mechanism underneath the barrel which, when unlatched, enabled the whole assembly to slide forwards; it very sensibly fired the standard .577in Enfield cartridge. Hans Busk, the self-appointed critic of British military firearms, reported on the results:

*"Prince… fired one hundred and twenty rounds in less than 18 minutes, and surely it is not easy to imagine any exigency of modern warfare requiring a soldier to deliver his fire much oftener than once in 9 seconds… it was certainly a perfect weapon".*

One wonders what Busk would have made of the rate of fire of modern small arms. The gun impressed all who saw it, including members of the trade, who were notoriously reluctant to be impressed by anything they had not invented themselves. In an event possibly unique in the history of British gunmaking twelve of them signed a testimonial vouching for its virtues. Regardless, the Small Arms Committee still rejected it.

Although the percussion cap was by far the best method of ignition yet invented, it was certainly fiddly to pick up and place on a nipple, particularly if a man's hands were cold. An American dentist, Dr Edward Maynard, had seen an early French system of "tape priming" invented by Baron Louis Heurteloup in 1834; this was a thin tube of soft metal foil (usually an alloy of lead, tin and zinc) with a priming compound sealed inside it. This continuous primer was detonated by a blow from the hammer, which also incorporated a cutter to snip off the expended portion of foil. Naturally, there was an inherent problem: if the primer were

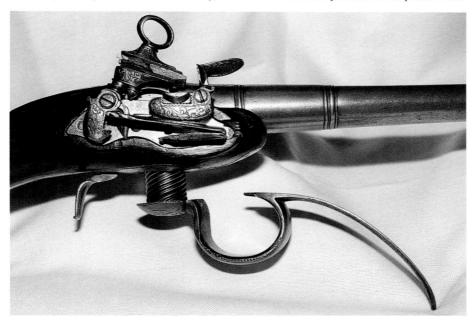

not cut off cleanly by the hammer at each shot then the compound, which had the same characteristics as matchcord, would continue to burn. If the shooter was not careful he could find that an already burned length of primer would appear on the nipple; or the entire tape might simply continue burning right through.

Maynard saw the tape approach as an excellent means of speeding up the priming process, but recognised its limitations. He produced an improved paper and fulminate tape, and a toothed wheel which rotated when the hammer was cocked to push a single pellet onto the nipple. It was cheap, convenient and reasonably weatherproof, and could be adapted for fitting into existing locks. The US Government incorporated the system into considerable numbers of rifles and carbines.

Although breech-loading appeared to cure all the ills that attended the black powder firearm, it did create its own unique problems. One of the major difficulties was that of obturation - the escape of propellant gas from between the chamber and breech block. (The Hall system was notorious in this respect). This was not only uncomfortable for the shooter, who received a faceful of hot particles with each shot, but also inefficient in that much of the power of the propellant gas was wasted. Finding a means of tightly sealing this gap taxed the ingenuity of many gunmakers, for it was compounded not only by the old problem of fouling but also by the tremendous heat and pressure generated. Leather or rubber seals disintegrated after a few shots, and while it was possible to manufacture chambers with very fine tolerances, fouling would eventually prevent the gun being loaded as it formed a thick crust around mating surfaces.

*The Ferguson-type mechanism on a Spanish miquelet pistol by Odal Le Med, c.1730-70. With the breech plug unscrewed the opening of the chamber can be seen, as can the complex threads required to ensure smooth functioning; once covered by powder fouling it would become increasingly difficult to close the breech properly. (XII.4856; The Board of Trustees of the Royal Armouries)*

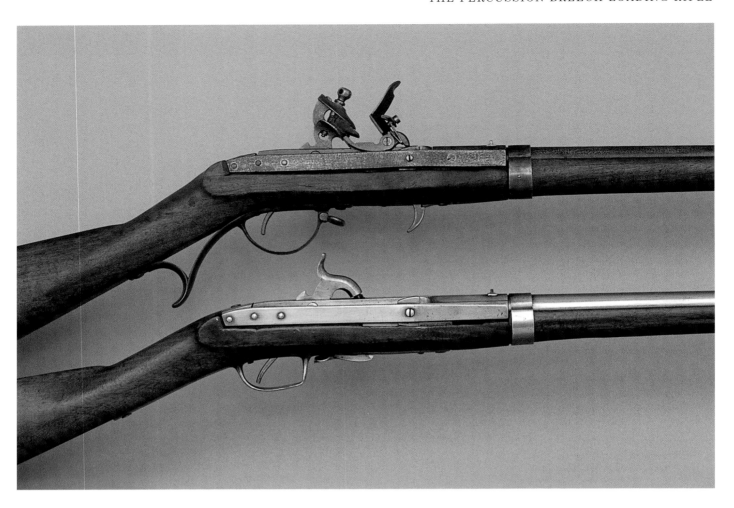

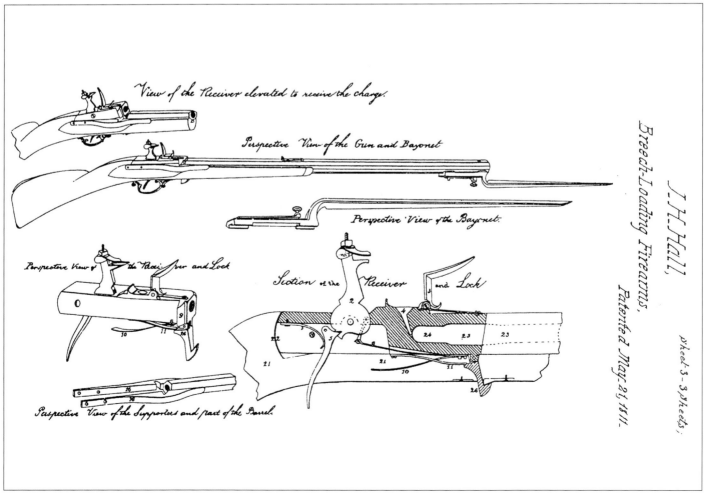

**LEFT** *Two Hall breech-loading carbines; although one is flintlock and the other percussion their basic mechanisms are identical. The entire breech block along with the trigger can simply be lifted straight out of the rifle. (XII.2396/2489; A5632; The Board of Trustees of the Royal Armouries)*

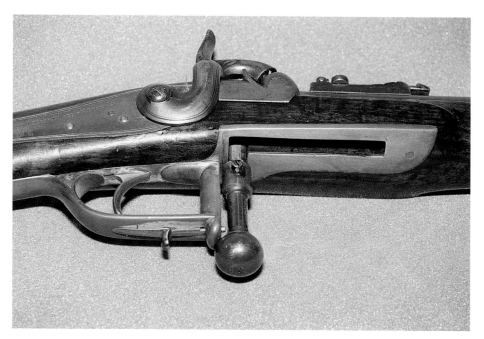

**THIS PAGE** *Prince's patent .577in rifle of 1859, a beautifully made but complex action. The sliding safety bar on the bottom of the trigger guard had to be pulled to the rear. This allowed the bottom-mounted locking bolt to be moved to the right, which unlocked the two retaining lugs from the breech; the bolt was then slid forwards in its brass guide slot. The bolt was attached to the base of the barrel, and this pushed the entire assembly forwards, giving access to the chamber. A paper cartridge was then inserted, and the procedure reversed. As can be seen in the closest view, any loose powder or fouling might prevent the finely machined breech mechanism from locking. (XII.451; The Board of Trustees of the Royal Armouries)*

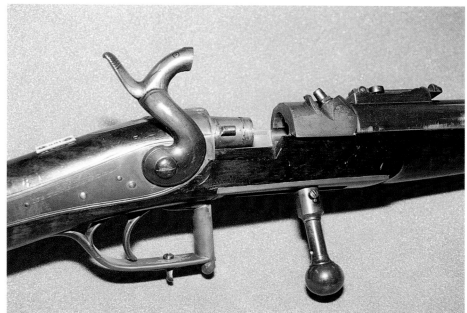

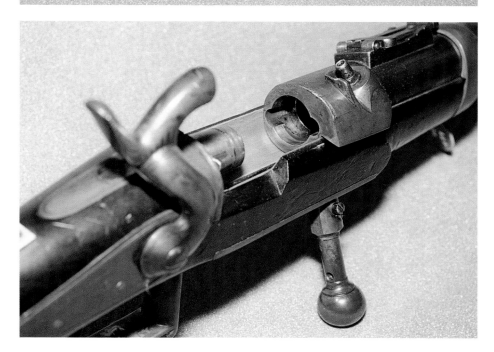

**LEFT** *A patent drawing of May 1811 for the Hall breech-loading gun; the self-contained breech block is shown at lower left.*

A Sharps breech showing a roll of original Maynard tape primers in position. Each time the hammer was cocked a metal arm pushed the reel up the feed channel by exactly the correct distance to ensure a fresh cap lay above the nipple. When in use the mechanism was covered by a hinged metal plate.

One rifle in particular was to become synonymous with the Maynard tape system, and that was the Sharps. Christian Sharps was born in New Jersey around 1811, and was initially employed at the Harper's Ferry Arsenal where, amongst other things, he helped manufacture Hall's breech-loading carbines. Blessed with a fertile and mechanically-inclined mind, young Christian believed he could improve on the breech-loading system. In 1848 he took out his first patent, for a "falling block" action operated by a hinged trigger guard. The breech mechanism was a solid block of steel which, when unlocked, dropped vertically on guide tracks machined into the inside of the receiver to expose the chamber for loading. It had the benefit of being immensely strong and able to handle almost any charge of powder; and, like all the best inventions, the system was simple, relying on the minimum of moving parts.

The earliest Sharps were manufactured by a Philadelphia gunsmith called Nippes in around 1849-50. By 1851 the Sharps Rifle Manufacturing Company had been formed, and a year later the first government contract was received. It was manufactured in greater numbers than any other weapon of its type, and was to prove one of the most enduring.

In Britain a number of trials had been held to see if there was a capping breech-loader suitable for adoption by the army. In particular, the government wanted to solve the question of the most effective weapon for issue to the cavalry. The use of a breech-loading mechanism and pre-prepared cartridges seemed to be an ideal solution to the age-old problem of reloading while on horseback. Dozens of experimental rifles and carbines appeared during the 1850s, but relatively few were of any real practical use. Of the breech-loading rifles tested by the Small Arms Committee only three proved to be acceptable: the Calisher and Terry, Westley Richards, and Sharps - each of which was adopted (in carbine variants only) for British service use.

Patented in 1856 by William Terry of Birmingham, the first was a complex design using a sliding breech-locking system not unlike that of a modern bolt-action rifle. The breech block locking handle had to be unhooked and swung backwards and upwards, the whole assembly then being pulled to the rear to clear the short slot in the right side of the receiver into which the cartridge was pushed. The cartridge was also unusual, being of the standard paper type but with a thick greased felt wad at its base against which the brass head of the bolt pressed. This formed a very effective seal to prevent gas leakage as well as acting as a cleaning wad, carrying accumulated debris with it as it left the barrel. In tests at the Royal Navy's small arms proving ground at Portsmouth it was noted that:

*"The Calisher and Terry performed very creditably, firing 1,800 consecutive shots without failure. Upon inspection, there was no apparent fouling in the breech or bore, the method of cartridge sealing being most efficient. The weapon was perfectly capable of being fired again without cleaning."*

An early "slant breech" Sharps, so called because of the way the breech angles sharply back towards the hammer. This .56 calibre example dating from c.1856 has the Maynard priming mechanism with its cover closed, and a brass patchbox in the buttstock. In general appearance this resembles the .577in model issued to British cavalry regiments in India. (XII.1044; A6/499; The Board of Trustees of the Royal Armouries)

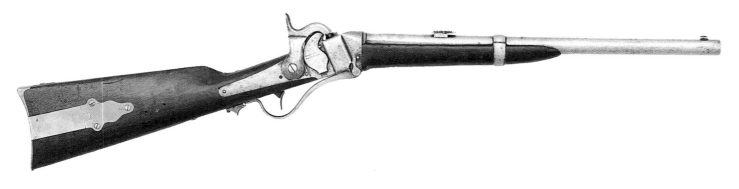

This was an incredible feat for a black powder weapon; yet the Terry was far from perfect. The port through which the cartridge had to be inserted was quite small, and loading with cold hands or while wearing gloves was difficult. In addition, any dirt or rust on the hinged part of the mechanism could prevent the breech being locked. Failure to use the correct ammunition would also cause problems with obturation and fouling. There were eventually two models of the Terry: the 1857, in .56 calibre, and the 1860 in .54 inch. The actual number manufactured is unknown, but probably amounted to no more than several hundred. The British army adopted it only in small numbers, and it was issued solely to the 18th Hussars (although a number were purchased by the Confederacy during the American Civil War).

By contrast its competitor, the Westley Richards, was widely regarded as the best percussion breech-loading system ever invented - which makes the eight years it took to gain final acceptance all the more puzzling. It used a very simple hinged breech mechanism which was simply unlocked and lifted to expose the chamber. Its curled shape when unlatched earned this carbine the nickname "Monkey Tail" by which it has been known ever since. Attached to the underside of the cover was a breech bolt which moved into the chamber as the cover was lowered; the front end of this bolt had a short brass plug attached which was a very close fit inside the chamber, helping to prevent obturation.

Like the Terry, the Westley Richards required special ammunition, firing a .568in bullet with a thick greased wad in its base. Unlike that of the Terry, this wad remained in the chamber after firing; when the next cartridge was loaded it was pushed up the breech by the bullet, being driven out of the barrel when the next round was fired. This was a very effective means of preventing fouling, and a Westley Richards was recorded as firing 2,000 rounds without requiring any cleaning. Its simple mechanism proved extraordinarily reliable, greatly assisted by the quality of workmanship; Westley Richards were one of the premier English sporting gun manufacturers, and this is clearly seen in the fine fit of the parts and quality of finish of the early examples. From 1866 the Royal Small Arms Factory at Enfield took over production, making over 19,000. The Monkey Tail was to survive longer in service than any other capping breech-loader, remaining with some Yeomanry cavalry units until the late 1880s when it was eventually replaced by the Lee-Metford magazine rifle.

The Sharps has arguably become the most famous percussion breech-loader in history, and deservedly so; it was remarkable for several reasons. It was produced in huge numbers both as a rifle and a carbine, and with minor modification spanned a time period from the introduction of the percussion cap right through to the modern centrefire cartridge era of the

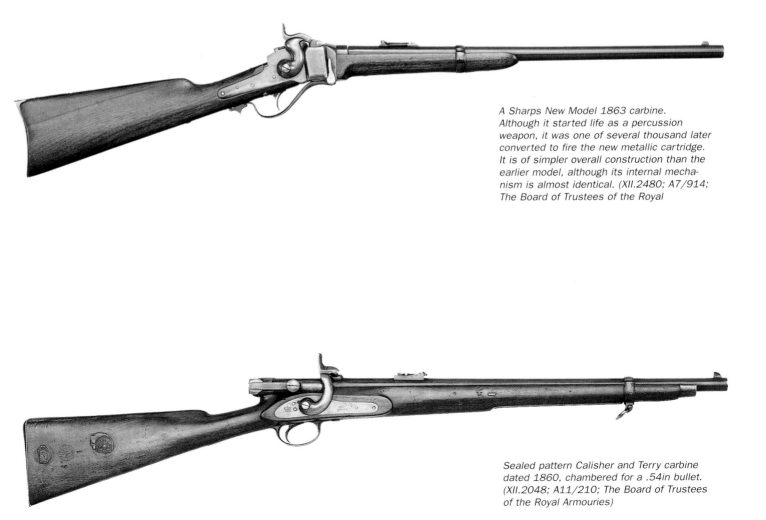

*A Sharps New Model 1863 carbine. Although it started life as a percussion weapon, it was one of several thousand later converted to fire the new metallic cartridge. It is of simpler overall construction than the earlier model, although its internal mechanism is almost identical. (XII.2480; A7/914; The Board of Trustees of the Royal*

*Sealed pattern Calisher and Terry carbine dated 1860, chambered for a .54in bullet. (XII.2048; A11/210; The Board of Trustees of the Royal Armouries)*

*The breech mechanism of a Calisher and Terry rifle. The locking lever is released and pulled back until it is at right angles to the breech. It is then turned upwards through 90 degrees, which disengages the locking lugs on the bolt. Finally it is pulled to the rear, allowing a cartridge to be placed in the chamber via the port on the right side of the receiver - the hammer must be forward to clear the port for loading.*

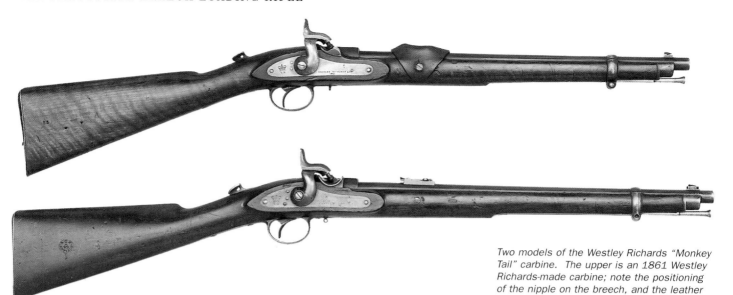

Two models of the Westley Richards "Monkey Tail" carbine. The upper is an 1861 Westley Richards-made carbine; note the positioning of the nipple on the breech, and the leather sight-cover. The lower example is an 1866 Enfield-made weapon, with the nipple recessed and protected by a curved shield. (XII.1043/3145; A11/212; The Board of Trustees of the Royal Armouries)

20th century. It was also manufactured in more calibres and charge loads than any other single-shot rifle. Extensive tests in Britain had also shown that the Sharps was exceptionally reliable, and the report of the trials held at the School of Musketry at Hythe concluded:

*"Sharpe's [sic] breech self-loading and priming carbine was tried at various distances, from 100 to 500 yards, the results proving it to be an effective weapon. 60 shots were fired in seven minutes [at 100 yards], of which 47 struck the bull's eye. 160 rounds were fired from the piece during the trial with the greatest ease, no oiling or cleaning from fouling being required. The same piece, after the trial, was loaded and left all the following day, when, after placing the carbine under water, and putting to other severe tests before firing it, it was discharged, after missing fire twice, the wet having got into the caps."*

With only two misfires due to faulty caps, reasonable accuracy and negligible barrel fouling, the Sharps appeared to be a soldier's dream. It did suffer from some gas leakage; but a flange across the face of the breech block almost eliminated this, and what did escape was not considered serious enough to warrant its rejection. It had been issued to the US Dragoons since 1854, where it was regarded as a very satisfactory weapon, Captain R. Ewell of the 1st Dragoons writing that: *"I have had five Sharps carbines on hand for six months, and have found them superior to any firearm yet furnished to the Dragoons."*

Prejudice towards new technology and political interference prevented the very widespread issue of the Sharps to British units. Nevertheless, between 1856 and 1858, 6,000 Model 1855 Sharps carbines were purchased (most of them fitted with Maynard's tape primer system), and supplied to British cavalry regiments serving in India. They differ from standard US issue Sharps in having either 18in or 21in barrels, and being fitted with a rear sight optimistically graduated to 600 yards for their .577in bullet.

If any proof were needed of the value of the capping breech-loader it was provided during the American Civil War of 1861-65, where the rapid action of breech-loaders gained them an enviable reputation for the weight of fire that they could pour into an attacking formation. As they could shoot at approximately three times the rate of a muzzle-loading rifle, this was hardly surprising. Yet the lifespan of the percussion breech-loading rifle in British military service proved remarkably short, from around 1855 to the late 1860s only. Even in America, as the Civil War was drawing to a close the end of the percussion ignition system was already in sight, brought about by the gradual introduction of the metallic cartridge.

The open breech of a Westley Richards. The plug-like brass breech face ensured that the cartridge was pushed firmly into the chamber, and also formed a gas seal to help prevent obturation.

**Technical Specifications**

**Sharps carbine:**

| | | |
|---|---|---|
| Overall length | 38.5ins | (976mm) |
| Barrel length | 22ins | (559mm) |
| Calibre | .52in | (13.2mm) |
| Weight | 7lbs 8oz | (3.5kg) |
| Charge | 60 grains | |
| Ignition | Percussion cap | |

Reconstruction: US Cavalry sergeant of the late 1860s, with a Sharps carbine hooked to a crossbelt by a swivelling clip engaged to a ring sliding up and down a bar on the left side of the stock. He also carries a revolver and 1860 pattern sabre, although by the end of the Civil War the sword had been almost completely abandoned as a sidearm.

**Firing the Sharps carbine**

Although we were offered an example of a second model .539 calibre Calisher and Terry carbine, it was rejected on both practical and historical grounds. Its mechanism had developed a considerable amount of play over the years, making a sound gas seal at the breech unlikely; even if it had been shot the leakage of gas would probably have invalidated any results. Historically, it was not a rifle of particular interest, having been issued only in very small numbers.

The Sharps which was used was of a slightly later model than those issued to British units, being manufactured in 1863, and of the type without the brass patchbox seen on British issue carbines. For this reason a US cavalry trooper was used for the photographs, as the Sharps saw considerable use not only during the American Civil War but also during the Indian Wars of the 1860s and 1870s.

It is a compact weapon, and considerably lighter than one first expects. The carbine is very well balanced, with most of its weight in the breech assembly; and an examination of the breech and block revealed no excessive wear, with a reassuringly close fit between the face of the breech block and the rear of the chamber. There was evidence of black powder corrosion in the barrel, which exhibited some signs of wear, but that was to be expected in a weapon of this age. Some original cartridges were produced for photographic use, but these are now collectors' items - besides which, 130-year-old black powder was unlikely to prove reliable.

We were determined to make up a selection of cartridges exactly as per the Sharps company's instructions. Having made a piece of wooden dowel of .52 in diameter, we struggled to take:

*"... proper cartridge paper or linen cloth of proper length, and of width sufficient to form a cylinder on the cartridge stick, with a lap of three sixteenths of an inch, secure the lap with gluten or paste, withdraw the stick, place a piece of thin paper or gauze three-fourths of an inch square on the reverse end of the stick, form it to size, apply the paste or gluten to the part which overlies the circumference of the stick and insert to form the rear end of the tube. When dry, charge with the requisite powder and insert the rear end of the ball moistened with adhesive preparation."*

I have to say that we failed dismally. Instead, we reverted to the usual method of rolling a piece of cartridge paper around a dowel and lightly gluing it together, one end being twisted closed as it would have been on a musket cartridge. A charge of 60 grains of coarse powder was poured into the cartridge, and the neck was snipped off to leave just sufficient space to enable the conical bullet to be seated. The bullet had three deep grooves, the lower two being coated with grease. It was inserted into the mouth of the cartridge and secured in place with button thread, which was wound tightly around the top of the cartridge paper and the top groove to prevent it slipping.

When loading, we were careful to ensure that the length of the cartridge was not less than the 2.06ins specified; if it were undersized the edge of the block would fail to cut the rear off the cartridge, and this could lead to a misfire or an air gap when the breech was closed.

With the hammer at half-cock, the loading lever/ trigger guard was unlatched by pushing backwards about one quarter-inch a small spring catch mounted in the stock just behind the end of the lever. The lever was swung down and forwards, and the falling block slid sweetly down its track to reveal the chamber. We inserted a correctly measured cartridge, the rear of which overhung slightly. Lifting the loading lever smartly brings the sharp top edge of the closing breech block up underneath this protruding tip, snipping it cleanly away as the lever locks into its catch. (One of the minor benefits of all capping breech-loaders was their versatility where loading was concerned. Should the breech block become jammed for any reason it was perfectly feasible to revert to muzzle-loading, leaving the problem to be sorted out at leisure. This method was often resorted to by buffalo hunters who had run out of components with which to reload their cartridges.)

All that remained to do was to place a percussion cap on the nipple, pull the hammer back to full-cock, and take aim. This proved to be one of the shortcomings of the weapon, for the sight picture is extremely poor. The foresight was a thick blade of German silver, which had, over the years, become worn down; and the adjustable rear sight has such a shallow V-notch as to be almost useless. The practical range of the Sharps carbine in the hands of the average soldier was reckoned to be 100 yards, and in the hands of an expert 350 yards, which actually seemed unlikely, as sighting on the target at 100 yards was difficult enough.

The trigger pull was heavy but the recoil quite light, the short barrel jerking somewhat and the target inevitably being obliterated by the smoke; the report is a fine, round "boom". At 50 yards accuracy proved to be very good; the Sharps achieved a four-inch group with ten shots, with one "flyer" which clipped the top right hand edge of the board. Muzzle velocity varied somewhat but averaged out at 984 feet per second.

At 100 yards it became a little more difficult, mainly because of the poor sights. Using a table to rest on helped considerably, and we were able to obtain a group of approximately 11 inches, although a couple of shots strayed outside this. The Sharps was quite quick to load and fire, nine shots in a minute being the fastest that we attained. At ranges of over 100 yards the sights again proved to be a problem, and shooting at 200 yards also showed up the limitations of the cartridge. In practical terms it contained about 55 grains, as some powder was always lost each time the breech snipped off the base of the cartridge. It certainly had a high trajectory, and bullet drop was quite noticeable; shooting at 200 yards with the rearsight adjusted to 300 yards, the point of impact was still half way down the target. The explanation for this could simply have been foresight wear.

Certainly, the short .52 calibre carbine has no place in any of the legendary tales of feats of accuracy with Sharps rifles at extreme ranges. The most famous and oft-repeated story was of a shot made by Billy Dixon, who fired at a mounted Indian at a range of 1,538 yards. But (and it is a *big* but) he was using a much longer .50 calibre heavy-barrelled rifle with target sights, and a cartridge with a charge of anything up to 110 grains of powder. Even he admitted afterwards that it was a very lucky shot.

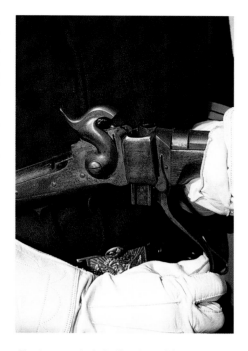

The hammer is in half-cock position; supporting the barrel with the left hand, he lowers the trigger guard/loading lever enabling the breech block to drop - it can be seen underneath the receiver. The elongated teardrop-shaped piece above the end of the lever is the hinge pin which holds it in place; removing it takes a few seconds, and permits the entire breech block to be dropped clear of the weapon.

As we reasoned that 1,500 yards was slightly beyond the abilities of the carbine, and we couldn't find any Sioux in Yorkshire, we compromised and set up a six-by-six foot target at 300 yards. The Sharps certainly proved it had the ability to hit it, but the shots were scattered, and velocity was down to almost one third of its original value. Clearly, the carbine was at the outer edge of its performance, which was predictable in view of its barrel length and relatively small charge. It was, after all, designed as a close range weapon for skirmishing or keeping attackers at bay until a swift departure could be made.

Some hunters insisted that their rifles were more accurate when a wad was used between the powder and bullet. This may well be true; we tried using a thick piece of card, and at 100 yards the group tightened up a little to 10 inches and all of the bullets struck home. It would really require a day of testing with a long rifle rather than a carbine to determine if the theory about the wad holds true consistently, but it appears to be promising.

There was quite an amount of blowback from between the chamber and breech, despite the apparent close fit of the components; all who used it commented on how unsettling it was when shooting, the tendency being to close ones eyes as the trigger was squeezed. It never became a real problem, but one was always aware of it (I have seen a photo of a much more worn carbine being fired which shows some fairly alarming pyrotechnics from this source). There was also some build-up of fouling which made the breech stiff to operate after about ten shots, and washing the block occasionally helped matters. There was some fouling of the breech and chamber too, but in practice it did not appear to make any difference to the accuracy or functioning of the rifle, and in view of its age it performed quite creditably.

**BELOW** The cartridge is slid into the chamber. The constriction of the breech prevents it disappearing into the barrel, and provided it is the right length a small part of the rear of the cartridge should remain visible once it has been fully inserted. **BOTTOM** As the lever is brought back up towards the stock the breech block closes, and its sharp upper edge cuts off the protruding end of the cartridge. Once it is fully closed, blowing hard onto the block gets rid of the scrap of paper and the few grains of loose powder, which could otherwise cause a build-up which could lead to fouling.

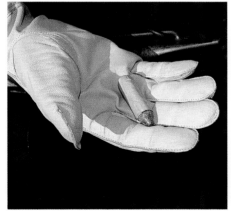

A cartridge is taken from the leather pouch worn on the left hip - this is an original linen example. They were always susceptible to damage, particularly when being carried on horseback, and this was one of the reasons for the rapid rise in popularity of the new metallic cartridges.

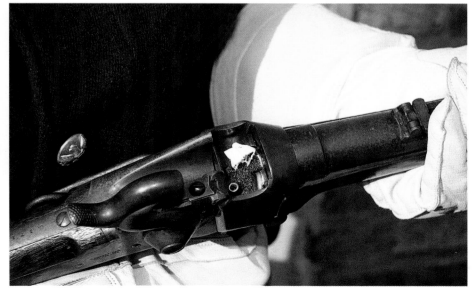

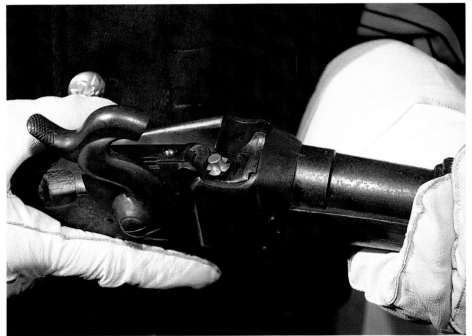

The breech block of the Sharps removed, looking from the "barrel side". The nipple on the top of the block is connected by a machined tube to the nipple in the face of the block, carrying the spark from the percussion cap straight into the now-exposed powder charge of the cartridge.

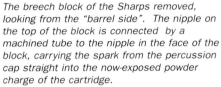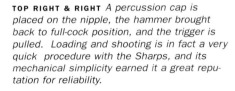

**TOP RIGHT & RIGHT** A percussion cap is placed on the nipple, the hammer brought back to full-cock position, and the trigger is pulled. Loading and shooting is in fact a very quick procedure with the Sharps, and its mechanical simplicity earned it a great reputation for reliability.

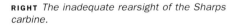

**RIGHT** The inadequate rearsight of the Sharps carbine.

**FAR RIGHT** At 100 yards or so - which was in fact a realistic battle range under most circumstances - even the short-barrelled Sharps carbine was adequately accurate. If a hit was achieved the impact of the heavy .52in bullet on human flesh and bone was shattering; these exit holes in the oak post, roughly four inches across, which we used as a target prop.

# THE CARTRIDGE RIFLE

Unlike the previous chapters in this book, this final section must, unavoidably, devote considerable space to the history of the cartridge rather than to a specific firearm.

From the introduction of the black powder firearm in the 14th century until the middle of the 19th century there had been no radical change in the slow, unwieldy process of loading. As we have seen throughout this book, the various improvements adopted had applied mainly to the type and speed of ignition, reaching a peak of efficiency with the percussion cap. The actual loading process had only taken a major leap forward with the introduction of percussion breech-loading rifles in the mid-19th century; but even then the combination of lead and powder with a fragile paper cartridge was not a happy one. The paper had to be thin enough to be completely combustible and easily inserted into the barrel, and that inevitably meant that it was never strong enough to withstand rough usage. Although later examples were greased to help repel moisture, the properties of gunpowder ensured that incorrect storage or long exposure to wet weather would render the powder useless. Neither did the breech loaded paper cartridge address the problem of obturation, which remained apparently insoluble.

As the century progressed firearms were being manufactured to much finer tolerances and rifling had become commonplace. Consequently, new standards of accuracy were being demanded; both gunmakers and governments began to look much harder at exactly what the small arms projectile was doing, and how well it was doing it.

It had been recognised since the Middle Ages that the use of a pre-prepared cartridge radically speeded up the loading process, but the cast iron cylinder that had been acceptable for medieval cannon was hardly suitable for the modern breech-loading rifle. Since the 18th century a number of inventors had tried to develop some form of self-contained cartridge, made of linen, animal intestine, metal foil, steel, copper and even rubber. The main hurdle inventors faced was in coming up with a reliable, weather-proof method of priming the cartridge.

Arguably the first to find an acceptable solution had been Johannes Pauly, a Swiss ex-soldier who had created a brass-bodied, rimmed cartridge in 1812. Not only did it provide a reasonably effective gas-seal, but it also had a self-contained fulminate primer, which although rather vulnerable to the elements was relatively efficient. In 1829 the design was taken up by a Frenchman, Clement Pottet, who manufactured a brass-based cartridge which could use either fulminate primer, or a nipple that accepted a standard percussion cap. Pottet modified this in about 1855 to create what was to all intents and purposes the modern shotgun cartridge, comprising a brass base and fibre body with a cap primer.

Casimir Lefaucheux had made an important contribution by patenting the **pinfire** cartridge in 1835. It was improved in 1846 by C.H.Houllier; his definitive version of the pinfire comprised a copper case with a black powder charge and lead bullet, and an internal priming cap which was detonated by striking a brass rod projecting at right angles from the base of the cartridge. It worked quite well, but was rather fragile; the rod was easily damaged, and banging it or dropping the cartridge could cause accidental detonation. There was also a limit to the size of charge that the copper could withstand without rupturing, a problem that was to recur throughout this phase of cartridge development.

Houllier's next contribution was a patent that employed a one-piece copper case with a small quantity of fulminate powder encircling the rim, which became the forerunner of the first rimfire cartridges. In America, Walter Hunt had patented his "Rocket Ball" cartridge in 1847; this contained a propellant charge in the base of a lead bullet. Like Houllier's early rimfire it was too low-powered to be very practical. It was left to a pair of Americans, Horace Smith and Daniel B.Wesson, to achieve a major breakthrough by perfecting the **rimfire** cartridge, which they began to sell in 1858. This took the form of a rimmed copper case with fulminate packed around the inside of the rim; when it was struck by the hammer of the firearm, the impact detonated the fulminate and set off the gunpowder charge. The practical rimfire cartridge was an invention of tremendous importance, which enabled the development of a whole range of breech-loading military and sporting firearms. Smith and Wesson had created an ammunition that was totally weatherproof, could be loaded and carried in a weapon indefinitely, and was easily stored and transported. One of the earliest and most significant weapons to make use of the new rimfire cartridge was the Spencer, which became the first breechloading cartridge repeater adopted by any country for military use.

\*     \*     \*

Christopher Spencer's design rose head and shoulders above most of its contemporaries. Employed as an inspector at a silk mill in Connecticut, Spencer was only 19 years old when in 1859 he presented his design to the US Patent Office for a rotary breech rifle with a tubular magazine contained in the stock. The idea itself was not particularly innovative, but the key to the Spencer's success was its self-contained ammunition. No such weapon could have been successfully produced before the invention of the metallic cartridge in the late 1850s. The Spencer rifle of 1860 impressed all who saw it, including a US Navy Department captain who test-fired one over a period of two days:

*"The piece was fired 500 times in succession… there was but one failure to fire, supposed[ly due to] to the absence of fulminate. The mechanism was not cleaned, and yet worked throughout as at first. Not the least foulness on the outside, and very little within. The least time of firing seven rounds was ten seconds."*

So impressed were the US Navy that they ordered 700 Spencers. Initially only the .52 calibre, 47in long Repeating Cartridge Rifle was produced, the carbine not being available

There had been many attempts to produce an efficient breech-loading rifle, and this .77 calibre example by Fvlick Sarvm is one of the better examples. It was made in England c.1690, and uses a removable iron chamber. The hinged mechanism is a practical touch, and it would doubtless have made an excellent sporting rifle. (XII.1457; A10/385; The Board of Trustees of the Royal Armouries)

A removable chamber and lock from a .62in Flemish-made flintlock sporting gun of c.1740 with a mechanism like that of the Sarvm gun. The system allowed rapid reloading, but was of course expensive; there is an example in the Dutch Royal Army Museum, Delft, complete with a fitted case with eight identical detachable lock/chambers. (XII.252)

until October 1863 (when it was at first inexplicably issued to an infantry regiment). In all some 46,644 Spencers were supplied during the American Civil War, 34,176 of them carbines; by 1865 it had been issued to no less than 38 infantry and 15 cavalry regiments.

The design of the Spencer was both compact and strong, but its unique feature was its firepower. It has been said that use of the Spencer was one of the more significant factors in turning the Civil War in favour of the North. That may be an overstatement - in the real world the results of wars usually turn on money, not technology. Nevertheless, many local tactical victories were certainly due to a Spencer-armed rifleman's ability to pour seven shots in as many seconds into an attacking force, and to reload in under a minute, all while lying prone and without exposing himself to enemy fire. In a letter to the Spencer Company dated January 1865, Union Major-General J.H.Wilson commented:

*"...There is no doubt that the Spencer carbine is the best fire-arm yet put into the hands of the soldier, both for economy of ammunition, and maximum effect, physical and moral. Our best officers estimate one man armed with it equivalent to three with any other arm. I have never seen anything else like the confidence inspired by it in the regiments or brigades which have it. I have seen a large number of dismounted charges made with them against cavalry, infantry and breastworks, and never knew one to fail. The confidence in the arm is so widely spread that I have now applications from every regiment in the corps, not already supplied with them."*

The earliest major demonstration of the power of the new rifle was on 3 July 1863 at a small homestead called Rummel's Farm near Gettysburg. As 1,200 Confederate soldiers advanced to within 100 yards of the dismounted troopers of the 5th Michigan Cavalry, they were met with a blast of fire which caused their front rank to reel. An officer, used to the slow ways of the muzzle-loading rifle, yelled, *"Now for them, before they reload!"*, but as the wave of Confederates rushed forwards they were met with another volley, then another, and another. As the still air cleared of the choking smoke a wall of bodies lay in the grass, and it became obvious that the rebel attack had been all but wiped out. Spencer's rifle had begun to claim its victims, and modern warfare was coming of age.

Ironically, it was the very success of the rimfire cartridge that was to lead to its demise. As the demand grew for larger calibres (.58in rimfire was the largest ever made) and more powerful cartridges, so the thickness of the case had to be proportionally increased to prevent its rupturing when fired. The rim eventually became too thick to be indented by the falling hammer, so a compromise in terms of power and calibre had to be reached; but the combination of a heavy bullet and relatively small charge did not give the power or range required for a military weapon. There were also problems with the calibre and quality of ammunition supplied. The Spencer was issued in both .50 and .52 calibres, which created considerable confusion; and the commanding officer of the 27th Infantry Regiment complained to the Chief of Ordnance that *"the ammunition furnished for this command is defective and unfit for service, of 473 cartridges expended in practice, 177 failed to explode, 250 would not fit the carbines. I request a supply of suitable ammunition."*

Questions were also raised about the design of the breech mechanism of the Spencer. After testing one in 1867 to determine its suitability for continued military use, General Augur reported that:

*"In a number of instances the base of the shell (at the rim containing the fulminate) burst out in firing and blew grains of powder and bits of copper out at the junction of the breech slide and barrel; in one instance when this occurred the quantity was sufficient to sting severely and blind me for a moment and I think if I had not had on spectacles to have temporarily injured the eye. In every instance it blew grains of powder into the face of the person firing."*

By the end of the American Civil War the rimfire had reached the limit of its development. Unfortunately the swivel action of the Spencer's breech was based entirely upon the rimfire cartridge, and it effectively limited the length of cartridge case that could be chambered, in this instance to the modest 45-grain load. Any attempt to use the newer, longer

An early Pottet-type cartridge of the second quarter of the 19th century: this heavy brass tube with a nipple for a percussion cap in the base was obviously too expensive for mass production.

The open breech of a Chassepot needlefire rifle. The tube extending into the receiver contains the long firing pin; behind it note the thick seal to help prevent obturation. (XII.2548)

Reconstruction: British infantry sergeant of the 24th Regiment, famous for their actions at Isandlwana and Rorke's Drift in the 1879 Zulu War. Sergeants were officially issued a so-called yataghan sword-bayonet; this Martini-Henry rifle has the other ranks' socket bayonet - which since the 1853 Enfield had had a secure locking ring much improved over that of Napoleonic days.

Ten .577/450in Martini-Henry cartridges in their original packet of issue; they were manufactured in 1887 at the Royal Laboratories, Woolwich. The single "bottlenecked" round shows the rolled brass construction of the cartridge case, which has a separate brass base cup and steel base washer. These were held together by a hollow rivet through the centre, into which the priming cap was inserted. After prolonged firing there could be extraction problems, with the base tearing away and leaving the thinner brass in a hot, fouled chamber.

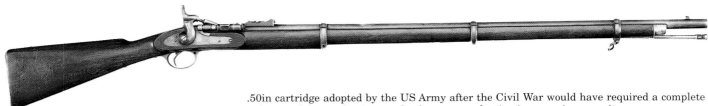

.50in cartridge adopted by the US Army after the Civil War would have required a complete redesign of the mechanism, and subsequent reduction in magazine capacity.

The US Board of Ordnance were also unhappy that the rimfire cartridge could not be reloaded; inserting the fulminate could only be undertaken under factory conditions. This also meant that the cartridge had a limited appeal for civilian hunters, whose remote locations made re-usable cartridge cases a necessity.

\* \* \*

Conveniently, it was around the middle of the 19th century that the technology to spin or draw brass into a shape began to become available; but there were still practical limitations with any system that used fulminate powder for ignition in the manner of the rimfire. In England, Charles Lancaster almost succeeded in creating the perfect cartridge by patenting the first drawn metal, all-brass case with a small fulminate charge in the centre of its base. Unfortunately the new brass cartridges were simply too expensive to be considered by the average purchaser, especially as they could not be reloaded once fired.

From the early 1860s there had appeared a rash of primitive **centrefire** cartridge designs from dozens of patentees. Amongst many others, messrs Benet, Laidley, Martin, Benton, Tibbal, Prince, and Crispin all produced self-contained ammunition, but all suffered from one or other form of shortcoming: their primers were too easily detached, or they were unreliable, or the vent from the base of the cartridge to the charge became blocked, or the cases themselves proved too thin and easily damaged.

It was another American, G.W.Morse, who solved most of these problems, producing a series of patents from 1856 to 1858 which incorporated most of the features of the modern centrefire cartridge; but practical perfection was left to a pair of colonels, one American, the other English.

Hiram Berdan and Edward Boxer each produced brass-bodied cartridges that were almost identical in form, although they used fractionally different methods of priming. Both types had a percussion cap set firmly into a recess in the base, and tiny holes led through into the body of the case. When struck by a firing pin the cap detonated to send jets of flame into the main charge. With hindsight it seems remarkable that the self-contained centrefire cartridge should have passed through so many convoluted stages before reaching practical perfection, but the usual rule of countless man-years of experimentation and failure applied. The new centrefire ammunition brought the 500-year-long muzzle-loading era to an end in the developed world.

Now gunmakers had to find a simple method of opening and closing a breech that was capable of safely resisting the high pressures generated in firing, and was reliable enough to withstand constant use without breaking. Dozens of types of experimental breech-loading longarms appeared in the latter half of the 19th century, some adapted from earlier designs and others completely novel. To examine all of them would require a book in itself, so we limit ourselves here to a brief glance at the earliest and most important types adopted for service in Europe and America.

In 1848 the Prussian army had adopted the **needle-fire** system which was, in technical terms, half-way between percussion and centrefire. Invented in Prussia in 1841 by Johann von Dreyse, it used a bolt-action mechanism (subsequently adopted by almost every rifle manufacturer), allied to a novel paper-wrapped black powder cartridge with a percussion cap which rested against the base of the bullet. A long, needle-like firing pin passed right through the base of the cartridge and the powder charge until it struck the cap. The Dreyse was effi-

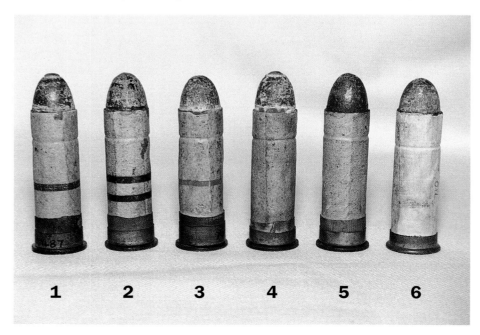

A selection of .577in Snider cartridges: (1) Mk VI of 1867, with exposed wooden plug in the nose of the bullet; (2) Mk VIII, with the wooden plug covered by a thin lead cap; (3) Mk IX, the last issue of the Snider cartridge, 1871; (4) Mk V of 1867, which was rejected as being too fragile; (5) Mk II, approved August 1866; (6) the earliest pattern, a Mk I with a solid head, approved July 1866.

cient, quick to load and fire, but still suffered from the problem of obturation, as well as having a fragile firing-pin. The 11mm Dreyse was followed in short order by an improved French model, the Chassepot, which had a more efficient primer in the base of the cartridge.

The success of these new weapons in the Austro-Prussian and Franco-Prussian Wars (1866, 1870-71) convinced the British government to look in earnest for a replacement for the old 1853 Enfield. Having adopted the percussion Terry, Sharps and Westley Richards, the introduction of the new centrefire cartridges of Boxer and Berdan had plunged the British military authorities into confusion. There were tens of thousands of P53s in store; so in 1864 they invited gunsmiths to submit designs that would enable their conversion to centrefire at minimum cost. Of 50 conversions offered, eight were selected for testing; and of these the system offered by the American Jacob Snider was selected.

It was a simple conversion, involving cutting away about two inches of the upper end of the breech just in front of the breech plug to leave a hollow trough. This was filled with a solid breech block, hinged on the right side and locked on the left with a thumb catch. A sprung firing pin passed diagonally through the breech block, emerging at an angle on top of it and looking at a casual glance exactly like a percussion nipple. The existing hammer and .577in calibre were retained. After unsuccessful trials with an Enfield-made cartridge in 1867 the new Boxer primed centrefire cartridge was adopted.

The Snider was exhaustively tested before being accepted in 1866. It could be loaded and fired at a consistent rate of ten aimed shots per minute, while the Pattern 1853 Enfield took four minutes to load and fire the same number of shots. Its bullet was also more accurate than that of the percussion rifle, its mean deviation at 500 yards being just 12 inches. Like all newly introduced weapons it did suffer from teething problems, mainly difficulty in extraction after firing. The coiled brass cases had a separate iron rim riveted to their base, and if the cartridge jammed in the breech the hapless soldier could find that the ejector had ripped off the iron base leaving the brass firmly stuck in the chamber. Mark I Sniders also had a tendency to unlock their breeches on firing, so a stronger spring catch was fitted.

The first recorded use of the Snider was by the King's Own Royal Lancaster Regiment in April 1868 against Abyssinian tribesmen. Standing in open order, the soldiers poured fire into the attacking warriors at 150 yards with devastating effect, the big bullet bringing down two or sometimes three men. As one Lieutenant W.Scott laconically wrote, *"How they did just about catch it... you never saw such a sight."* The Snider was issued to all Regular infantry and mounted units, last seeing service in the Ashanti campaign of 1874 before being gradually phased out in favour of the Martini-Henry.

As a postscript to the story of the Snider rifle, despite the fact that over 150,000 were manufactured the Ordnance Committee steadfastly refused to pay royalties due to Jacob Snider. The grounds given were that *"A (commercial) patent has no legal force against the Crown, and that any compensation claimed for your invention would be considered as 'bounty'."* In 1866, in desperate financial straits and poor health, Snider eventually accepted £1,000, all of which promptly went to his creditors, and he died soon afterwards in penury. Sadly, this episode is entirely typical of the treatment of inventors by governments of every period and nationality.

*   *   *

In America, a similar need to modernise the issue Springfield rifled musket was met with a system not dissimilar to that of the percussion "monkey tail" which was designed by Erskine Allin, the master-armourer at the Springfield Armoury in Massachusetts. He was granted a patent in 1865 for a breech system which was hinged above the chamber and locked by a spring catch under the nose of the hammer. Originally chambered for the standard .58 calibre musket bullet, the "Trapdoor" rifle was rechambered to accept a new .50in cartridge invented by Colonel S. Benet. It was an unhappy choice, as the Chief of US Ordnance, General Dyer, tersely pointed out to the commander of the Springfield Arsenal in 1866:

*"It is observed that the .50 calibre musket sent to this office... allows the cartridge to be exploded when the breech piece is not in place and locked. This is a serious defect which should be corrected. A centre-primed cartridge is preferred to the rim-primed, if one suitable for the military service and equally sure of fire can be devised. You will direct your attention particularly to getting up a proper cartridge, but the conversion of the arm will* **not** *be delayed in order that you may determine whether centre-primed cartridges may be adopted."*

Fortunately, by this time the perfected Berdan cartridge was available; and in 1870 a new .45-70in cartridge was adopted. Using 70 grains of powder, it proved exceptionally accurate, giving a mean point of aim deviation at 500 yards of only 8.5 inches - at that time the most accurate shooting ever recorded from a service rifle.

The .58 Trapdoor's baptism of fire had come in July 1867, when a small force of 28 soldiers and four civilians under the command of Major James Powell were attacked by Indians while collecting wood near Fort Phil Kearny, Wyoming. Using a mixture of Spencers and the

**BELOW** *Breech of a Snider rifle showing the simple conversion from the Enfield 1853 muzzle-loader. It was opened by pushing upwards on the thumb latch at the left side; the cartridge was pushed into the chamber, and the block snapped closed. After firing, the block was opened and pulled sharply backwards to allow the ejector to pull the cartridge clear of the chamber.*

new Springfields, the soldiers faced a force estimated at as many as 1,500 Indians under Chief Red Cloud. Sergeant Sam Gibson of the 27th Infantry later recounted how the newly issued Springfields performed. Boxes of cartridges had been opened and placed at strategic places around the barricade of wagons hastily prepared by the soldiers:

*"Instead of drawing ramrods, and wasting precious time, we simply threw open the breech-blocks of our new rifles to eject the empty shell, and slapped in fresh ones…our fire was accurate, coolly delivered and given with most telling effect, but nevertheless it looked for a minute as though our last moment on earth had come."*

The losses to the soldiers were six dead and two wounded, while the Indians suffered about 60 dead and 120 wounded. Red Cloud was later to concede that he had lost the flower of his warriors to the new cartridge guns of the soldiers.

\*     \*     \*

Britain, meanwhile, had continued to plan the modernisation of its service rifle, the Snider only ever having been regarded as a stopgap measure. Trials had continued to find a suitable system to replace it, and by the late 1860s there were a number of good British and European breech-loading mechanisms available commercially. After trials of no less than 120 different types of action and 49 different cartridges they decided on the .450 calibre Martini-Henry. This was actually a mating of separate barrel and lock systems combined in one rifle.

The breech system was devised by a Swiss-Hungarian named Friedrich von Martini, and comprised a very simple locking mechanism, hinged at the rear, which dropped to expose the chamber when a lever behind the trigger guard was lowered. This action automatically ejected the spent cartridge case, and a new one could immediately be inserted; as soon as the lever was raised the action cocked itself, and the rifle was ready to be fired. The rifling used on the Martini was the invention of a Scottish gunmaker, Alexander Henry. Henry's barrel had shallow seven-groove rifling which provided a very flat trajectory for the bullet.

Initially the Martini used rimfire ammunition, which suffered the inevitable problems of ruptured cases and failure of the extractor to remove the soft copper case. Eventually the Ordnance Committee settled on a Boxer-designed "bottlenecked" centrefire cartridge with a heavy 485-grain hardened lead bullet of immense penetrative power. The term "bottleneck' simply referred to the tapering of the top half of the cartridge, enabling a combination of small bullet and large charge. In practical terms Henry's form of rifling meant that even at long range the target was more likely to be hit, as the rifle did not have to be aimed high to compensate for bullet drop. At 500 yards bullet trajectory was 8.1 feet, as compared to 15 feet for the Enfield rifled musket, allowing even a poor shot a better chance of hitting a target. When it was tested against a .577in Enfield in 1870 Captain Vivian Majendie, Superintendent at Woolwich Arsenal, wrote of the new design:

*"At 1000 yards range, for instance, a fresh wind which carried [the .577] from 40 to 50 feet to the right only threw the former [the .450] from 20 to 25 feet in the same direction… and the accuracy of shooting is great. The following are the best figures of merit obtained… being the averages of 100 shots, without cleaning the barrel: .47 feet at 300 yards, 1.06 feet at 500 yards, 1.85 feet at 800 yards and 3.12 feet at 1000 yards. Penetration is very great, it penetrates the following: 14$^{1}/_{2}$ inches of elm planks, or 3 x three-inch fir balks dry, in addition to one wet, at 100 yards; 1 x .26 inch plate of iron at 200 yards; 4 x thicknesses of 3 inch rope at 350 yards."*

For a lead bullet, propelled by black powder, these results were indeed remarkable. Tests using skilled marksmen showed the Martini to be accurate to 1,000 yards, and Sergeant Bott of the Royal Marines fired 20 aimed shots in a fraction over one minute. It was estimated that in action a rate of 12 shots per minute was realistic, and even in the hands of a relatively unskilled shot a hit at 300-400 yards was regarded as feasible.

*(1) .58in pinfire cartridge; (2) .52in Spencer rimfire; (3) early centrefire .45/70in cartridge tested in the US "Trapdoor" Springfield rifle; (4) .50/70in Benet cartridge, not adopted for service.*

**1**      **2**      **3**      **4**

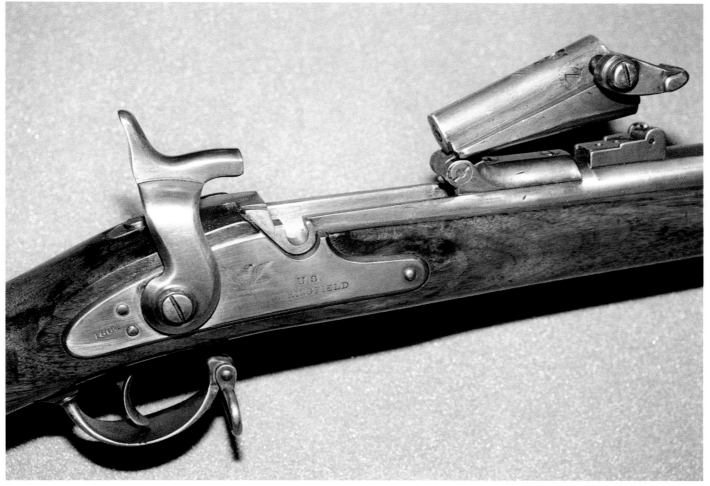

There was still much debate about the standard of shooting in the Regular Army, and E.De Cosson, who accompanied troops to the Sudan, commented that the average soldier could hit a target only *"if he has the distance measured out for him and is allowed to take his position and his own time... but ask him to find his own range in an unfamiliar country, to hit a moving object or to shoot at a mark after running a hundred yards, and you will not find ten men in a hundred who will hit a haystack."*

These comments are reminiscent of those made after the introduction of the 1853 Enfield, and are probably equally unfair. Target shooting had become a very popular pastime in the Volunteer Regiments, and the quality of marksmen this had produced had not been lost on the Regular Army. Although the army may not have been able to produce many long-range sharpshooters, with disciplined use the Martini proved to be more than a match for the tactics that the British faced during the innumerable Colonial wars of the late 19th century. During the Sudanese campaign a square of Guardsmen faced over 2,500 Mahdist warriors. An anonymous eyewitness later commented:

*"At no point were the Arabs [sic] able to close with the British, the rapid fire of the rifles preventing them from gaining any ground closer than 20 yards. Their [the Guards'] rifles became so hot that they wrapped cloth around them to prevent burns, and continued to fire coolly, and without hesitation. The natives were beaten back with tremendous losses."*

The power of the bullet inflicted terrible wounds, and Lieutenant John Chard VC recalled after Rorke's Drift that:

*"Some of the bullet wounds were very curious. One man's head was split open as if by an axe. Another had been hit between the eyes, the bullet carrying away the whole of the back of his head, his face perfect as though it were a mask, only disfigured by a small hole made by the bullet..."*

Modern readers sometimes find these tough-minded, unreflective accounts of Victorian Colonial blood-letting a little hard to take. It is perhaps worth commenting not only that the past was "another country where things were done differently"; but also that eyewitness descriptions - some by doctors - describe the almost incredible ability of charging non-European warriors to keep on coming after suffering horrific wounds. Detailed accounts of the battles - and aftermaths - of Isandlwana (1879), Adowa (1896) and Anual (1921) are recommended as an antidote to any suspicion that white troops enjoyed unchallengable advantages.

The heat generated by rapid fire with the Martini-Henry was quite considerable, and there are many accounts of infantrymen during the Zulu Wars sewing sacking or even wet rawhide around the forestocks of their rifles to provide some protection against the burning steel. There were other problems with the Martini, that which attracted the most frequent comment being its vicious recoil, which worsened as the bore became fouled. To give some idea just how severe this was, it was noted that after the battle of Rorke's Drift in 1879 the men's trigger fingers were bleeding, and their shoulders and biceps were red raw. In fairness it has to be said that each had fired several hundred rounds almost non-stop, which would be punishing with any full-bore rifle.

The barrel fouled easily, and although it never prevented the weapon firing or seemed to affect accuracy it did not improve the recoil problem. The Martini's mechanism could also be jammed by infiltrating dust and sand. Overall, though, these were minor problems that would affect any service weapon. The reliability of the action coupled to its accuracy and power won the Martini great respect, among both those who used it and those against whom it was used.

*Four variations on the Martini-Henry. The top rifle is an 1886-dated Enfield-made Mk I with the long cocking lever. The second rifle is an LSA Co. Mk II with the shorter lever. The third is a Mk I carbine manufactured at Enfield in 1879. Although the bottom carbine was made in 1880 it has been chambered to fire the new .303in cordite cartridge, and also has provision for the shorter knife pattern bayonet. (XII.1940/1944/1734/1756; A7/500; The Board of Trustees of the Royal Armouries)*

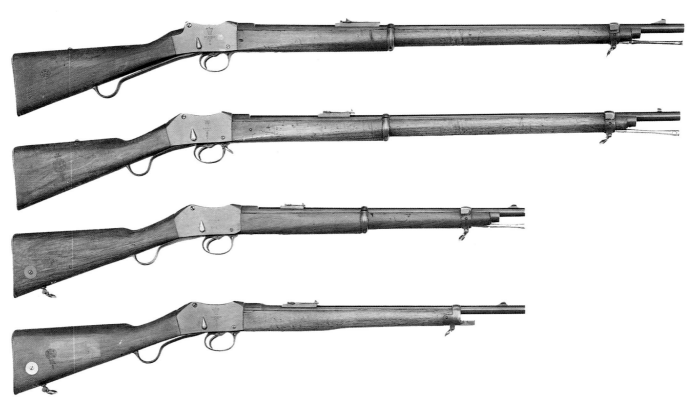

**Technical Specifications**

| Spencer carbine: | | | Martini-Henry Mk II rifle: | | |
|---|---|---|---|---|---|
| Overall length | 39ins | (990mm) | Overall length | 49ins | (1244mm) |
| Barrel length | 22ins | (558mm) | Barrel length | 33.25ins | (844mm) |
| Calibre | .50in | (12.7mm) | Calibre | .455in | (11.5mm) |
| Weight | 8lbs 4oz (3.7kg) | | Weight | 8lbs 8oz | (4kg) |
| Charge | 45 grains | | Charge | 85 grains | |
| Ignition | Original, rimfire cartridge; centrefire for test | | Ignition | Centrefire cartridge | |

### Firing the Spencer carbine & Martini-Henry rifle

The author has to admit to a certain degree of compromise during the test on the **Spencer**, since large calibre rimfire cartridges have not been commercially available for decades. Those that survive are collector's items which, even if they worked, would render test firing for a morning more expensive than buying a yacht. Fortunately a centrefire breech block has been produced which enables the .50 calibre Spencer to shoot the short .50-70 centrefire cartridge similar to that used in the later Sharps carbine. Cartridges were filled using 450 grain lubricated bullets, and 45 grains of coarse powder - the same specifications as for rimfire cartridges manufactured for issue during the Civil War. The smaller charge being used meant that a small amount of airspace in the case had to be filled with corn meal before seating the bullet. This ensured that the bullet packed the powder down firmly, and seated the bullet at the correct height in the case.

The magazine tube was removed by turning its heel through 90 degrees and withdrawing it from the butt. Seven cartridges were then slid into the tubular recess, the tube being replaced behind them. Another cartridge can be placed in the breech, giving a useful eight-shot capacity. To chamber a round was a simple matter of lowering the trigger guard lever, which rotated the breech block and allowed the magazine spring to push a cartridge into the breech. Raising the lever closed the breech behind the chambered round. The hammer then had to be manually cocked, and the rifle was ready to fire.

In skilled hands a rate of fire of about 10 to 12 aimed shots per minute was possible, assuming there was no fumbling with the magazine tube - easier said than done, especially with cold hands. Our test was carried out on a chilly morning, and we found that in practical terms shooting one full magazine per minute was realistic. The Spencer was equipped with a device known as a Stabler cut-off. This closed the magazine, and enabled the rifle to be fired in single-shot mode, saving the loaded magazine for emergencies. At least one group of US 4th Cavalry troopers owed their lives to this device when holding off a war party of Comanches in Texas. They fired their rifles single-shot until about to be overwhelmed, then unlocked the Stabler device and let loose a devastating rapid fire which destroyed the Indians' charge.

The process of reloading could be speeded up by employing an early "speedloading" device called a Blakeslee Cartridge Box. Patented in 1864, this was simply a leather case which held six metal tubes each containing seven cartridges. With the magazine tube removed from the rifle, the soldier simply poured the cartridges in from the Blakeslee tube. A later ten-tube version was supplied to the cavalry, and 13-tube boxes to the infantry.

To a modern shooter, the performance of the Spencer was frankly disappointing. As with the Sharps, the sights are rudimentary and give a poor target picture. Nevertheless, the carbine was actually very pleasant to shoot, mainly because of the modest power of the cartridge; and at shorter ranges of 100-150 yards it was tolerably accurate. We were able to register seven hits out of seven on a man-sized target at 100 yards, which is arguably good enough for any short-barrelled cavalry weapon. It must be said that the bore of the particular example used had clearly suffered from years of wear; it showed some rust pitting and the lands of the rifling were visibly worn, factors which certainly affected its accuracy.

Muzzle velocity was about 860fps, but it was clear that the large bullet was running out of steam at 200 yards. Shots aimed at the bullseye at this range were kicking up dust at the foot of the target, and raising the point of aim resulted in a random spattering of hits around it. In fairness, some of the poor performance can be blamed on the cartridge which, like the original Spencer rimfire round, was woefully underpowered.

Cartridge ejection was not particularly positive, and care had to be taken to ensure the fired case actually cleared the breech. On several occasions the carbine had to be turned upside down to allow the empty to drop clear; and it was easy to see how cases covered in verdigris (inevitable in a hot climate when they were in contact with leather) could become cemented into a hot breech. The lever action was quite smooth, aided by a liberal smearing of copper-based lubricant, and there were no misfires. Penetration of the bullet was quite good at closer ranges. At 100 yards it went through a solid oak panel one inch thick, but it predictably lost power at longer range. Even so, although travelling slowly it was still a deadly projectile at 300 yards. Over all, we were not surprised to find the Spencer similar in handling and accuracy to the Sharps percussion carbine; it did not have the versatility of accepting the wide range of different cartridges that the Sharps rifles could be chambered to fire, but its unique rate of fire undoubtedly made it a great improvement on its predecessors.

Despite its removal from military life the Spencer lived on for decades after the Civil War, being carried across the West by Indian and settler alike. At least one example was recorded still in regular use for hunting in the Appalachians in the late 1930s! Its adoption was a giant leap forward in military technology, although it was quickly overwhelmed by the remorseless march of progress. It is interesting to note that no other army adopted a breech-loading repeating rifle until bolt-action magazine rifles began to proliferate in the last years of the 19th century, when within a decade every major world power would embrace an invention which was by then 30 years old. Probably the Spencer's greatest epitaph was the quot-

ABOVE *A .50in rimfire Spencer cartridge shown next to one of the modern .50/70in cartridges used in our test. Although they look like different calibres the modern .50in bullet is almost identical in dimension to the original.*

BELOW & BOTTOM *Loading the Spencer. The heel plate of the magazine tube is turned to the right, and the tube is withdrawn. The tube does not hold the cartridges, but houses the spring which keeps them held firmly against the rear of the breech.*

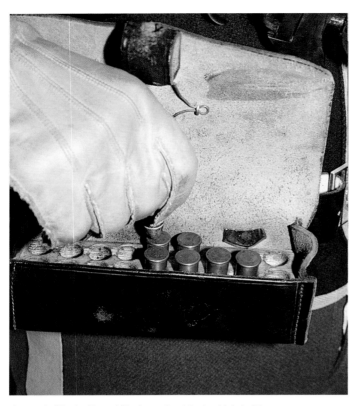

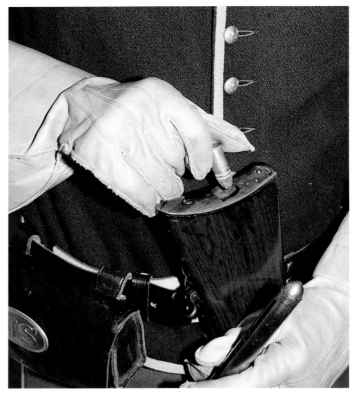

A pouch fitted with a drilled wooden block which holds 18 cartridges.

The first of seven cartridges is dropped into the tubular recess in the butt. The end of the magazine tube is also visible, bottom right, showing the conical, sprung steel cap that ensured a fresh cartridge was pushed into the breech once the action was unlocked. The tube is reinserted after the seventh cartridge, and turned to lock in place.

Cocking the action by dropping the loading lever allows the first cartridge to be pushed into the chamber; raising it again closes the breech.

The hammer has been pulled back to the full-cock position, and the Spencer is now ready to fire. The mottled colouring on the receiver is the result of case hardening. This occurs during the manufacturing process when the hot steel is hardened by immersing it in oil,

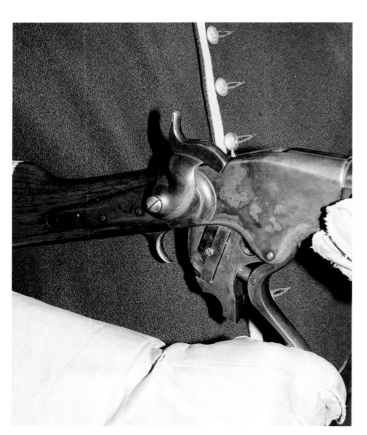

ed tribute by one disgruntled Confederate to the rifle that "You'ns load on a Sunday and fire all week".

\*       \*       \*

The Mk II **Martini** tested was an utterly different weapon from the Spencer, although the breech unlocking method by means of the lever underneath the stock was quite similar. It was undramatic to load, requiring the loading lever to be lowered and a single cartridge to be placed onto the dished breech cover, then pushed into the chamber with the finger.

At this point I would like to challenge the assertion made by an anonymous British soldier that "the Martini kicks like a mule". In point of fact it kicks like a carthorse, and one can only wonder at the stamina of the soldiers who fired hundreds of rounds in the course of an action. The cartridges we used were modern solid-drawn copies of the original brass foil type, using the same 85 grain charge and 485 grain bullet. The sights were quite good, being graduated up to 1,400 yards. The first shot at 100 yards was a bullseye, and at that range, without using a rest, a three-inch group was achieved - good by any standards. Muzzle velocity was a reasonably consistent 1480fps, and although this naturally dropped as the range increased it did not fall anywhere as rapidly as with the muskets. Ejection of empty cases could also be slow, and on a couple of occasions a knife point had to be used to prise a reluctant cartridge out, but by and large its action was quite positive.

The range was increased to 500 yards, and it was found that the Martini did indeed have a very flat trajectory. After 20 shots, firing from a prone position (where the recoil made itself very unpleasant), the rifle was able to manage a ten-inch group, with one flyer two inches outside the rest. The power of the bullet was indeed awesome, with easy penetration of a six-inch wooden post at that range. It was little wonder that the .450 calibre cartridge became so popular with hunters in the late 19th and early 20th centuries; there were few big game animals that could not have been brought down by one. It was difficult to obtain accurate figures for the velocity at the longer range, but from those that we did get the bullet appeared to be still travelling in excess of 950fps, so being struck by one would have been a memorable experience. There was no doubt in anybody's mind that even today the Martini is a very potent weapon, although shooting it is hard work physically.

The Martini was to soldier on in service long after the introduction of the bolt-action .303 calibre Lee-Metford rifle in 1888. Many thousands were rebarrelled to accept the new cartridge, and it was even re-issued for training purposes during the First and Second World Wars. It was the last black powder rifle used in military service in Britain, and when its .450 cartridge was eventually replaced by the new smokeless cordite ammunition an era ended which stretched back five hundred years.

**BELOW LEFT** *Loading the Martini-Henry. When the lever is dropped to open the breech the teardrop-shaped cocking indicator on the right of the receiver swivels back from the vertical position, showing that the weapon has been cocked. It remains in that position until the rifle is fired.*

**BELOW** *Opening the cartridge pouch, and extracting a .577/450in round. Each pouch held 20 cartridges in their ten-round packets of issue; common practice was to empty them loose into the pouches, so more could be carried.*

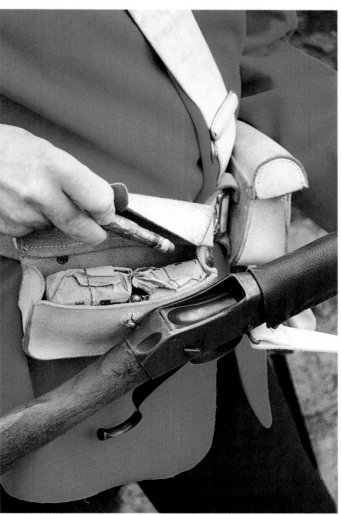

**ABOVE** *Inserting the cartridge into the chamber. This rifle has a leather cover sewn around the forestock and barrel to protect the left hand from the rapid heat build-up during sustained firing.*

**RIGHT** *Locking the breech closed by squeezing the lever up again with the right hand. The loading procedure is extremely quick, allowing this single-shot weapon to be fired 12 times a minute.*

**BELOW** *The Martini was the last British rifle to use a black powder round, so this was the last generation of redcoats to be unsighted and pinpointed by the usual cloud of smoke and glowing powder grains blossoming from the muzzle. With its flat trajectory even moderate marksmen were generally able to hit a man-sized target out to 300 or 400 yards, and the impact of the bullet was devastating.*

# FURTHER READING

There are hundreds of books relating to firearms, many of them very specialist, but for general information on the development and history of firearms and ammunition I can do no better than recommend the following:

De Witt Bailey, *British Military Longarms*, Arms & Armour Press
De Witt Bailey, Pattern Dates of British Ordnance Small Arms 1718-1783, Thomas Publications
Claude Blair (gen.ed.), *Pollards History of Firearms*, Country Life
David Blackmore, *Arms and Armour of the English Civil War*, Royal Armouries
H.L.Blackmore, *British Military Firearms*, Greenhill Books
H.L.Blackmore, *English Pistols*, Royal Armouries
G.Boothroyd, *The Handgun*, Cassell
G.Embleton & J.Howe, *The Medieval Soldier*, Windrow & Greene
Ian V.Hogg, *Weapons of the Civil War*, The Military Press
G.Hoyem, *A History and Development of Small Arms Ammunition, Vols 1-3*, Armory Publications
J.Lugs, *Lugs Firearms Past & Present*, Grenville
Majendie & Browne, *Military Breech-Loading Rifles*, Arms & Armour Press
Dr C.H.Roads, *The British Soldier's Firearm*, R & R Books
J.Rosa, *Guns of the American West*, New Orchard Editions
J.Rosa, *Colt Revolvers*, Royal Armouries
I.Skennerton, *List of Changes in British War Material*, published by the author
F.Wilkinson, *The World's Great Guns*, Hamlyn

# CONVERSION TABLES

**Mass**

| | |
|---|---|
| 27.34 grains | = 1 dram |
| 16 drams | = 1 ounce |
| 16 ounces | = 1 pound |
| 7000 grains | = 1 pound |
| 1 milligram | = 0.01543 grains |
| 1 gram | = 15.43 grains |
| 1 gram | = 0.03527 ounces |
| 1 grain | = 0.0648 gram |
| 1 dram | = 1.772 grams |
| 1 ounce | = 28.35 grams |

**Velocity**

| | |
|---|---|
| 1 mile per hour | = 88 feet/min |
| 1 mph | = 1.467 feet/sec |
| 1 mph | = 0.447 metre/sec |
| 1 foot/min | = 0.5080 cm/sec |
| 1 foot/min | = 0.01136 mph |
| 1 foot/sec | = 0.6817 mph |
| 1 metre/sec | = 2.237 mph |
| 1 cm/sec | = 1.967 feet/min |

# BORE & CALIBRE SIZES

The relationship between bore size and calibre is calculated by the number of lead balls that could be cast from a pound ingot. Thus 3 bore equated to three lead balls, each being 1.325 inches in diameter. The term "calibre" is now generally used only for rifles and pistols, bore being the accepted term for shotguns or other smoothbore weapons - although until comparatively recently either term could be used irrespective of the type of weapon.

| Bore | Calibre | Bore | Calibre | Bore | Calibre |
|------|---------|------|---------|------|---------|
| 1 | 1.669 | 51 | .450 | 101 | .358 |
| 2 | 1.325 | 52 | .447 | 102 | .357 |
| 3 | 1.157 | 53 | .444 | 103 | .356 |
| 4 | 1.052 | 54 | .442 | 104 | .355 |
| 5 | .955 | 55 | .439 | 105 | .354 |
| 6 | .919 | 56 | .436 | 106 | .353 |
| 7 | .873 | 57 | .434 | 107 | .352 |
| 8 | .835 | 58 | .431 | 108 | .350 |
| 9 | .803 | 59 | .429 | 109 | .349 |
| 10 | .775 | 60 | .426 | 110 | .348 |
| 11 | .751 | 61 | .424 | 111 | .347 |
| 12 | .729 | 62 | .422 | 112 | .346 |
| 13 | .710 | 63 | .419 | 113 | .345 |
| 14 | .693 | 64 | .417 | 114 | .344 |
| 15 | .677 | 65 | .415 | 115 | .343 |
| 16 | .662 | 66 | .413 | 116 | .342 |
| 17 | .649 | 67 | .411 | 117 | .341 |
| 18 | .637 | 68 | .409 | 118 | .340 |
| 19 | .629 | 69 | .407 | 119 | .339 |
| 20 | .615 | 70 | .405 | 120 | .338 |
| 21 | .605 | 71 | .403 | 121 | .337 |
| 22 | .596 | 72 | .401 | 122 | .3365 |
| 23 | .587 | 73 | .399 | 123 | .336 |
| 24 | .579 | 74 | .398 | 124 | .335 |
| 25 | .571 | 75 | .396 | 125 | .334 |
| 26 | .563 | 76 | .394 | 126 | .333 |
| 27 | .556 | 77 | .392 | 127 | .332 |
| 28 | .550 | 78 | .391 | 128 | .331 |
| 29 | .543 | 79 | .389 | 129 | .330 |
| 30 | .537 | 80 | .387 | 130 | .3295 |
| 31 | .531 | 81 | .386 | 131 | .329 |
| 32 | .526 | 82 | .384 | 132 | .328 |
| 33 | .520 | 83 | .383 | 133 | .327 |
| 34 | .515 | 84 | .381 | 134 | .3265 |
| 35 | .510 | 85 | .379 | 135 | .326 |
| 36 | .506 | 86 | .378 | 136 | .325 |
| 37 | .501 | 87 | .377 | 137 | .324 |
| 38 | .497 | 88 | .375 | 138 | .323 |
| 39 | .492 | 89 | .374 | 139 | .322 |
| 40 | .488 | 90 | .372 | 140 | .3215 |
| 41 | .484 | 91 | .371 | 141 | .321 |
| 42 | .480 | 92 | .370 | 142 | .320 |
| 43 | .476 | 93 | .368 | 143 | .319 |
| 44 | .473 | 94 | .367 | 144 | .3185 |
| 45 | .469 | 95 | .366 | 145 | .318 |
| 46 | .466 | 96 | .364 | 146 | .317 |
| 47 | .463 | 97 | .363 | 147 | .316 |
| 48 | .459 | 98 | .362 | 148 | .3155 |
| 49 | .456 | 99 | .361 | 149 | .315 |
| 50 | .453 | 100 | .360 | 150 | .314 |